Nick lots of love &
very best wishes for a
happy birthday, 2002

Jock & Moira

xx

RICHARD & JUDY

RICHARD & JUDY

The Autobiography

Richard Madeley and Judy Finnigan

Hodder & Stoughton

Copyright © 2002 by Richard Madeley and Judy Finnigan

First published in Great Britain in 2002 by Hodder and Stoughton
A division of Hodder Headline

The right of Richard Madeley and Judy Finnigan to be identified as
the Authors of the Work has been asserted by them in accordance
with the Copyright, Designs and Patents Act 1988.

1 3 5 7 9 10 8 6 4 2

A CIP catalogue record for this title is available from the British Library

ISBN 0 340 82093 4

Typeset in Sabon by Palimpsest Book Production Limited,
Polmont, Stirlingshire

Printed and bound in Great Britain by
Mackays of Chatham plc, Chatham, Kent

Hodder and Stoughton
A division of Hodder Headline
338 Euston Road
London NW1 3BH

Judy

For my mother

Richard

For my children, Tom, Dan, Jack and Chloe

Prologue

Judy: We decided to write this book after a period of thirteen years which changed our lives.

Before *This Morning* we were two regional TV journalists, each with a fairly turbulent emotional history. Both of our first marriages had broken up; we had found each other, married, and added two more children to my existing family of twin boys. We were very happy, very ordinary and very broke. Two divorces and two more children in quick succession do not tend to lead to a comfortable financial position. But, although money was a major worry, we enjoyed our lives, each other, and our family, in relative anonymity. Yes, we were both on television, but only in the north-west. People there tend to take their regional presenters very much for granted, and that suited us just fine.

On 3 October 1988 we found ourselves zipping up the M62 from Manchester to Liverpool for the very first episode of a brand-new daytime television programme called *This Morning*. We were both nervous, and matters didn't improve when we were stopped for speeding by a (fortunately) friendly policeman. That slight hitch was, perhaps, an indication of the turbulence to come. Over the next thirteen years our money problems became a thing of the past. But we were about to learn the cost of fame – with a vengeance.

As the viewers discovered *This Morning*, so the press discovered us. I think we've been accused of pretty much everything over the years except, as Julie Goodyear once told us in an interview, bestiality and arson. Our marriage has been described as a sham for the cameras; smearing rumours accused me of being an alcoholic and Richard of beating me up; calls from newspapers said they had it on the highest authority (whose? God's?) that we were about to get divorced; Richard was falsely accused of shoplifting; and perfectly normal intimate female health problems gave rise to the rumour that I was terminally ill. Oh, and the press took it as a given that we were desperately unhappily married, and absolute nightmares to work with.

None of it's true. We are, essentially, exactly the same as we always were: a close family, a happy couple who do a very strange but hugely enjoyable job. We're very lucky that our marriage is as strong as it is – it's needed to be – and we're much wiser, too. This autobiography is the story of how we got some way along the path of wisdom and came to understand the whole business of celebrity for what it is: a hologram, a chimera, with the power to deceive and destroy. The trick is to survive, and stay sane.

———

Richard: Writing an autobiography reveals a number of things to the author or, in this case, authors. One is the almost horrible acceleration of time that develops as you grow older. I don't think that Judy or I have quite reached terminal velocity yet, but the years are flashing by so fast now that we can't be far off. I optimistically reckon that if I'm roughly halfway through my life – in other words, if I live to be ninety – the next forty-five years will, in my own perception, be over in about twenty. That's not so much depressing as alarming.

Another revelation, and a far more soothing one, is how much more trusting one gets as the birthdays pass. I haven't read any of Judy's chapters and she hasn't read mine; a mutual act of faith that would probably have been impossible even ten years ago. We both decided at the outset of this enterprise that we were entitled to our own take on the past – obviously about the years before we met, but in the period since, too. There's nothing worse than couples who bicker at dinner parties about who actually said what, when, where and to whom; and little more tiring than a husband and wife who cannot agree whether the holiday from hell happened in Madeira or Miami.

So what you are about to read is a paradox: an individual yet joint account of two lives, both singular and intertwined.

That doesn't mean there hasn't been some mutual cross-referencing as we wrote. 'Was it me or you who said . . . ?' or 'Who was that bastard who once told us that . . . ?' But, for the most part, these are memoirs written in mutual isolation. I hope there won't be too many discrepancies, but such as there are will intrigue and annoy us more than they will you.

Judy and *Richard*
London, 2002

1 : RICHARD

Anyone who walked into my bedroom when I was ten would have known exactly what I planned to be. The ceiling was strung with hanging model aeroplanes – Spitfires, Hurricanes, Lancasters and their successors, the Lightning, the Vulcan. Dotted among all these were little biplanes – the Sopwith Camel, the SE5A. I had them all, and my bedroom could have handled any overspill from the RAF Museum at Hendon, provided visitors didn't mind coming in only two at a time. Then, in an instant, my ambition to be Richard Madeley, fighter pilot, evaporated.

One schoolday morning, while we were all in class, a kid came into the room with a note for our teacher. The teacher read it, looked very shocked and, turning to the boy, said, 'Right. Tell Mr Williams I will see him at break.' He folded the note and put it in his pocket. I instinctively knew the boy who had delivered the note had read it. He knew what the message was. I didn't. And I wanted to be that boy, wanted to know what was going on. I realized, for the first time, that this was actually my permanent state: I was incredibly curious, greedy for information about anything and everything, always desperate to be the first to know what was going on, so I could tell everybody else. The classroom incident was a pivotal moment – an unexpected awakening. The seeds of my real ambition had pushed up their first shoots. I wanted to be a reporter.

All these years on, it's strange to be writing my own story. It's tempting to leap to the turning points, the moments of personal drama that are my own private headlines. But this isn't a news story; it's a feature. We need some background stuff.

I never knew my maternal grandmother, but I vividly recall the events surrounding her death. It was my first – and only – experience of extra-sensory perception. My mother, Claire, is Canadian and was born in the west of Canada. When she emigrated – re-emigrated as it were – to England after she met and married my father, my grandparents remained there. My mother was very close to her mother and, because we didn't have a phone in those days, used to write to her on an almost daily basis. I can still remember my grandmother's blue airmail letters dropping through our letterbox by return of post.

One night, when I was about five years old, I was woken up by a huge commotion on the landing outside my bedroom. It was the early hours of the morning, but all the lights were on in the house. I opened my bedroom door to see my mother pacing rapidly up and down our narrow landing, my father alongside her, his arm around her shoulders. Mum was in a terrible state and I was frightened. I could see my older sister, Liz, who was nine, standing outside her bedroom, crying. I had never seen my mother in near-hysterics. She kept saying she was seeing dreadful images, that something terrible was happening, that my father's mother, Kitty, was seriously ill. She was so convincing that my father put on his dressing-gown and walked up the road to a nearby public telephone box to call his parents. When he got through to them in their Shropshire farmhouse, his father – who must privately have wondered what on earth was wrong with my mum – said everyone was fine, and we should all go back to bed.

Fat chance. When Dad returned to the house, Mum remained inconsolable. Something terrible, she kept insisting, had happened to someone in the family. Don't think my mother was prone to this kind of thing; it's never happened before or since. She was beside herself. In the end Dad had to go to the phone box again to call out our family doctor. When he arrived, he gave Mum a sedative. And finally, at about five or six in the morning, she drifted off to sleep and everything calmed down.

A couple of hours later, there was a knock on the front door. It was a boy with a telegram for Mum from Canada. Her mother, it said, had collapsed and was desperately ill. The message – from my mother's kid brother, Bailey – didn't mince any words. The gist of it was, 'She's dying. Get on a plane.'

Today I don't have a shred of doubt that my mother picked up a human distress call that night, transmitted from one brain to another. It crossed three thousand miles of Atlantic Ocean and got a little scrambled along the way, but it was a full-on case of ESP all right.

Mum flew to Canada that day and remained there until her mother died just two weeks later, of cancer. A few years after that Mum's father died of it too. But as I never saw them except as a tiny baby, they were effectively unknown to me, sweet-faced strangers looking out from a photo album.

It was very different with my paternal grandparents. They lived in England and I was very close to them. My grandfather was one of six children who lived in Worcestershire. Long before the First World War, soon after the turn of the century, his family decided to emigrate to Canada. But they didn't have enough money for everyone's passage. So a deal was struck between my great-grandfather and his brother who owned and ran a farm with a sister in Shropshire, about ten miles from Shrewsbury. The farm-owners would come up with the cash for the journey but, in return, they would get to keep one of the family's six children to help them on the farm. That was my grandfather. Only when he was grown up would he be free to join the rest of the family – assuming he wanted to. It was, in effect, selling a small boy into a form of serfdom or bondage.

My grandfather, just seven at the time, was the youngest. He had no idea about what was to happen to him. On the weekend when the family was due to sail to Canada they travelled from Worcestershire and slept at the farmhouse, halfway to Liverpool. Then, in the dead of night, when my grandfather was fast asleep, his family crept out of the house and headed north for the port.

Granddad woke up to a very quiet farmhouse. Where had his family gone? Years later, he told me he'd never been consumed by such choking panic, not even in the trenches during the First World War. His uncle and aunt were brusque. They told him he was now going to live with them and wouldn't see his mother and father or brothers and sisters again for many years. There wasn't a shred of sympathy or affection. Just strait-laced, hard-faced pragmatism. Poor Granddad. He somehow got through that first day and decided to run away that night and walk to Liverpool. He was too little to know how impossible that was. But he stayed awake until the house was still and dark, dressed and crept to his bedroom door. It was locked.

And so his new life began. He somehow accepted his fate and knuckled down to life on the farm with two adults who, although never cruel to him, never showed him any affection either. So, deprived of his mother, father and siblings, my grandfather spent his childhood making the best of things. He went to the village school and helped out on the farm. But secretly he kept the memories of his family bright and burning in his mind.

When the Great War broke out, Granddad lied about his age and joined the army. He was originally in the cavalry, but horses weren't much good against machine-guns and he ended up in the infantry, and in the thick of it. He rarely spoke about his experiences in France. Like so many of his generation, he came home and shut up. But I do remember him telling me that his position came under such sustained attack from the Germans that the bolt on his rifle literally glowed with heat. His fingers and palms were covered with blisters when the shooting stopped. Another time a friend coming back from a patrol in no-man's-land had his arm cleanly severed by a burst of machine-gun fire.

My grandfather told me that the poor guy ran around in tight circles, spouting blood, before collapsing and dying of shock. I always remember the words he used to close that story: 'Believe me, Richard, that wasn't anything like the worst of it.'

God knows how men like my granddad came home sane.

But he did, and at last sailed for Canada to find his long-lost family. He succeeded in tracking them down and knocked on a door which was opened by his mother. He recognized her at once, but she had no idea who he was. Nevertheless, there was a reconciliation and rapprochement. I think he came back to Britain with what we would now describe as 'closure'.

His now elderly aunt and uncle promised him that if he returned to work with them, he would inherit the farm when the old man died. But when that happened, and the will was read, Granddad discovered that his aunt had inherited the farm. Disappointed, he put on a good face and continued to run it with her.

After he met and married my grandmother, Kitty Edwards, a dairy girl, the old aunt agreed to move out of the farmhouse into a cottage, and my grandparents lived in the main house. But the old lady exerted a tremendous hold over them, because it was up to her whether or not to leave them the farm. By now totally blind, she used to visit the farmhouse every week and would walk around it, feeling for all the furniture and paintings to ensure that every item was exactly where she had placed it. Before these visits, my grandmother used to run around the house putting everything, including horrible furniture that should have been burned years ago, back exactly where it used to be.

Finally the old lady died – and guess what? The whole estate went to the Madeleys in Canada. No one ever really found out what was in the old girl's mind. For my money, it was a kind of perversity, a strange almost wicked capriciousness.

Granddad was absolutely winded. Through no choice of his own he'd invested all his energies in the place – indeed his entire life – had toiled to build it up, only now to find himself disinherited. And his brothers and sisters, who had left for Canada with his parents all those years ago, were to reap the harvest sown in the season of his childhood misery. But an older sister in Canada would have none of it. Furious at the injustice, she called a family conference. She told her brothers and sisters that the will was iniquitous, that none of them deserved his or her share of the farm and that they should all sign it over to my grandfather. This was eventually agreed, but only with the proviso that, over time, he should pay them their share of what the farm was worth. My grandfather had no option but to agree. He spent years working to pay off the debt, and finally succeeded in doing so after the last war.

In the years between the wars, he and Kitty had three sons. Their first, John, died, at three, from pneumonia.

I can remember when I was small, playing in my grand-parents' living-room, coming across a small screw-topped jar with tiny balls of gold and silver paper inside – a dozen or so of them. After a while my grandmother came into the room and gently took them from me and put them back in the jar. 'It was John's money,' she said. 'He was too little for real money, and anyway we didn't have much, so he made these little balls and called them his money.' Half a century on, her eyes were full of tears.

My Uncle Jim was born in 1924, followed by my father,

Chris, in 1928. Strangely enough, although my grandparents were always demonstrative in their affections towards me and my sister, I don't think they found this so easy with their own children. My father once told me that he couldn't remember his father actually telling him he loved him, or cuddling and kissing him. He put it down to Granddad's own cold, remote upbringing.

But the pattern was decisively broken by my dad, and indeed by my Uncle Jim. I know it's said that parents repeat their parents' behavioural traits with their own children, but my dad didn't. He was very affectionate towards us, loving and generous. I think that through me and Liz he enjoyed the childhood he never had; gave us the fun and warmth he felt he'd been denied.

The latter years of his schooldays were pretty miserable, too. The family fortunes were improving, but Dad was becoming rebellious and difficult at his grammar school in Wem. He wouldn't do his homework and his parents thought he was being distracted by girlfriends. He probably was. At fifteen, he found himself packed off to what was then a forbidding and minor public school: Denstone, in Staffordshire. He hated it there. Perhaps if he'd gone at the age of seven, he would have adjusted better, understood the public-school culture more. But at fifteen he was too old for such an abrupt change. At a stroke, he'd lost all his friends; he spoke with a country accent, and consequently was picked on. In fact, Dad was generally traumatized by the whole experience. He thought Denstone was a ghastly place and always said that his subsequent National Service in the RAF was, by comparison, a light-hearted, upbeat and liberating experience. My mother told me that on the rare occasions when my father unburdened himself, it was obvious that his three years at boarding school, with ancient teachers (the young ones had been called up), the truly terrible wartime food, and the severing of his adolescent relationships back home, were shrivelling years that damaged him. He was a sensitive man who remained scarred by the experience, and in later years he responded to pressure or stress by internalizing everything, just as he had learned to do at school. I've always been convinced that this was a strong contributory factor to his death, at forty-nine, from a heart attack. The other was that he smoked like a chimney. When I was small I can remember him smoking three packs of untipped cigarettes a day.

Dad and Jim helped on the farm as they grew up, but my father really had no interest at all in farming. He had twin obsessions: classical music and literature. He had no talent for making music, but he could write and decided to be a journalist.

When he was demobbed, he did a couple of years on the *Shrewsbury Chronicle*. But the greyness of post-war British life was stifling, and the old familial tug towards Canada stirred in him, too. The clincher was that newspapers there were not subject to newsprint rationing and had many more pages than the savagely restricted British press. So Dad took a boat for Quebec, and a job with the Thomson newspaper group. But a stormy voyage meant he was very late and by the time he arrived, the job was gone. He ended up selling underwear in a department store. To make ends meet, he bought a camera and snapped holiday pics of kids on donkey rides across the beaches of Lake Ontario. One of them was published in a local newspaper in the tiny tobacco-growing town of Tillsonburg, and Dad pushed hard for a job there – and he got it.

That was where he met my mother. He was sent to review a local amateur play in which she was playing the lead. Within three weeks he had proposed, she accepted, and inside three months they were married. A year later my sister was born. Then some quack dentist told Mum she needed a thousand dollars' worth of dental treatment. 'To hell with that,' said

Dad. 'We've got a national health service in England. I'll take you back there.'

Mum, a secret anglophile, was thrilled and within a month they were home here. Incidentally, the NHS dentist who checked her teeth said she needed one filling. So the dodgy Toronto tooth-man meant I was born in Essex, not Ontario, and that Mum kept the gnashers that God gave her.

Dad got a job with Ford in the press office. His boss was one Colonel Buckmaster, the former head of the SOE, who ran Britain's wartime secret agents in occupied Europe. Dad was in awe of him. When Ford's head office moved from its huge Dagenham factory to leafy Brentwood, we left my first home, a three-bedroomed semi in Romford opposite a launderette, for another three-bedroomed semi in Brentwood. This one was opposite a wood. My hunger for the countryside, awakened by tantalizing interludes at the farm in Shropshire, was satisfied.

My father was six feet two and, given that my mother is petite, I obviously inherited my height from him. He was always very well turned out and, when we teased him into removing his glasses, he looked oddly like the actor Robert Wagner. He was a very private man. I talk to my kids – Dan, Tom, Jack and Chloe – all the time, I chunter on about the nightmare day I might have had, and they tell me about theirs, but I don't ever remember my father telling me that he was under pressure at work, or unhappy about anything. One of the few things he taught me by bad rather than good example was not to bottle things up. He was easily stressed and had quite a short temper (which I too have inherited).

We were not particularly well off. Dad didn't earn a huge amount and my mother, except for a brief period as a teacher, didn't work. We didn't have central heating until I was about eleven, couldn't afford a phone for many years, but we did have a small black and white TV and a car that came with Dad's job. We didn't really fit any specific social category. Financially we were, I suppose, at the lower end of middle class, and yet Dad's public-school education and Mum's Canadian classlessness challenged that classification. To this day I'm not at all sure where my inherited social roots lie. Agricultural, emigrant, journalistic: my background isn't really defined by class and, on the whole, I'm glad not to carry that particular baggage.

My happiest childhood memories of Dad and Mum were my birthdays. They took these occasions very seriously. If he could, my father always made a point of taking these days off work and there was always much consultation about what I most wanted to do. For me, it was either a picnic in Epping Forest, which I thought a magical place, or the thrill of a visit to London Zoo, Madame Tussaud's or the Planetarium. On the whole, I usually plumped for the zoo where, in those days, you were allowed to feed the elephants with buns.

But most ordinary days ended in tremendous fun. Dad and I called our favourite rough-and-tumble game the Play, and it became a twenty-minute nightly ritual. It must have started when I was about four and carried on until I was ten or so. It consisted of five rounds of wrestling on the parental bed. The winner was the one who could push the other off the bed, and the subtext was that my father didn't try too hard – just hard enough to fool me he was doing his best and make it a scrap worth having. You couldn't hit, yank or pull, but you could give sharp pushes with the flat of your hands or feet. Dad, of course, let me win and I loved this game. I remember a cousin coming to stay and, when he peered through a crack in the door while my father and I were engaging in the Play, he was gobsmacked at the lunatic display.

Having said that, Dad wasn't without his faults. He could be over-strict and inconsistent. Some days you could get away with things which, on other occasions, would bring down the wrath of God. Whenever I did something he thought was really beyond the pale, he used to cane me on the leg or bum, but never in a 'bend over' ritualized way. Nowadays, when even smacking a child has virtually become a criminal offence, this probably sounds terrible. But that was how my dad had been punished at home and by the corporal punishment system at his school. 'Spare the rod and spoil the child.' He didn't see anything wrong with this form of punishment, although I think Mum had doubts. Once every six weeks or so, I would do something that Dad felt merited a whack with a stick. But it stopped when I was about eight when something in the enlightened culture connected with my parents; and, after a final episode concerning some Rolos bought to be shared around after tea but which vanished down someone's throat beforehand – mine – the bamboo stick was returned to the garden and enjoyed a retirement supporting runner beans. I think my mum had 'had a word'.

Mum took her responsibilities towards us very seriously and seemed to enjoy her role. She was very pretty: a Debbie Reynolds type, with that star's build and soft features. At school functions – plays, sports and open days – my friends would always say, 'Isn't she pretty; isn't she nice?' She was a redhead, but more on the spun gold side of that colour. She was a fantastic, mumsy mum and Liz and I had a very relaxed, cuddly childhood with her. She was completely focused on us, never left us in any doubt that we were deeply loved and treasured, and that gave us a very stable and happy upbringing. She and my father were clearly devoted to each other and they remained so until the day my father died. Looking back, I think I was enormously lucky.

Their parenting days, though, could not have been easy. My sister, Liz, and I were responsible for that. Liz, born in Canada in July 1952, is nearly four years older than me. Our life together began well, but it was not to last. She was thrilled to bits when she was first told I was on the way, and kept running to Mum asking, 'When is the baby coming? When will it be here?' Because I was due on 12 May 1956 – I actually arrived on the 13th – and because we had a lovely big laburnum tree in the garden, which flowered in the first or second week of May, my mother always used to say, 'When the laburnum is out.' Ever since then, whenever it's a cold spring, my mother always calls up on my birthday and says, 'It can't be your birthday – the laburnum isn't out.' But that first year, the laburnum did blossom on the Saturday. I was born at home on the Sunday, and Liz was thrilled.

Once her initial excitement wore off, however, we had an incredibly adversarial relationship. All my early memories of Liz and me are of fights: real punch-ups, tempestuous bouts in which no quarter was asked for or given. Although she was bigger than me, I was a strong boy, and we were pretty evenly matched. She was bossy – still is, she's a teacher – so I used to feel over-marshalled by her and she felt, entirely understandably, wound up by me. I was very good at that. One night, when she was about twelve, our parents went out and left her in charge for an hour or so. At this time, I used to get six pennies a week pocket money, and I used to polish them until they looked like gold, before putting them in a cigarette box. Liz always spent her pocket money on the day she got it; I saved mine. That night, she asked if she could borrow some of my money. In a position of sudden power, I instantly chose to refuse it. 'No,' I said, with a sickly smile. She persisted, I resisted, all smirks and little-brotherish taunts like: 'If only you *saved*, Liz, like I do.' Provoked beyond endurance, she picked up the cigarette box, emptied all my money into her hands, and threw it at me. Her timing was terrible. My parents simultaneously walked through the door to find their younger child with blood streaming down his face and a frightened big sister in floods of tears, guilt and remorse. Secretly, I felt I had scored a triumph.

Although we still continued to row incessantly throughout our childhood, Liz and I never really doubted that we loved each other. That's how it is with some brothers and sisters. When she left to go to teachers' training college an extraordinary change took place in weeks. When we met up again, we stopped tormenting each other and almost overnight became close confidants. From then on, instead of fighting me, Liz fought many a battle on my behalf. She got my curfews put further back, argued brilliantly for my right to grow my hair longer, and when I wanted to change schools, because of a miserable interlude of bullying, she was in my corner.

Ever since then, we've been very close. We don't see each other as often as we would like, but we talk on the phone and we are always there for each other. Today, she is Curriculum Manager in the European School, near Chelmsford, Essex, and she lives just outside the town, quite close to where we lived in Brentwood. She's married to another teacher, Peter, and they have two lovely daughters, Charlotte and Claire.

Looking back, I seem to have spent a lot of my early years in punch-ups. At five, when I went to the local junior school, Rush Green, Romford, Essex, I had a fight the moment I arrived. We were all with our mothers in the assembly hall. I was standing next to a boy and, because Mum had taught me at home, I could read his name badge. 'You're Glen,' I said and, to my astonishment, he hit me. We had a spectacular rumble and our mothers had to prise us apart. Glen and I were never friendly, but I've never forgotten his head. To me, it seemed to be the shape of a rugby ball, on its side. Years later, I thought I must have imagined that. But then, when I was eighteen and doing my rounds as a cub reporter, I saw him on a bus and his head *was* shaped like that. I hope he never played rugby – he'd cause a lot of confusion in the scrum.

When I moved on to junior school at seven, I went through a long phase of silliness and not doing any work. I was the class joker, I mucked around, and I can't remember getting a good report for years, but somehow I scraped through my eleven-plus.

I was sent to Coopers Company School in the East End of London, just off the Mile End Road in Bow. It had had a good reputation, but by the time I arrived it was going downhill fast and was pretty rough. The headmaster was due to retire, there was no real school spirit, and a lot of serious bullying. It was the late 1960s and the classrooms were full of skinheads. Most of them acted much harder than they really were, but there were a few genuine nutters. It was a very aggressive atmosphere, and some boys ended up hospitalized. One was shot in the mouth with an air pistol, another was beaten unconscious with a metal chair leg outside the school gates.

I felt pretty much an outsider at Coopers. Most of the boys there were from the East End proper. I was part of a minority from further out, in Essex. We had to commute in by train and tube, and when the other boys were socializing after school and at weekends we couldn't be around.

The outsiders were often picked on. I was okay for a couple of years because I played in the school rugby and cricket teams, and was part of what school culture there was, but eventually my turn came. It was fairly standard stuff – a lot of threats and taunts, leading to regular bouts of being kicked and punched. I think the reasons for it were pretty standard too: I was one of the tallest boys in my year; I didn't have the strong Cockney accent the others did and, fatally, because I knew I didn't fit in, that sent out a signal. A couple of boys who had been badly bullied had left the school and suddenly I was an isolated target. This happy interlude lasted six months.

Some of the boys carried knuckledusters and knives, but nothing really life-threatening happened until the last day of the Easter term. Then I was tipped off by one of my few remaining friends that I was going to be 'rumbled' with knives after school on my way back to the tube station. Whether that was true or not – and I suspect it wasn't – I had no intention of finding out. I went straight to the school secretary and insisted on phoning my dad at his office. When he got the gist, he called the headmaster and they had a massive row. I can remember the head furiously denying that the school had problems with bullying, or that I was in any danger. Then things went very quiet at the school end. I don't know what Dad said to him, but the headmaster slammed down the phone and turned to me. 'Your father has told me to keep you here in the office until he comes to pick you up,' he said. Then he sat me down and wanted the names of the ringleaders. As I wanted to keep all my teeth I explained this wouldn't be something I could help him with. This wrangling went on until my father turned up.

Once we were in the car driving away Dad astonished me by saying, 'It's okay, Richard. You're not going back there. But why the hell didn't you tell me or your mother what's been going on? Your sister's been speaking to us for weeks saying she's positive there's something wrong. If only we'd known, we would have done something.'

I still don't know why I hadn't spoken out, but I suppose it had a lot to do with shame. Most of us have been bullied some time or another and, as well as fear and loneliness, it also brings real embarrassment. You feel ashamed not to be fitting in, and you don't want to tell anyone about it. Anyway, Dad was as good as his word. I never went back to Coopers.

By this time we had moved even further away from London to a semi in Hartswood Road, Brentwood. My new school was Shenfield Tech, and the huge difference from Coopers was that it was coed. Girls everywhere. And not a knuckleduster to be seen. It took me a while to fit in and get used to being with girls. They were a shock to my system. I was incredibly shy of them.

As for asking one of them on a date, that was only marginally less terrifying than the thought of going back to Coopers. Compared to the boys in my year, I was a very slow mover at parties and school dances and I didn't have a girlfriend until I was fourteen or fifteen. I was so nervous about asking her out, so convinced I wouldn't be able to think of anything to say, that before ringing her up I actually wrote down some key words and subjects as prompts. Sad, but true.

Rather more disconcertingly, before I managed to get my hands on a girl, the odd bloke tried to get his hands on me. The first time was when I was about thirteen, on a packed tube train. My face was jammed into the back of the man in front of me, and the sly bastard tried to cup his hand over my groin. As soon as I realized what he was up to I managed to clear some space and brought my school briefcase down hard to knock his hand away, telling him, 'Fuck off!' He did, and I didn't see any point in reporting it to anyone. The second incident was a year later. I was returning from a scouts' meeting on a hot, thundery night. While I was waiting for a bus in Romford High Street a man tried to pick me up. He said he could tell I smoked cigarettes and if I liked we could share one round the back of the pub across the road. It was pretty blatant stuff, and he had a very nasty look about him. When I said no he tried to grab me and hustle me across the road anyway, but I kicked him in the shins, ran out from the bus shelter into the now pouring rain and stood in the centre of the road. Luckily the bus came round the corner and he ran off.

Coopers had given me rudimentary sex education. It didn't connect the sexual act with pleasure (and not a word was said about homosexuality). I approached adolescence with a highly romanticized idea about love, relationships and marriage. By the time I was eleven my friends and I had a disjointed, scanty knowledge of sex. I remember one conversation when I was ten when it became clear that none of us had the faintest idea why we had erections. We agreed it must be a sign you needed to pee really badly. Sex, we thought, was all about groping and perhaps looking a bit. Then one evening my father decided to tell me the facts of life. I remember him sitting on the edge of my bed, with a face that, even in the half-light, I could see was crimson with embarrassment. But, although he described why men had erections and what they did with them (but only to their wives, he underlined several times), once again the pleasure principle was completely ignored. I was left with the image of my parents meeting very formally on the landing or in the bathroom, somehow connecting up, and then sort of – well, *standing* there for a while. They would then part company, get dressed and never talk about it again. This image remained until a year or so later when I was at last enlightened by older boys. Someone brought a porn magazine they'd stolen from their dad's secret stash and three of us spent an astonished and mostly silent twenty minutes turning the pages, until a teacher found us and confiscated the mag.

Then, when I was about fifteen, I was conclusively enlightened during a game of sardines at a teenage party. I found myself squashed into a wardrobe next to an older girl I fancied. When all the other 'sardines' were fished out, we decided to stay in. Drink had been taken, and my virginity left me in a happy blur. I think it was over pretty fast, but I didn't care. As we stumbled out of the cupboard, I knew that, clumsy though it had been, all was going to be well. I could 'do it'. I was initiated.

But I was still shy with girls, and I thought I'd do better if I learned to play the guitar. A few of my friends played and even if they only knew three chords there was always a little knot of girls sitting around them as they strummed away, cross-legged on a desk. So I got one, too. By a fantastic stroke of luck, our music teacher had actually once toured with Paul Simon when he'd come to England unknown a few months before his and Art Garfunkel's *Sounds of Silence* album took off around the world. So our Mr Patterson, for it was he, knew all the Paul Simon finger picks and chord progressions, including the formidable 'claw hammer', and he was able to teach us them. All for free, too.

I quickly became friends with another boy in the guitar class, Paul Dedman. We formed a duo together, Alchemy – how seventies is that! – and played at local folk clubs. Crap at first, we slowly improved and our finest hour was performing at the 1974 Windsor Pop Festival, the one that was comprehensively raided and shut down by the police. When we came off stage, an A&R man gave us his card and told us to send him a tape, mentioning something about a contract. Paul and I were very excited. But Paul was just about to go to university to study medicine, and I was already working as a newspaper reporter. We talked about it for a few days, but decided to stick with our career plans.

I have no regrets, but most men fantasize about being a rock 'n' roll star, and Paul (who is now a psychiatrist) and I often wonder if we would have got anywhere. I still play the guitar at home, and I did this occasionally on *This Morning* for a laugh. Once Justin Hayward of the Moody Blues and I did a duet. But on the whole I've become extremely embarrassed about singing in public; only if Judy and I have a party – and I get reasonably hammered – will I sing; but I haven't done that for a while now. These days, if Judy is reading and the kids aren't at home, I'll go into the back room, shut the door, pick up my guitar and sing away happily to myself. It's very cathartic. I've moved on now from Simon and Garfunkel, though not too far. I'm with the Eagles now. We seem to get along okay, as long as there's no one else in the room.

———

My first ambition, as I said, was to be an RAF fighter pilot. I was very up to speed in the 1960s on aircraft. I dreamed of little else but flying and was about to join the local ATC (Air Training Corps) when two things brought me down to earth. First, my eyes let me down. I was slightly short-sighted and was told military pilots had to have 20:20 vision. Second, I was hopeless at maths, and you can't fly if you can't navigate.

But by now my whole mind was becoming fixed on how to become a reporter. My father had told me about his experiences as a young journalist on newspapers, here and in Canada, and I found them incredibly exciting. He had obviously had a great time. But – and this was a huge plus – it didn't sound like work to me. I could imagine myself doing it. My favourite subject was, luckily, English, and I was near the top of the class. I loved reading, anything from classics to pulp fiction, and usually had two books on the go. I enjoyed writing. Suddenly the lost boyhood dream of flying fighters didn't seem to matter any more. My careers master at school sensed my excitement. 'Never mind the RAF,' he said, 'fly a typewriter instead.'

The plan was simple. I would continue at school and take A-levels, hopefully go to university, read English, then join a graduate training scheme on a regional paper or, if I was really lucky, a national. But my schooldays and further education came to an abrupt end. When I finished my O-level GCEs in the summer of 1972, I tried to get some journalistic work experience. I wrote to our local paper, the *Brentwood Argus*, and asked if I could make tea, sweep floors, run messages, clean the toilets, whatever during the summer hols. The editor, Brian Davies, wrote back: 'You're obviously very keen. If you want to come and see me one afternoon, after we have gone to press on a Wednesday, I will happily give you an hour of my time but sorry, we don't do work experience.'

So off I went. We talked for a while. Then he suddenly sat back, smiled and said, 'Okay, Richard, I'm going to do something I had no intention of doing before this meeting. The *Argus* actually has a cub reporter's job available this August. I was going to advertise, but I'd like to offer it to you.'

I was totally flabbergasted. 'I really don't know,' I said, realizing, even as I spoke, that any would-be reporter was supposed to sound crisp and decisive. 'You see, I've got to go back to school to do my A-levels, and then take my degree.'

Brian shrugged. 'Well, it's up to you,' he said. 'But if you're sure you want to be a reporter then join us. You'll get on-the-job experience and we'll send you to college to learn shorthand, law, etc., and after three years you'll get your proficiency certificate – and you'll be set up. We will pay you peanuts but, by the time you are nineteen, you will be ahead of the game.' He went on to say that my would-be journalistic contemporaries would still be in their first year at university. 'So, mate,' he finished, 'if this is a race you want to win, I suggest you do it my way.'

When I told my parents, they were as confused and surprised as me. Dad, who had dozens of contacts thanks to his job in the Ford press office, spent the whole of that evening on the phone. 'This is the situation,' he kept saying, 'if it was your son what would you do?' Without exception, every journalist he contacted said, 'If he's sure that's what he wants to do, tell him to go for it. After all, if it doesn't work out, he can always go to university later.'

The next morning I wrote a letter to my headmaster explaining what I was planning to do, then I phoned the editor, accepted his offer, and went on a short holiday with my parents to Wales. Around mid-August, I put on a suit, climbed on to a little Honda moped my parents had bought for me – I was too young to drive – and stuttered off to the *Brentwood Argus*. I was sixteen.

On the one hand, I felt very important. The dream – this thing I knew I wanted to be, had romanticized about – had

24

come true. There I was in a real newspaper office, phoning people up and going, armed with pen and notebook, to their houses. It was amazing. On the other hand, I was a fraud. I was still a boy – what did I know? My first by-line which, true to every other cub reporter before and after me, I could not stop gazing at, was 'Church Notes – by Richard Madeley'. Wow. But that was weeks after I joined. First, I had to learn to type. 'There's no point in writing copy in longhand,' I was told. 'It'll take you for ever and the subs won't be able to read it.' So, two-finger style, I learned on an old Underwood typewriter dating from 1930. As for shorthand, I had to get by with a personal version that would probably have given Pitman, whoever he was, a double coronary.

My first jobs were to write up weddings and funeral notices which came in from photographers and undertakers. As there was a house style for this, that was simple enough. I just copied earlier articles and changed the names and dates. Next, I was promoted to the Church Notes column. This involved leafing through all the parish magazines – there must have been about a dozen – and phoning up the vicars, priests, rectors and curates if there seemed to be anything worth following up. That, as I said, led to my first by-line. I was as proud as someone who'd just won the Pulitzer.

I soon learned that being a local newspaper reporter was sometimes not unlike being a local bobby: you saw and heard things first, all right. One day we picked up on a fatal accident involving a Mini and an articulated lorry. Back in the seventies articulated lorries didn't have safety bars along their sides and the Mini had gone underneath one at a roundabout. When I got there, they had just winched the lorry off, and the tangled, spherical mass of metal underneath was riddled with human remains. It was breathtakingly horrible, and the smell of death filled the air. The poor man's flesh had made contact with hot engine parts. It was like a human barbecue. I was the first to throw up, followed by our photographer. Then, still feeling nauseous, I interviewed some witnesses and the snapper took photos that of course would never be published.

Why, I have sometimes wondered, do photographers do that: take such grisly shots? It must be some kind of reflex reaction. I've seen it again and again with newspaper photographers and TV cameramen, even though they know the images they're recording won't be used. As the accompanying reporter I frequently encouraged them to do it. I think it is a kind of impulse to do a complete, competent job; get everything on film just in case, and let someone else make the judgement on what can and can't be shown, later.

Gradually I gained experience. I learned when to make notes during an interview and when not to bother. I also learned the hard way what not to write down. A local politician had died and I was sent to interview his widow. After half an hour I had all the background information I needed, but the old lady was enjoying talking about her husband so I stayed on, pretending to make notes. I finally jotted down the words 'Same old stuff – ignore last two pages' and got up to leave. Before I could stop her the woman took my notebook, saying, 'Can I just see what you've written?' She flipped through my fractured shorthand and arrived at the terrible last page. Her eyebrows lifted slightly and she handed the notebook back to me without another word. When I got back to the office, I slaved over that copy as if it were the Pope who had died. I wanted it to be the best obituary ever. It was a salutary lesson. I never made the same mistake again.

Another time someone's widow led me into a dark front room where the curtains were drawn. I sat down on the edge of the sofa, making my notes and drinking the cup of tea she had made for me. Just as we were wrapping things up, she said suddenly, 'Would you like to see him?'

'That's very kind of you,' I said, 'but there's no need, really.'

'Oh,' she said, 'it's no bother at all. He's just there, next to you.'

He was too; the corpse had been laid out on the sofa I was sitting on and covered with a rug. I was sitting next to the head. What I had thought in the darkness was a bundle of cushions and blankets was in fact her dead husband. So I viewed the body with the kind of muted enthusiasm I felt the occasion demanded, and made a rather clammy exit.

By the time I was seventeen I knew I had made the right decision. I was incredibly happy as a cub reporter for the *Argus*. My colleagues were kind and put up with me, suffered all my mistakes and remained loyal even when I landed the paper with a writ for libel. It was during the second general election of 1974 and one of the local candidates was accused by two others of fiddling his expenses. They said his adverts for the business he ran had very similar wording to his election adverts, and he should have declared them as election expenses.

Frankly, it wasn't a huge story, but we ran with it – after the lawyers had passed it – and with rather unfortunate timing it made the front page on polling day itself. The 'legalled' copy was clean – but the headline above it wasn't: ELECTION MAN IN EXPENSES CHEATING ROW! The damning word 'cheating' didn't just make for a libellous headline, it completely coloured the whole carefully constructed piece. Worse, the two complaining candidates backed away from the case, and refused to be defence witnesses.

Our publishers wisely decided to settle and the *Argus* handed over £15,000, a lot of money for a local paper in the seventies. The editor took me out for a beer the day the cheque went off. 'Never mind, laddie,' he said. 'You're not really a journalist until you've been sued for libel.' He was kind enough not to add that it's generally considered to be a more successful rite of passage when you actually win the action.

By now, I was a fully paid-up member of the NUJ (National Union of Journalists) and was the immensely proud owner of a press card. I moved to the biggest paper in our group, the *East London Advertiser*, whose offices, by coincidence, were a stone's throw from Coopers school. But my return to the East End was a much happier experience. It was a great news beat, and lots of the stories we covered were strong enough to run in the national papers. By now I was on a really steep learning curve, and shortly after my nineteenth birthday I got the job of assistant editor, which in effect meant I was chief reporter, chief sub and deputy editor to the editor, Bob Hutchins.

I loved multi-skilling, but it caused an atmosphere in the office for a while. One day I was one of the lads, the next I was telling them what time to come in, allocating jobs, subbing and rewriting their copy. It was the last bits that didn't go down so well. Bob had always had a fairly relaxed attitude to rewriting and the paper had had a very eclectic mix of writing styles up to then. My brief from the group editor, Terry Hopley, was to sharpen it all up into a more tabloid house style. So I'd sit at my subs desk, furiously rewriting stories under the frozen stares of my colleagues. After all I was only nineteen, the youngest person in the office, and if I'd been them I'd have been pretty hacked off, too. But things gradually settled down and the atmosphere improved.

I did that job for a year but never actually took my National Certificate for Journalism exam. I was meant to sit it in November, but there was the massive 'Free George Davis' story breaking. Eastenders were convinced Davis, who already had 'form', had been fitted up and wrongfully imprisoned. It was a huge story at the time; his supporters dug up the cricket pitch at Headingley during a test match, which caused a furore.

The editor called me into his office. 'Look,' he said, 'this exam doesn't really matter now. You're assistant editor of the biggest-selling paper in East London and, anyway, I need you here. No one's ever going to ask you if you have the damn certificate or not.'

He was dead right. To this day, no one ever has.

So all that agonizing over the indenture stuff and about whether I would qualify at the end of it all, and whether I had made the right decision to give up my education, had all been for nothing. Things had turned out fine.

While I was working on the *Argus* I was still living at home, but there were growing tensions between my father and me: the usual teenage stuff about coming in late or going to the pub after work and rolling home a bit drunk. I knew Dad was becoming very keen for me to get myself a flat, so I did. I was desperate to get into my own space and loved being independent. Most of my mates at work were the same. It's amazing today that so many kids, in their late twenties, still want to live at home. We were a very different generation.

Anyway, after I'd moved out, relations with Dad and Mum got back on an even keel. It was a good move.

My sister's then boyfriend, Brian, was a teacher who had a house in Leytonstone that he shared with two other teachers. Leaving home coincided with my move to the *Advertiser*, so I rented a bedsit on the ground floor. The two girls, Brian and me got on really well and had a great time. Then, as my salary improved, I rented a flat in a house owned by one of my old *Argus* colleagues, John Craske and his lovely wife, Annie.

I quickly became very close to John; he was the older brother I'd never had. Annie and he were incredibly kind to me and took a close interest in my career. I was now well set up and beginning to put down my London roots. I had a terrific network of friends, and had made lots of contacts in the national dailies. I assumed the next move would be to Fleet Street (this was long before Wapping and Canary Wharf), but one night at home, Annie asked me if

I had ever thought of getting into radio news. Her question would change everything.

These were the tremendously exciting early days of LBC and Capital Radio in London, and elsewhere BBC local radio was mushrooming across the country. The immediacy of radio news appealed to me and thoughts of Fleet Street began to fade.

I started writing hopeful letters to local radio stations. The first to reply, in November 1975, was BBC Radio Brighton, saying, 'We're interested – send a tape.' I did and heard I was on the short list. Something told me I'd get the job. On Christmas Eve, I stopped by my flat on the way home to Mum and Dad and there it was on the mat – and it was a big fat 'No'.

With falling hopes I kept on trying stations, but got no replies. Then, in the spring, I finally got a letter from BBC Radio Carlisle saying it had a vacancy for a one-year contract reporter. Would I send a tape and go and see them?

I was totally ignorant about the north and thought that Carlisle was in Scotland. But I drove up for my interview anyway and on the day sat outside the station manager's office with six hot-shot candidates, all older than me and better qualified. In those days a lot of people wanted to make the break from newspapers into radio and this bunch all talked impressively among themselves. I felt very pessimistic. My turn came and I found myself facing a very solemn BBC board and the station manager, Tim Pitt. I told them I knew I was very young and made a feeble joke about the boss's namesake Pitt the Younger only being twenty-four when he became Prime Minister. He pretended to laugh.

I drove back to London, had a shunt on the North Circular and took it as a bad omen. Next morning I was back at my desk subbing copy. My phone rang. 'News desk.'

It was Tim Pitt. 'You're too young to be an MP, let

alone Prime Minister, but you've got a job here if you want it.'

It was a seminal moment not just for my career but for my personal life. The move to Carlisle led to a career in broadcasting, my first marriage, and a dreadful blow that would coincide with my honeymoon.

2: JUDY

I never knew my father's father who, like my dad, was called John. He died when Dad was about a year old, but his story is a strange one. He and my paternal grandmother came from Dublin, and Granddad died of TB in 1914, a year after my father was born. But my granddad actually died in what was then called the Prestwich Mental Asylum, Manchester, because he had had a terrible nervous breakdown linked to politics. He was a very ordinary working-class man but, during the build-up to the First World War, had become manically depressed about the state and future of the world. Admitted into the asylum, he contracted TB and died.

I only found out about this a few years ago when my younger brother, Roger, was digging into our family history after my father, who had never once mentioned it, died. So, my dad was an only child, brought up jointly by his mother, who never married again, and her sister, my Great-Aunt Leah. They were very poor and lived in Beswick, one of the most socially deprived districts of Manchester.

My grandmother and Great-Aunt Leah were devout Catholics, true Finnigans. All I remember about them is that they always seemed terribly old; and their house terrified me. It was a dark, two-up, two-down terrace, with heavy brown velour curtains and a lavatory in the back yard. I hated it and dreaded going there. It was full of religious artefacts and everywhere I turned there was a crucifix with a plaster Jesus hanging on it. One I particularly loathed and have never forgotten was a bust of Jesus, hooked up on the wall, displaying an open heart with

33

droplets of blood running from it. My grandmother also had phials of holy water in almost every drawer. These fascinated me and I looked at them with enormous awe. I thought they had magic properties and could do miraculous things.

My brother Cal, who is ten years older than me, had much more to do with my grandmother than I did. This was because, during the Second World War, when my father was away fighting, my mum had to go to work and Cal was virtually brought up by our gran. After the war, we only saw her and Great-Aunt Leah on Sundays for tea. Gran, I thought, was fearsome.

My dad, having grown up in this rather over-poweringly religious household, with no brothers or sisters, was a very disaffected Catholic. He went to the local school where times were so hard that many of the kids didn't even have shoes. The headmaster, however, was a fantastic man who believed that shoes gave kids dignity and pride, and he used to work all the hours that God sent to get them a pair and then encourage them to keep them polished. To the end of his days, my father was also obsessed with clean shoes and used to polish his and ours every day. There was a special cupboard where he kept all the shoe-shine materials and brushes. For him, decent shoes, with no holes or scuff marks, remained a mark of rising above your poverty.

He was very bright, my dad, and did exceptionally well at school. When he was eleven he won the Lord Mayor of Manchester's prize for essay-writing. Given his dirt-poor background that was an amazing achievement. He left school when he was thirteen. His teacher tried very hard to persuade my gran to let him stay on; said he could organize scholarships and thought my father should go to university. But there was just no way my gran could let him. They had to get some money coming in and, at thirteen, my dad was considered a young man, capable of earning a much-needed wage.

I don't think Dad ever got over his lack of education and this continued to depress him in later life. I also think he may have inherited a depressive nature from his father. As an adult, he never did manual jobs. He had beautiful copperplate handwriting and always worked as a clerk. His first 'proper' job was with a manufacturing firm, Failsworth Hats, Manchester. At one stage, together with Dunns, the men's hat firm in London, it was doing really well. Dad started as tea and office boy but, having caught the eye of the boss as a clever young man, was made company secretary after the war. So he did really well and ended up being joint managing director.

He met my mother, Anne Dudley, a Protestant, when they were both eighteen and they married at twenty-two. She was also very working class, lived in a terraced house, with lavatory in the back yard, but was from a completely different background. Her father had a skilled job in engineering, so they were respectable working class, never short of money. Her mother, Louisa, a very Edwardian-looking woman, died of liver cancer when my mum was ten, which was very hard for my mother and the rest of her family. Mum was one of five children; Louisa, Ada, Arthur and Eric, and was then brought up by her father, Bill Dudley, whom she adored, and her elder sisters, Ada and Louisa, and her older brother, Arthur. They were all remarkably strong characters in their own way.

She left school at sixteen and my grandfather sent her to Lucy Clayton Secretarial College, Manchester. She was very family-orientated, close to all her brothers and sisters, and they went around together in a big gang. At first, my father loved all this large, close, family-unit stuff, because he had grown up as a lonely only child. But, by the end of his life, I think he found it all too oppressive.

Because of my paternal grandmother's Catholicism, there was certainly a big problem about my parents marrying.

She and my mother never got on, really hated each other, something that was apparent to me very early on in life and one reason why I found going to my grandmother's house so oppressive. I always knew my mum disapproved of all those religious artefacts. There was also a big hoo-ha, which my mother often mentioned, about the parish priest coming round and making her promise to bring up any children she had as Catholics. She did promise, but told me she had absolutely no intention of raising us in that way. My father and mother were not churchgoers and, if we were brought up as anything, it was Church of England. There were endless rows about this, and the mutual resentment between my grandmother and mother never went away.

My gran died when I was about eleven. I remember my father, as an only son, always feeling very guilty about her. When she and Great-Aunt Leah both went blind, he thought it was his duty to give his mother a home, but my mum resisted that. This became a source of great tension between my parents, and that was why I remember those Sunday teas, when incidentally we always had boiled ham, limp lettuce, tomato and cucumber, tinned peaches and evaporated milk, as very tense occasions. To this day, I loathe evaporated milk.

My memories of my grandfather are much jollier. He was kind, smiley and always correctly dressed. Very much a father figure, he always wore a waistcoat and a fob watch. Mum told us that when she was young and my Auntie Ada was his housekeeper, her father always had fillet steak and a soft-boiled egg for breakfast. We were awestruck, but this was considered the right breakfast for the man of the house.

We used to go to see Granddad a lot, and I especially remember Easter Sunday teas when all the cousins would be there, too. But the really big day was Whit Sunday. We would always, a real working-class thing, get new clothes to take part in the Whit Walks. I wore a feathered alice-band thing, and long white frock, and my mum is fond of mentioning how excited I was when I put these on for the first time. Apparently I told a friend that it went 'all the way down to my gollies', galoshes (or pumps today). We would all parade around town and then end up back at the church hall where we were given a sticky bun with icing on the top, and milk. It was quite an occasion; a big deal in Manchester. I wasn't remotely aware that the walks were anything to do with religion. To me it was simply a time when your parents could be proud of you; and you had to be squeaky clean and beautifully turned out in lovely new clothes. After the procession, we would get changed into another new outfit and go round to my granddad's where we would prance around for him and be given a sixpence. I really enjoyed all that.

My father, having had such a weird upbringing, was a rather strange man. I knew he loved us, but he wasn't in the least bit openly affectionate and rarely showed his feelings. The only time he did was when I was going to the Saturday morning pictures. I'd ask him for the threepenny bit to get in and he'd say, 'Only if you give me a kiss,' and I'd get all bolshie. I don't think his lack of displayed affection was anything to do with his relationship with us, it was just his nature. He was a very sensitive, clever, vulnerable man and, to be honest, a depressive. That was why I was so intrigued when my brother found out about my grandfather.

My mother is a very different character who doesn't know what depression is. Completely wrapped up in herself, her children and her sisters and brothers, she has never looked elsewhere. She was also always totally certain that she was right. My father was a soul-searcher who would sit and brood, but Mum acted spontaneously as she thought fit. As a home-maker, she couldn't be faulted, was fantastic. She was also a very good full-time mum. She only went out to work during the war and again when I was in my early teens. Her marriage wasn't going brilliantly well then and she thought she was being taken for granted. She got a secretarial job, which she hated and only stuck it out for a week. She was never happier than when pottering around her house, decorating and furnishing it the way she liked, preparing meals the way she liked to cook them. She was a really contented housewife.

The year of my birth, 1948, coincided with a baby boom and the publication of the highest birth-rate figures for twenty-six years. It was also the year when Mahatma Gandhi was assassinated in India, Prince Charles was born and post-war footwear rationing ended. But what I remember Mum telling me about the day I arrived on 16 May was that she hadn't had a cigarette all the way through her pregnancy, and the moment I entered the world she asked for 'a cup of tea and a cigarette – *now*'. Before me, she had an ectopic pregnancy, which ruptured and she almost died. She remembers coming round and the night sister saying, 'Well, you knocked on the door that time, Mrs Finnigan, but He didn't let you in!' She was then told – which proves the ignorance of those times – that because she had had an ovary removed she would find it very hard to get pregnant again; and that, if she did, she would only be able to have children of one sex because the ovaries determined the sex of the child. She then disproved this nonsense by having me and, two years later, Roger.

I lived all of my early life in Amos Avenue, Newton Heath, north Manchester. Like the grandparents' houses, it was a two-up two-down terrace, no bathroom, no garden and a lavatory in the back yard. But it didn't have quite the same air of poverty as Beswick, the area where my dad was born. It was a step up from that, a bit less *Coronation Street*-ish. My mother was very houseproud and did as much as she could with our rented house.

She's eighty-eight now and has a flat near Colchester, Essex.

She lived with Richard and me for two years when we moved from Manchester to London, but she's a very independent woman and needed more space. She's blind now. But, because her flat is in the grounds of a residential home, she has the same level of care as the other residents, has an intercom, and is very happy there.

I'm her middle child, which some psychologists say is the most difficult position in a family because you are neither the eldest nor the baby. I was born in a place called Beech Mount Nursing Home. I don't know much about the birthing facilities of that time, but Mum has always been very proud that she managed to have Cal, me and Roger in a nursing home. She loved to be, and wanted us to be, 'a cut above'. I have always teased her about this, but I don't blame her. She was the one who made sure we all got a good education, the one who was really ambitious for us. We may have got our brains from Dad, but it was Mum who pushed and motivated us. Nobody in her or my father's family had been to university, but Cal, Roger and I did. She was very determined about that and, unlike many, never differentiated between the boys and me. She wanted the best for all of us.

I had pneumonia when I was five and very nearly died. The reason I remember this so clearly was that my mother brought my bed downstairs to the living-room, and the custom then was that this only ever happened one step before death. This was why when my father was dying of cancer, he refused right to the end to have his bed downstairs. When I was ill, I couldn't sit up and had this thing with a long thin spout which I had to drink from. One day, very alarmed, I said to my mother, 'Mummy, am I going to die?' This must have been on my birthday because I remember Mum had made a cake with candles on it, and I was too weak to blow them out. Then, a few years ago, when I had a chest X-ray, I was told this had shown scarring and calcification and that I had had

TB. Perhaps, I thought, it was TB not pneumonia that nearly killed me.

I also remember a childhood game where we used to tie a rope to two metal rods at the top of a lamp-post and swing around on it. Once, when I was going very fast, my hands slipped and I fell off, crash-landing on my spine, and was totally winded. Since then I've had back problems and have been told that my vertebrae are fused together. Was it that accident, I have often wondered, that caused this problem?

Up until eleven, we kids always played in the street and there was never a hint of danger: no worries about paedophiles, of being assaulted, abducted or murdered. Our only minor problem, if you could call it that, was that there was a passageway running along the back of our houses, 'the back entry' as everyone called it, and just opposite our back door lived a man who enjoyed his drink and who used to come out with a big brown jug to go to the off-licence. Adults talked about him in whispers, so I knew there was a problem. There was always a feeling that, although we were all living in identical economic circumstances in identical houses, some people were all right to talk to, others were not.

My brothers and I went to the same local primary school, where I had one very good, best friend, Joan Harris, whom I still see. She ended up being head girl and I was deputy head girl. Apart from Joan, whose parents had similar aspirations to my mother, I became a bit of a target for the other kids for being bright. The headmistress, Miss Wareham, who had also taught and adored Cal, was thrilled to bits when I came along ten years later. She was a very strict woman who, although she didn't exactly single me out, always expected me to know the answers. Sometimes she would summon me to her office, when she was with somebody, and would say, 'Judy, do you know how to spell Tarmacadam and asphalt?'

'I think so,' I'd say and spell the words. 'Why?'

'Oh, we were just having an argument about them,' she'd reply.

I was blessed really. She was great, demanded good results and got them.

My favourite teacher was Mr Parrot to whom I owe a great deal. He used to set us incredible general-knowledge holiday assignments. Completely fazed by these, I would leave them to the last minute, just before returning to school, then my father would do them for me. He loved going to the public library to find out all the answers. So, all I had to do was to copy them out. Nevertheless, I picked up a lot of general knowledge while doing this.

I did very well in the eleven plus, but there was a lot of jealousy from the other parents when I got a scholarship to Manchester High and their kids didn't. I was very sensitive about this. When I took the exam to go to the school my mum was on tenterhooks, and like a cat on a hot tin roof while we were waiting to hear whether I'd got in or not. I remember my father bringing in the envelope with Manchester High School written on it, just before I was going to school. When he opened it the first para he read out began, 'I am sorry to say that,' and my mother immediately flipped, exclaiming, 'She's not passed!'

I felt dreadful and wanted to die. In fact, I had passed. The letter simply went on to explain that I hadn't got the scholarship which meant that everything was paid for, including the uniform and games kit. But I still had a free place. My mother's first reaction, though, left me feeling ever after that my life would not be worth living unless I succeeded.

Cal also got a scholarship to Manchester Grammar and then went to Leeds University; Roger got a scholarship to William Hulme. At that stage these were direct-grant not independent grammar schools, and without the scholarships my mum and dad would not have been able to afford the uniforms and games kits. My uniform was the full Monty, black and yellow, with a black divided skirt, a horrible thing that chafed your thighs, white shirt, black and yellow tie and blazer, and black felt hat. I was always getting told off for not wearing my hat, but I felt such a fool walking home in it. The school is still there and doing very well; but the uniform is much more casual now with Aertex shirts.

My parents moved house from north Manchester to Birchfields Road, Fallowfield, south Manchester, the year I started at Manchester High. By now, they were in a position to buy their first house. This was a semi-detached, which looked out on to a busy main road and was within walking distance from my school. It had three bedrooms *and* a bathroom *and* an inside loo! Before, I had always shared a room with my brothers, and the bath was a tin one which, having been filled from a copper, was placed in front of the kitchen fire. The new house felt such a size, and so luxurious. It also had a long garden which meant that my parents became fanatically green-fingered. Best of all, its fence backed on to my school's playing fields, which was great because it felt like living in the country. I was so happy. Before we moved, I had had to go to school from my old house for a few months, a long journey involving two buses, and I was the only person wearing that awful school uniform.

Cal went to university when I was about eight, met and married Ro and never really came home again. He started working as a journalist at the *Pudsey News* and then went to Paris and got a job with Agence France Presse. He and Ro lived there for ten years, and both my nephew and niece were born in Paris. I used to go over for weekends, which felt fantastically sophisticated. Cal's life there seemed very glamorous, frequenting pavement cafés with his expat journalist friends.

Then he came back to London and worked on the *Guardian*, where he was head of the parliamentary desk. Having taken early retirement, he now lives in Suffolk.

Like Richard and his sister Liz, Roger and I used to fight like cat and dog until I went to university. Then we suddenly started to get on.

As a child I wasn't at all extroverted. I was quite shy; a bookworm who would rather spend the whole day curled up in a chair reading. My father was the same, but reading was not something that appealed to Mum. She was a doer and we irritated her. She used to get really cross with me and say, 'There's nothing clever about spending the day reading books.' I was also very dreamy, away with the fairies most of the time; I daydreamed non-stop; dreamed up stories in my head, wrote them down and won a *Sunday Express* writing competition. My contribution was pure imagination, about a pony I would have loved to have had. I wasn't really turned on by dolls and such like, although I do remember getting one for Christmas and Cal making a cradle for it out of Meccano. Mum, who was a very good dressmaker, then made a lovely blue hood and matching counterpane for the cradle. That was a great thrill on Christmas morning.

My dad was a really good pianist who used to sit for hours at the piano picking out his favourite tunes, and playing them by ear. We used to, a very Irish thing this, have great big family parties at home, their numbers swelled by Mum's huge family. We never had to have an excuse for these, but the Christmas and New Year ones, when Dad played the piano all night, were especially wonderful shindies. His all-time favourite tune was a song called 'Chloe'. I haven't a clue who wrote this number, and the name didn't even feature in the lyrics, but that's why many years later Richard and I called our daughter by that name. It was a very unusual choice then, but it's actually become the most popular name for a girl now, and Jack has become the most common name for a boy. I wonder why!

These parties, then, were a huge part of my childhood. In fact, the reason my mother can't remember what time I was born one Sunday is because her sister, my Auntie Louie, was having a party at the time which Mum, to her annoyance, had to miss. When she phoned my father at Aunt Louie's party to say that she had had a little girl, she was so overwhelmed by all the whooping and singing in the background she completely forgot the time of my birth. When I asked her, she couldn't even remember whether it was a lunchtime or evening party, and neither can anyone else in the family, which just shows how drunk they all were.

Throughout my early childhood I can remember being carted around to innumerable aunties and uncles and very close friends, who were called 'aunties' and 'uncles'. My Uncle Harold, who was my dad's best friend, was a really larger-than-life man, who became a publican, and we were always going to his pub for parties. We kids would just be bundled around and sit there until we collapsed; then we'd be taken upstairs and put in a bed until the shindy finished in the early hours of the morning, when we'd be scooped up and taken home. It was great.

That was the time when things were at their best between my mum and dad. Before he became quite reclusive, Dad loved parties. He'd play away at the piano, accompanied by my brother Cal; and my Uncle Arthur and Uncle Harold, his friend, were also brilliant pianists. My father would play all the well-loved pub songs, 'When Irish Eyes are Smiling', 'I'll Take You Home Again, Kathleen', the lot, while everybody sang along and danced around. My Auntie Ada's favourite song was 'The Old Rugged Cross'!

It was all very good-humoured and everybody drank a lot. It was the absolute norm for this to go on until dawn and, once my brothers and I were in our teens, we stayed up, too. It was all very exhilarating and we'd always end up watching the sun rise. The parties were, though, somewhat intimidating for my boyfriends. John, my first one, used to sit hiding in a corner because it was quite difficult for him to get into the mentality of it all. My family was quite overbearing, and my mother in particular despised anyone who couldn't get into the swing of it.

Much later on, when I was married to David Henshaw and hugely pregnant with our twins, Tom and Dan, we went to my mum's and dad's for Christmas where there was a huge party. I was just so exhausted I went upstairs to bed, but it was so noisy downstairs I couldn't sleep and was getting quite tearful and distraught. When my mother came upstairs for something, I asked if she could quieten things down a bit because I was so tired. She just looked at me and said, 'Absolutely not. I'm not asking my guests to quieten down just so that you can get to sleep.' I was really angry. I know if my daughter, Chloe, ever made that request to me, I'd say, 'Of course, darling, you must get some sleep,' and I would tell everyone to make less noise. But that was my mother! She was very loyal to her own family, and I swear her brothers and sisters were sometimes more precious to her than we were. In fact, she always liked us best when we were contributing something to the parties and joining in all the singing and dancing; she hated it if we sat in a corner, not feeling well or with a boyfriend, because she took this as a criticism of her way of life.

That aside, the parties were tremendous fun and my best memories of my dad stem from those days. When he died, we all came back to the house after the cremation, and Uncle Harold started to play the piano and everybody sang his favourite songs. When they got to 'Who's Sorry Now?', one of Dad's great favourites, I just completely blew it by bursting into tears and having to leave the room and go upstairs. But I just couldn't help it.

————————

We also had some really good family holidays, and went to all the obvious seaside places like Blackpool. Holidays were very big things in my family. Dad would apply for all the brochures immediately after Christmas and we would spend wonderful evenings with these laid out all over the room, choosing. Mum, who was very fussy, would not stay bed-and-breakfast; she wanted a hotel, even if it was a small one. We also went to Cornwall, and my love affair with this area began then. It was such a long car drive, it was like going to a foreign country. I was always so excited because we broke the journey and had an extra night in a village pub before going on to Newquay. And I had new clothes, which my mother made and started to pack a month before we went away. This premature packing drove me barmy because it was such a big deal and, during those weeks, we couldn't wear anything that had been washed, ironed, folded and put into a case.

Two other abiding memories are of my mother having insurance with the Co-op which was collected by a man and entered into a paying-in book every week; and Dad always doing the football pools and dreaming of a big win.

When I was growing up as the only girl in a typical working-class, male-dominated household, I used to get upset because I knew I was every bit as clever as my brothers, and I resented the different ways in which the two sexes were expected to behave. My problem was that I didn't really fit into the traditional mould. My father, for example, would watch football every Saturday afternoon, if not at Old Trafford then at home on the telly with my brothers. That was sacrosanct. The curtains would be drawn in the living-room to block out the sunshine, and my mother's answer was to go out shopping, which she loved. But, as I hated football and shopping, I used to get very wound up and feel deeply resentful on Saturdays. I've never been particularly interested in fashion, and I think my mother found me a bit frustrating because my interests were so different from hers.

I also felt the same at Christmas when my mother invited all the aunties and uncles for Christmas Day dinner, and it was taken for granted that the men would go out to the pub while the women did the cooking and laid the table; it was also taken equally for granted that when the men returned they would be waited on hand and foot, and served first with all the best and biggest portions. Worse from my point of view was that, while my brothers, Roger and Cal, were allowed to go to the pub with the blokes, I had to miss out on this because I was expected to stay behind and help my mum and the aunties!

I know some of my attitudes, especially after I'd tuned in to women's lib, antagonized my mother. She was a full-time housewife and rightly proud of her home-making achievements, cooking, decorating and sewing. She worked hard and was very good at it. But I always knew that that would never be enough for me, and that I wanted a career. When I kept saying this my mother took it personally and felt I was criticizing her, which put her on the defensive and this, in turn, made my father angry with me.

The general feeling was that I was being stroppy and stupid and, although I knew this was unfair, it did get me down. Then when I came home from uni for the holidays, my mother's sisters and sisters-in-law would disapprove of my 'attitude'. I distinctly recall one of them coming into the kitchen and saying to my mum, 'Well, you've made a rod for your own back with that girl.' This simply meant that they thought I was spending too much time on my studies and I wasn't any good at housework. I was incensed. My brothers didn't do housework, so why should I be criticized?

I used to get very aerated about all this, but life has knocked a few corners off me since then. Now, from a more mature perspective, I can accept that in oblique ways I was criticizing my mother because I had so little experience of life. Like many women, I needed to have children of my own before being able to appreciate her qualities fully; and now that my attitudes have softened I often wish I was as half as good at home-making as she was. I'd love to be one of those women who can move into a complete wreck of a house, dismantle what's there and transform it within weeks into an oasis of warmth and calm. My friend Emma Bowe can do that, and I really envy her. I've no eye whatsoever for decor and I can't sew for toffee, but both are talents I now admire. When men have this ability, they are called 'talented interior designers'; when women have it, they're called 'housewives'!

The worst thing that happened to me in my early years was having to wear glasses. I was just approaching nine when I started to have difficulty in seeing the blackboard, but I didn't tell a soul. I think this was because I always wanted to be perfect for my mother. But my sight got worse and eventually I told my best friend Joan, who then read out to me what was on the blackboard. All was fine until one horrible day when the teacher asked me to stand up and read from the board. I couldn't. The teacher was baffled at first, but it soon dawned on her what the problem was and she informed the headmistress who then told my mother I had an eye problem.

One of the reasons I was so horrified about this was because my grandmother and Great-Aunt Leah were blind; and I was convinced I was going blind, too. Even now, I dread going for eye tests just in case I'm told my sight has got worse. Also, when I got my first pair of glasses my mother was desperate for me not to wear them. She didn't think I looked very nice in them and was embarrassed. When we left the optician's, though, and I put them on I could see all the numbers on the buses; it was amazing as I hadn't been able to see these for ages. And when we got on a bus I sat there raving about what I could see. Very disapprovingly, my mother said, 'You mustn't wear them all the time.'

'Why not?' I asked, deflated. 'I can't see without them.'

'If you wear them all the time, your eyes will get lazy. And then you'll have to wear them all the time.'

The truth is, I have chronic eyesight, always have had. I inherited this from my father's side of the family. I wear contact lenses now, having given up glasses when I was about fifteen. But, in those days, I really couldn't see. I was a danger to myself and others. When I was eleven and going for my Manchester High exams, these tests were in two parts: written and, if you passed, oral. I remember Mum asking me how I had got on and me replying, 'Well, I don't really know.' I stood there looking in the mirror over the fireplace. I had my glasses on, and was very aware that I had an extremely round face, was dressed in my awful school uniform and had my hair tied, screwed up in ringlets. I thought I looked dreadful.

'Mum, do you think I'm pretty enough to go this school?' I asked. 'Do you think they will only go for the pretty ones?'

'Of course not,' my mother snapped. 'Looks don't count. It doesn't matter what you look like.'

It was not quite the reassuring answer I had hoped for!

I don't much remember birthday parties before my thirteenth but, once we were in the new house with the long garden, these suddenly became possible. My birthday is in May and we had a garden party for which my mum worked really hard. Lots of girls from my new school came and that was terrific. It was like living a different life. But I was always aware that Mum was desperate for me to fit in with girls who had not come from my kind of background and who had an affluent privileged lifestyle I'd never known. Having gone to the same prep school, they also knew each other very well. I, however, had to make friends from scratch. Although I did make some very good friends in the end, there were times when I felt like a fish out of water. I remember one particularly nasty lesson just before we moved house. We had to stand up and describe the kind of home we lived in, whether it was a semi or a detached house. I was the only girl living in a terraced house. I felt a bit humiliated. But I don't think I would have been so sensitive about this if I hadn't been so aware of how my mother felt. She was very proud, and always wanted to feel that everything that was hers, including her children, was as good as anybody else's.

I can't say I really enjoyed Manchester High. Founded post-suffragette time by liberal-minded philanthropists and pioneers of women's education, it was single-sex, had a high Oxbridge success rate, and its pupils were generally regarded as the *crème de la crème*. It provided a rigorous academic education where you were expected to do well in exams and to be a high achiever in your later career. I'm not sure I would want to subject Chloe, my daughter, to all that. There wasn't much joy in the school, which was ruled by fear, but that was the ethic around at that time. Architecturally, it was a very grand-looking school, with large playing fields and excellent facilities. Our teachers were mostly elderly and, being of the First World War generation, had had fiancés killed in the war. Most of them were single, but not unfortunately *The Prime of Miss Jean Brodie* type. They had no fashion sense, wore sandals and their hair in buns, and some of them were very strict. As I got older, I became more and more rebellious, although I did get through everything; I was a good linguist, did well at O-level German, French and Latin. I then took French at A-level, but didn't want to take German. At a parents' evening, my German teacher told my mum and dad, 'Judy could have been a fine linguist but, sadly, she has fallen by the wayside.' Along with other girls, I had sunk even lower than this by talking to local boys, the very worst of crimes in some of our teachers' eyes.

Girls at my junior school used to talk about the facts of life in the most lurid, graphic terms. But my mother never talked to me about sex. Roger and I used to come home for a cooked lunch and, one day when I was about eight and we were sitting around the table, I remember saying to Mum, 'How do babies come out, then?' Her answer I thought was horrendous and completely shut me up: 'They come out through your bottom,' she replied. So, all I really knew at junior school was that we had 'periods'. But I'd got hold of the wrong end of the stick by being told – and believing – that boys had these, too.

When I was eleven, just before I started at Manchester High, my mother, who had obviously been screwing up her courage, suddenly said, 'Judy, put down that *Bunty*, there's something I want to talk to you about.'

'What?' I said, looking up from my comic.

'I want to talk to you about periods.'

Going bright red, I said, 'I know all about them.'

'You need to,' she added, looking doubtful, 'because obviously when you get to your new senior school, some girls will—'

'Yeah. It's all right, Mum, I know.'

'Well, there's one other thing I have to tell you – and that's how you know when you are pregnant.'

'How?' I said, suddenly interested.

'Your periods stop.'

And that was it; that was our 'facts of life' talk. Mum didn't tell me *how* I got pregnant; but then it was the same for all my friends. Around eleven, we thought that even if we kissed a boy in a game of Postman's Knock we could get pregnant. Then at Manchester High, when we were twelve, the medical department handed us a booklet, *You Are Becoming A*

Woman, which explained everything in a very biological way. The whole thing was pretty joyless, and very alarming.

I lost my virginity at sixteen to my first real boyfriend. He went to the same school as Roger, so we knew each other vaguely before meeting at school dances and then at a party. He was tall, blond and gorgeous. By then, I had a big circle of friends, a really good crowd, and we used to go to parties every Saturday. After we had gone out alone together for the first time, I realized I was mad about him. I remember a friend saying, 'What's the matter with you? You're looking very glum.'

'I've just got a horrible feeling that this is too serious and I'm going to get very hurt,' I replied. Much later, this insight proved to be spot-on.

Boyfriend aside, I had become desperately interested in English and drama and wanted to be an actress. I used to watch wonderful series, such as *Elizabeth R* with Glenda Jackson, on television and dream away. My parents were also interested in drama, and Dad in particular was very literary. Although I wanted to act, I never really believed I would. But I wanted to be involved in that world. To me, it seemed the most exciting thing that could happen. What I didn't want was a nine-to-five job, working as a secretary or a teacher. I was very impressed by Cal's life in Paris and wanted to do something glamorous and meet interesting people.

When I went to Bristol University to do drama and English, it was the first time I had lived away from home. I was miserable, desperately missing my boyfriend with whom I had now been going out for two years. I was a typical sixties' teenager, really into music, especially the Beatles. John Lennon was my favourite. Mum always says the whole world changed during the sixties when the oral contraceptive pill became available, the sex laws and abortion were made more liberal, we had the Profumo, Christine Keeler and Mandy

Rice-Davies sex scandal, and Mods and Rockers running riot in the south coast resorts. And, given what has happened since that so-called 'permissive age', perhaps she's right.

My relationship with my boyfriend was very serious, and continued throughout my first year at university. He was the same age as me but, having had glandular fever, was still in the sixth form when I started at Bristol. Even though he visited me there, and I used to go home to see him, I could hardly bear life without him. Then, when he also got into Bristol, when I was in my second year, we got engaged. We were nineteen. We both thought everything would be wonderful, but it was an absolutely ghastly year. My friends and I were very end-of-sixties: we had long hair and wore hoop earrings and bead necklaces, all conforming to the hippy scene. He could not have been more different. He was a scientist, a physicist, totally involved with political protest. I adored him. But it was hopeless. He was going on anti-Vietnam marches and was really into the whole protest scene. It was all so strange. We began to have lots of rows and it became a very volatile relationship. Finally, at the end of his first year, and after hundreds of rows, he sent me a note saying he had gone to see his sister who was at university in Bath. He did not, he said, know what to do about his life any more.

Reading that filled me with sadness, but he survived this crisis, stayed with his sister for a bit, then worked all that summer on a farm owned by a friend of hers. At the end of the vac, we met and he said our engagement was off. I was devastated. I knew he was right, but I was still shattered. And it was so difficult going back to Bristol for my final year with this completely different set-up. I had started off not giving as much to university as I should because he was all I was really interested in. Now suddenly the present and future had changed and fallen apart. It was very traumatic, but somehow I got through the year, met lots of people, went out with other boyfriends, but there was no significant relationship. I continued to dream about him for ages, even throughout my first marriage. The dreams didn't actually stop until I met Richard.

That first relationship was a very formative influence on my life. It meant I didn't enjoy university as much as I could have done, and affected the next few years because, subconsciously, I was looking for marriage. The end of our engagement did not make me feel, Right, I've got to go off and see the world; it made me think, I want to be married, want to have a family. It was this that propelled me into marriage when I was still too young emotionally, at twenty-five. I had spent so many years thinking about it, I thought the only way to be happy was to find a similar relationship.

On the academic front, having done English and drama at university, I discovered I enjoyed the English far more than the drama. This was partly because a lot of the other students were very extrovert and from posh, well-connected families. Bristol University itself was also posh, and the English and drama course there was tough and demanding. It only took five students from three thousand applicants. The drama department was regarded as an elite and many of the students were the sons or daughters of actors or directors and, having been brought up in theatrical circles, they were supremely self-confident. I was just a girl from Manchester, with no experience of the theatre or moving in up-market circles. I found it all very intimidating.

Now, of course, I can see I was my own worst enemy. Having a boyfriend in Manchester, I would rush off at every opportunity and, therefore, not socialize. Nevertheless, I did find the set-up overwhelming, didn't think I could act and, although I did eventually make some firm friends there, a lot of the drama students were very precious. By the end of the degree, I had definitely decided I did not want to be an actress, but knew I wanted to work in a related field, like the media.

With everything in disarray, I left university, returned to Manchester and did a telephone sales vacation job which lasted nearly a year. I had run up an overdraft of £40, and my dad, who was very money-conscious, was furious and said I had to pay it off. The job didn't need any of my qualifications, so I was always thinking, What do I do now? Shall I go to London? Shall I try to get into journalism or television?

Having done the vac job and paid off the overdraft, I did the best thing I could have done. I went to a college of further education in Manchester, learned how to type and do shorthand and qualified with all the RSA diplomas. I then went down to London where I shared a nice three-bedroomed flat with two schoolfriends in a lovely old terraced house in St Peter's Street, Islington. With house prices being what they are now, I don't know how today's youngsters could possibly afford that but, even though we were only earning peanuts then, we could.

Just before I left to go to London, I had joined a temping agency in Manchester which, by sheer coincidence, had sent me to the BBC in Manchester as a temporary secretary in the children's department. I loved the people and the atmosphere, and found it all so exciting and exhilarating, which confirmed me in my thinking.

So, when I went down to London, although I took a temp job in a chemicals factory to keep body and soul together, I applied for jobs and eventually at the age of twenty-three got an interview with the BBC at Kensington House, Shepherd's Bush. I got a job straight away as a production secretary. It seemed like a dream come true, but it wasn't. I hated the work and soon became very disillusioned. I am just not tidy-minded enough to be a secretary. I didn't mind the shorthand, quite enjoyed that in a funny sort of way, but I loathed the filing.

Anyway, I was desperate to get on the creative side. That was my plan, to get a foot in the door as a secretary, then start applying to boards for a research job or whatever.

Little did I know that every secretary at the BBC had the same idea. Like me, they were all university graduates and, like me, they were all desperate to become researchers and producers. Every time a vacancy came up they would apply to the board, but they hardly ever got an interview. It was senseless trying really. The male graduates always got the jobs and, however bright you were, and especially if you were a secretary, you were overlooked. I only ever met one woman who had made it from secretary to producer, and it had taken her ten years. Good God, I thought, I'm not going to spend the next decade waiting for this.

In despair, I started looking for something else. A school-friend back in Manchester, who had a degree in psychology and was also very interested in TV, had managed to get somewhere. At that time, there was a very good theatre club called the Stables, attached to and funded by Granada Television. A smashing little theatre, with lots of very exciting productions, it was also the Granada bar. My friend, having got a job as a box-office girl, had met lots of people associated with TV and had got a job with Granada on a trainee scheme as a production assistant. Having told me about this, she then wrote again, saying she was leaving, that there was therefore a vacancy, and suggested I get in touch with Mike Scott, the Programme Controller. I applied and got an interview with him in London, at which he said, 'Great, yeah. Go up.' He then set me up with the people in Manchester, and they gave me a job. So I left the BBC, went back to live at home with my parents, then, shortly afterwards, shared a house with some colleagues.

It was a very interesting training scheme which, unfortunately, is no longer in existence. It was for people Granada thought had potential, but no relevant experience in the various fields such as research, vision mixing and so on. It would employ you on a nine-month, non-renewable contract. During this time you were basically used as a runner, a 'gofer', on all the different programmes, doing what the directors and floor-managers told you to do. I worked mainly on drama as the aide between the floor-manager and cast, making sure the actors were on set at the right time. Within those nine months, you had to learn as much about TV production as you possibly could. It was totally unstructured. There were no lessons and it was up to you to talk someone into giving you a job during or at the end of the contract. Six months in, having persuaded a producer to take me on as a researcher on *This is Your Right*, a high-profile consumer affairs regional programme, I started work on that.

The presenter was Michael Winstanley, a well-known local Liberal MP, who later became Lord Winstanley. I was thrilled and found it fascinating. I had to research all aspects of the law and benefits side, put together a programme, which would have all the correct facts to hand, and find the right interviewees. This job also meant I went straight into TV rather than radio work. The first time I came to Hampstead, where Richard and I now live, was to check out a lady from Cruse, the bereavement counselling service. She was very intellectual, but rather scatty and weird. I thought she was absolutely wonderful. I also thought Hampstead was gorgeous, almost countrified, and thought – prophetically as it turned out – I'd love to live there one day.

I was then employed to do some research work for *Granada Reports*, a Granada TV programme, which was where I met David Henshaw, my first husband, in 1973. I was a researcher on *Granada Reports* and David was working in the same building as an on-screen reporter for the same show. We became part of the same circle, were good friends for a while and then our relationship became more serious. I had a lot of admiration and respect for him, as he did for me. He was a clever man with socialist ideals. We believed in the same things, shared a lot of the same values, and just became closer and closer and decided to live together. I knew our relationship was not as intense as the one with my first boyfriend four years before, but I had never expected to feel that way again. I had bought into the whole agony aunt thing when they'd reply to readers' 'I don't know if I'm in love or not – what shall I do?' with, 'A relationship/partnership/marriage is based on much more than love. It is not just a question of sexual attraction and fluttering hearts, it's . . .' This was sort of right, but also rather misleading and *not* right. I had also gone along with 'everybody has one great love in their life and can't really expect another to match up to it'. I thought I had had mine.

I did love David, though, and, initially, we were very close and happy. He was quite adventurous and loved travelling, and I was perfectly open to all that. When he was at Cambridge, he had spent a year lecturing at the University of Vermont and, having thoroughly enjoyed that, had always wanted to go back to Canada and the US. So, once we were living together, we decided to leave our jobs at Granada and go and see, despite the green card situation, if we could get work there.

First, we flew to Toronto, where David had friends; then we went to Vermont and Boston; then to New York. Our living conditions in the 'big apple' were absolutely horrendous. We were staying in Manhattan with a girl whom David had known only briefly, and the two-roomed flat was squalid and infested with cockroaches. We were also broke, reduced to living on five dollars a day and only able to afford the most basic of burgers. We then went to Washington, but I was getting fed up. We were nearly out of money, still unemployed and I realized it wasn't going to work out. So we returned to New York for Christmas, then came back to England.

Once home, David didn't want to go back to Granada in Manchester, but to Norwich. His mother lived on the Essex/Suffolk border and, having done his degree at Cambridge, he knew the area well. He applied for a reporter's job on Anglia Television, and got it. So we bought a house in the centre of Norwich, between a church and the cathedral, and I found work as a secretary in the town hall. But I was not happy. I loathed the work and applied for a researcher's job at Anglia. When I went for the interview, though, I was told they were not looking for a researcher, they were looking for an on-screen reporter. They had never had a woman in this job before, but rather liked the idea.

'How would you feel about that?' I was asked.

'I haven't really thought about it,' I replied, astonished.

So, an audition was suggested, and the upshot was my first really big break. Anglia offered me the job and I was appointed as its first on-screen woman presenter.

By now, although David and I had been very discreet about living together, our parents were desperate to know when we intended to get married. I also wanted to get married, and had always seen myself as married. So, as we were both agnostics, we decided against a church ceremony and had the service at Manchester Registry Office on 23 March 1974, followed by a reception at Manchester's Midland Hotel. I was twenty-five.

Three months after the wedding, I started work at Anglia. The next three years, learning on the job, were incredibly useful. It was very special and, to this day, I still think a television news reporter's job on a local station is one of the hardest and most intense learning curves in existence. Every day at eight thirty there was a news conference with the news editor, and we had to be up to scratch on current affairs and come up with ideas. Once our suggestions were accepted, we had to set it all up, probably by spending an hour on the phone getting people for interviews and then organizing the camera crew.

Anglia covered a huge area and it was not unusual to go from Norwich to Southend and back in a day. I'd dash down, do the interview, write the script in the car and do my pieces to camera. I was lucky. I have an extremely good memory. Then I'd come scooting back and, in those days of film rather than video like now, I'd take the film to the lab to be processed, at least a fifty-minute job. Then I'd dash to an editing room, sit there with the editor constructing the story, do the voice-overs in the booth and then, having got my three- or five-minute piece passed, would go and write the script for the links. It was absolutely exhausting but, by God, it was brilliant training. You had to learn how to make silk purses out of sow's ears because, however disappointing the story when you got there, however grim the interview, you had to make it entertaining, both in language and pictures.

I loved this work, and don't think I ever envisaged giving it up to become a full-time wife and mother, but when I was twenty-seven my maternal instincts really kicked in. I don't know where these ideas come from! David was kind of 'okay', but I think he found the thought of having children a lot more daunting than I did.

I definitely wanted several children and wanted to spend time with them. I also remember, though, being very glad that the Employment Protection Act had just come into force and that this meant pregnant women couldn't be forced out of a job.

When, aged twenty-seven, I did become pregnant, I was thrilled. I had the normal GP check-ups and my young doctor would say things like, 'Hmm, you must be having a big baby,' but there were no routine scans as there are now. I didn't want to have the baby in hospital, and had decided on the 'domino scheme' where you went into a nursing home for the birth and returned home the same day or day after. It wasn't until I was thirty-two weeks' pregnant, when I went to register at the home and the midwife checked me over, that anybody said, 'Umm, are you sure you've got the dates right?'

'Yes, I'm absolutely certain,' I replied.

'Umm, just a minute, I'm going to fetch one of my colleagues.'

Oh, dear, I thought, panicked.

When she came back with another midwife, they both palpated my stomach, looked at each other and the first one said, 'D'you see what I mean?'

'Yes, I think I can feel two heads,' the second one replied.

I really flipped then, nearly fainted, didn't twig they meant two babies; I thought they meant one with two heads.

Then the first one said, 'We think you're having a multiple-birth pregnancy.'

'How many?' I asked weakly.

'Twins,' she replied.

I sank back, at least comforted by the thought that two babies would account for the two heads.

'You'll have to go to the hospital to have an X-ray but, first, we'll refer you back to your GP.'

So, off I went carrying a card that said, 'Query twins?'

When I arrived in the Anglia newsroom where David was working, he said, 'Everything all right?'

'You'd better sit down,' I replied. 'They think we're having twins.'

His reaction was really quite funny. I'd never actually seen a person go white before, with beads of sweat literally breaking out on the forehead. But the thought of twins was a tremendous shock for both of us.

When I got home, I tried to persuade myself that the midwives were wrong. It was my first baby; I had fantasized for months about what it would be like, how it would feel to hold my son or daughter for the first time, and I couldn't adjust that quickly to the thought of two. It was an alien concept. I couldn't believe I would love them both in the same way that I would have loved one; I couldn't believe I would be able to cope. The next time I saw my GP, I thought the problem was resolved. Having looked at the referral card, he said, 'Twins? Ridiculous.' He then got out his ear-trumpet, listened and said, 'I can only hear one heartbeat.' He felt my tummy again and added, 'There's only one baby in there. I'll stake my reputation on that.'

At the Norfolk and Norwich Hospital, however, where, having been X-rayed, I was sitting waiting for the results, the consultant came over to me and said, 'Come in. Would you like to sit down?'

'Why? What?' I said.

'Just take a look at that X-ray,' she replied.

And there, unmistakably, were two babies. One, which turned out to be Dan, was lying in the breech position, his bottom, spine and head clearly visible; the other one, Tom, was lying arched over Dan's head, the two of them forming a distinct T-shape.

'Clearly,' the consultant said, 'you will need to come into the Norfolk and Norwich very soon. I've hardly ever diagnosed twins this late, and with twin pregnancies we have to be careful you do not go into labour early. So we'll book a bed for you at the end of this week.'

Well! I hadn't even left work, and had planned to stay on until thirty-six weeks. Now I had to leave in a huge hurry. My colleagues gave me a good send-off, bought me a twin pushchair, and the Head of News said, 'We all agree here that you are by far the best woman reporter on the ITV network.' I was really touched; I thought that was great, wonderful.

I then went into hospital. I had been to all the National

Childbirth Trust classes, where the big thing was natural childbirth, no drugs. If you had pethidine, you were a wimp, not doing the right thing by your baby. But, suddenly, the resident consultant told me that, because of the way the babies were lying, I would have to have a Caesarean. It was silly to be upset, but I was. When I protested, he didn't help by making me feel really stupid: 'I am sure that you will want to do what is best for your babies,' he said, and strode off leaving me feeling horribly selfish.

The twins were due on 10 March 1977, but the hospital decided to do the Caesarean on 2 March. Epidurals, the spinal-block injections, were in their infancy then, but the anaesthetist said, 'This will be much better for you than a general anaesthetic and you will be able to see the babies born.' But he couldn't get the needle in. It was absolutely agonizing. When I said, 'Please, I just can't take any more,' he replied, 'Okay, we'll put you out.' And I knew nothing after that.

When I came round, I remember David saying, 'We've got two little boys and they are both perfect.' The next morning when I woke up, I was aware that something momentous had happened, but there were no babies beside me. Where were they? I rang the bell and said, 'Please can I see my babies?' And, when they brought them, they were gorgeous, perfect.

I had a horrible time in hospital and really loathed it. I was in a main ward and the only mother with twins. The nursing staff never put twin-birth mothers together on the same ward because it was too much work for one team. The problem was everyone else was getting bathing and feeding done in half the time I was. I was struggling to do all the right 'Sheila Kitzinger' things, such as breastfeeding. I knew this doyenne of the natural childbirth movement had had twins and I had read all her books, and remembered her saying, 'There's no reason why you shouldn't be able to breastfeed twins at the same time.' But it was ridiculous; as fast as I'd get one fixed, the other would slip off the nipple. I found it very upsetting and felt inadequate. But, then, all new mothers do. I also ended up having nothing to eat because every meal was brought in when I was doing something with the babies and taken away before I'd finished.

Doctors kept saying, 'Don't lift anything heavier than the baby,' but I was given no choice. The water for bathing them was in plastic buckets, which I had to lift and empty into a plastic bath. I got very low and tired, and just wanted to get out, especially as my mother was coming down to help. It was a panicky time. The twins were both absolutely adorable, but I was getting so distressed caring for two that I used to go for ten-minute walks in my nightie and dressing-gown, only to find a very disapproving nurse waiting by my bed.

Perhaps maternity wards are not so bad now, but that time was the height of the baby-bonding era and it was considered politically correct to have your babies with you all the time, including the night, even when you were recovering from a major operation. It was awful. When I finally got out, Mum and Dad came down from Manchester and my mother stayed for a month. I honestly don't know what I'd have done without her. She was great. It's all hands on deck when you have twins, and I have to say David was very good about helping to feed them during the night but, like most men, he found the reality of having twins a bit of a shock. He certainly always admitted that he wasn't the world's most marvellous father when Dan and Tom were babies, but he's been a very good father to them ever since.

There was no history of twins in my family or David's. My theory is that I'd been on the pill for such a long time that when I came off it my body took a long time to get back to normal and my ovaries released two eggs, allowing me to conceive fraternal twins. On the other hand, Dan and

Tom could be identical twins from one egg splitting into two. I've never had the blood test to prove this. There was some dissension about whether their placentas were fused or not. Identical twins have one, fraternal twins have two. But then again, fraternal twins can have placentas that are fused together so they look like one. My twins, though, are so alike in height, build, hair colouring, walk and the way they stand, that sometimes even I have to look twice before saying their names.

When I first became pregnant with the boys, the plan was for me to take maternity leave and return to Anglia Television after six months. But a month before I was due to go back, David got a new job back in Manchester. This was good for me because the twins were such hard work I needed my parents and friends. David's job was with the BBC's *File on Four*, the first edition of what was to become Radio 4's flagship political programme. He was thrilled to be asked to launch it, wanted to travel, and I was happy to go back to Manchester.

I didn't work then. We stayed at my parents' house until we found our own in Fallowfield, just a short walk away from their home in Birchfields Road. David's career was now going very well, and he was away a great deal. At first he was a radio reporter, then a radio producer, then a TV producer and was often abroad for several weeks at a time. He loved it. But I was lonely and in tears a lot of the time, and found being a full-time mum very restrictive. I joined a mother and baby group and made some good friends there, but I was still on my own too often. I'd intended to stay at home with the twins until they started school but, because I was so lonely, I couldn't stand it any more.

The last straw was Easter 1980, when the twins were just three. David was in Rome for three weeks, all my friends were away with their children, and even my parents had gone on holiday. I was home alone with Tom and Dan who were going down with German measles, and I was getting no sleep at all. The only adult I saw during this time was the milkman when I paid his bill. I was at the end of my tether and remember that when David rang up, I told him I couldn't bear it, I was getting so claustrophobic I had to go back to work. That same weekend I sat down and wrote to Mike Scott at Granada, saying, 'Remember me? I have had my babies and I would like to come back.'

Nowadays, I don't regret my time at home with the twins one jot. It was enriching. We became incredibly close during those years and still have a very strong bond. I just wish I'd done some basic things, such as learning to drive, because it was so hard managing two babies in a double pushchair on public transport. I did learn to drive eventually, but not until the twins were seven and not before I had failed my test six times. I enjoyed the local mother and baby group meetings in each other's houses, but the evenings, when I was on my own so much, and the nights, when the boys were not sleeping and I was getting up all the time, were awful.

When I had left Granada I was a researcher but, thanks to Anglia, I now had on-screen experience. Fortunately, when I got in touch with my former boss, he asked me to come in for an eight-minute audition, talking to camera. Despite the fact that I hated football I chose Manchester United as my subject. I'd grown up listening to Dad and my two brothers rhapsodizing about their beloved team, the Red Devils, and Old Trafford, and could have talked the hind legs off a donkey on that topic.

I was then told that I would not hear anything for some time. So we went to stay with friends in Norfolk. This meant nobody was answering the phone at our house and, one day, my mother rang to say that she'd called in and there was a telegram for me from the Head of News at Granada. It said: Please, please, I can't get anybody to answer your phone. Mike

Scott is desperate to see and talk to you before he goes on holiday. So we drove home and the next day I went to see Mike Scott. After three and a half years off the scene, I could hardly believe my luck. He offered me a job as a news reporter on *Granada Reports*.

The biggest shadow towards the end of that year, 1980, created a shock wave not only throughout the world of entertainment and the media, but worldwide among all the people who had ever loved the Beatles. John Lennon, whose music had inspired an entire generation, was shot dead at point-blank range on 8 December by Mark Channon, a mentally disturbed fan to whom, earlier that same day, he had given his autograph. This tragic event had occurred as John was walking into the Dakota Building, New York, with his wife Yoko. It was astonishing how upset my generation was, how we bonded in grief.

After so long away, I was very nervous when I first returned to work, but David was fantastic with me. On my first day I had to do a farming story in Cheshire and, the night before, David sketched it all out for me, the interview, pictures, speaking to camera, script. And, with that kind of template under my belt, I was fine.

At first, I wanted to work part-time but, given the nature of the job, that didn't work out. Granada, though, was very understanding and said I could do a four-day week. I had a six-month contract and comforted myself with the thought that if this didn't work out with the boys, if they were not happy, I would not renew the contract. But it was fine. Tom and Dan were already going to playgroup and nursery by then, and had settled in really well. I watched them like a hawk though because, like most working mothers, I felt guilty about leaving them. My first nanny left after six weeks because her husband was offered a job in another part of the country. She just wrote a note one Friday, saying she wouldn't be turning up on the Monday morning. That was difficult! But Mum was a great help. She took the twins to playgroup, had them in the afternoons, and I picked them up on my way home.

Sadly, my hope that being back at work again would take the pressure off my relationship with David was not to be realized. He was away so much we were becoming strangers, and drifting further and further apart. Also, despite the fact that I had gone back to work, I very much wanted more children. People, including David, couldn't understand this and kept saying: 'Why? You've got a ready-made family, two at one go.' My answer was: 'I never wanted a ready-made family, never wanted to get it all over and done with.' I wanted several more children and I wanted to have them over a number of years. But David didn't and this became a big issue between us. I tried hard not to give up on our marriage, but it proved impossible. Later, after he remarried, he had two more children.

We were also very short of money. We had bought the house in Manchester, but David wasn't earning that much. In fact, to my immense surprise, when I got the letter offering me the job at Granada, the salary was as much as David's at the BBC. Considering his experience, this was ridiculous. But ITV in those days had a lot more money. I felt empowered to be earning and it was the best thing all round for me to be back at work, but our marriage continued to flounder.

When I was promoted from news reporter to on-screen presenter on Granada's network programme *Reports Action*, where Joan Bakewell and Anna Ford had preceded me in the hot seat, I found working in a live studio a very different kettle of fish. It was very nerve-racking. Sometimes the only way I could get through a programme was to go to the ladies' loo, sit there and say to myself, 'Look, nobody has forced you to do this job, and there's no point in doing it if you're so nervous you can't enjoy it. You want to do it, you want to do it well, so you've got to stop being so stupid and enjoy it. Get out there and *do it*.' Giving myself a good talking-to worked, and it's something that, along with deep breathing and relaxation exercises, I still do when faced with a particularly testing situation. I love live presentation and really enjoy talking to people and being a communicator.

Then, one day on *Granada Reports*, when I was now aged thirty-four and well into my stride as a senior on-screen presenter, the Head of News came in and told me that John Huntley, one of my co-presenters, was leaving and was about to be replaced by a new guy. Would I be his 'mummy'?

'Of course,' I said. 'What's his name?'

'Richard Madeley,' was the reply.

3: RICHARD

I blew what savings I had – about £500 – on a second-hand white Triumph Spitfire, and headed north to start the Radio Carlisle job. It was the early summer of 1976, and I was just short of twenty. I drove out of London with everything I owned stuffed into the tiny boot and space behind the two seats. It was a scorching hot day, and the top was down.

I had no idea then how traumatic this leap into the north was going to be for me. My family were all in the south; so were all my mates and girlfriends. I began to realize I was leaving behind a very nice little number. I knew my way round London, was growing up fast and had made lots of useful contacts. It was a good life and an exciting time: supersonic travel had just taken off with Concorde's first commercial flight from London to Bahrain; the Liberal leader, Jeremy Thorpe, had resigned after weeks of Westminster gossip about his homosexuality; the National Theatre was scheduled to open on the South Bank. Meanwhile, my paper had had a great month for stories and, as I swung on to the M1 and left London behind, I suddenly asked myself what I was doing. I was headed for a city of which I knew nothing. I didn't know a soul there, and didn't know the first thing about radio.

Somewhere near Birmingham I had a blow-out and the tyre couldn't be repaired. The new one cost me almost every penny I had, and I remembered I wouldn't get my first pay-cheque for another month.

I rolled into Carlisle at about seven on a May evening. In my shirt pocket was an address for some digs that Radio Carlisle had fixed up for me, but there was only breakfast on offer – no evening meal. I was starving, and didn't even have enough money to pay for the petrol back to London. In the space of one car journey, my optimism had evaporated and I felt miserable. I found a corner shop, and bought some bread and milk, and asked for a jar of peanut butter.

'You want some what?' asked the guy in the shop.

'Peanut butter, please.'

He looked troubled. 'Right,' he said. 'I'll . . . be right with you.'

He disappeared behind a screen of plastic strips. I waited for about five minutes, then pinged the bell on the counter. Nothing happened, so I called out a couple of times. Finally, he shuffled slowly back and I realized he'd been hoping I'd gone.

'Peanut butter?'

'Right,' he said lamely. He went round to the fridge and got out a pack of Anchor.

'That's not peanut butter. What's the matter with you?'

He blushed deeply, and muttered that he'd never heard of it.

To this day, I do not believe that Carlisle was a stranger to peanut butter. I think my shopkeeper must have had a screw loose. But it was the perfect end to the perfect day!

Fuck me, where have I come to? I thought, as I left the shop.

I went to my bedsit and tried to feel excited about the next morning. Then I gave up, and went to sleep.

The really big problem for me to begin with at Radio Carlisle was that, although the people were lovely and really considerate, the senior ones were all *very* BBC – the 'old school' – a breed apart. Some had been with the corporation for years. The station manager had worked for Radio 4, producing the *Today* programme in its sedate days before Brian Redhead and the feisty John Humphreys came on to the scene. Others had been with British Forces Broadcasting. All of them were completely unlike the young London journalists I was used to. In their thirties and forties, they had a different code, different values.

The station was called Radio Carlisle, but it felt like an outpost to Radio 4. Or so I thought at first. In fact, I had misjudged them all, but I was very nervous and out of my depth. I tried to keep up a confident, cheerful front, but actually I was not waving, I was drowning.

In the first few weeks, depending on shifts, we all used to go over to a hotel to have lunch together. But I was still feeling awkward and isolated. I had no conversation; couldn't think of a thing to say. They were trying hard to make me feel welcome and involved, but I couldn't keep rattling on about my local newspaper days, and most days I'd slip away with my beer to the gents and sit in the loo reading a paper. Pathetic, really. Two things pulled me round. One was the rapid arrival of two other young reporters who, like me, had started on newspapers, Chris Conybeer and the wonderfully named Tony Nutter. We learned the ropes together.

The other was the patience and kindness of the older producers. I began to realize that most of them were very skilled technically and editorially, and I could learn a lot from them. By the late summer my crisis of confidence was over and I began enjoying myself.

I was a contract reporter. I came in at nine in the morning as the station's desk journalist. I would news-gather by phone, talking to police, fire stations, and follow up stories in that day's local papers. I'd write them up, then read them out on air for the hourly news bulletins. As the clock headed towards one o'clock and our main news programme of the day, I'd work with the producer and news editor to develop stories for that. Before when I was covering news, I'd have to wait days to see the story published. Now I was working to hourly deadlines and it was fantastically stimulating.

I was given a crash course in how to drive the programme desk and to edit tape. By the end of the first week I was given a big Uher reel-to-reel tape recorder (about twenty times bigger and heavier than the tiny digital units radio reporters use now). And, although I hadn't quite mastered the desk, I could use it efficiently enough for mixing my reports. I loved all that, enjoyed editing, found the whole thing fascinating. Best of all, I was allowed to get behind a live microphone. I could hardly believe that I was now 'a broadcaster'.

In radio you are absolutely front line of breaking news, and I loved that. Radio's the fastest and simplest medium of the lot. It beats television, the internet, everything, and my new job more than compensated for my continuing personal loneliness in Carlisle.

Then I nearly got the sack.

As anybody who has ever met me – or seen me on telly – knows, I speak very quickly. You should have heard me when I was twenty. Words sprayed out like bullets from a Uzi. Every day the news editor – my line boss – would pull me up and say, 'Richard, you're still reading too quickly. We have a lot of oldies phoning in to say, "Who is that new newsreader? We can't understand half of what he says. Tell him to slow down, for God's sake." Play your transmission tape back, then read literally at half speed. You've simply got to crack this.'

'Okay, okay,' I muttered. I listened to recordings of myself and tingled with embarrassment. I sounded like someone who had just swallowed a handful of uppers and drunk thirty cups of coffee. Totally wired. I tried to slow down but, within a couple of bulletins, I would slowly but surely slip back to top speed again. My friend Chris called me Ferrari Madeley: 'You go from nought to sixty words in five seconds, Rich!' But it was no joke and, after one particularly fast delivery,

I was summoned to a formal meeting with the news editor and – worryingly – the Personnel Officer. My boss, Stuart Campbell, could be terrifying when he was on the warpath.

'You're still on three months' probation,' he said coldly. 'We know you're trying, but you're not succeeding. You're just too damn fast. We can't just keep you on to compile copy and not read the news. You have to do both. If you can't do this by tomorrow, you're sacked. It's as simple as that. We don't want to do this, Richard, but I promise you we will.' He leaned forward. 'If you don't fix this here and now, bonny lad, you're out on your ear. Go home and think about it.'

One of the reasons I had joined the BBC was because I thought it would give me better training and better career prospects than the then fledgling commercial stations. And the career move had pleased my parents. They were proud that their son was working for the BBC. Now it looked as though he was going to be sacked.

So I went back to my bedsit with a tape recorder and a sheaf of old stories and for the rest of the day read at the prescribed speed of three words a second. Inside my head it sounded about the right pace for announcing the death of the Queen, but on playback I could see Stuart was right. Next day I nervously sat down to read the ten o'clock bulletin. On top of every page I had written in huge black letters: 'Slow! Slow! Slow-Slow-Slow!' I did the same all day. Stuart called me in before I finished my shift.

'Right,' he told me. 'That's better. But if you ever go back to your Formula 1 delivery, I'll personally kick your arse all the way back to London.'

He nearly didn't have to. That week I charged off to Carlisle railway station to doorstep Willie Whitelaw, who was then MP for Penrith and the Borders. When I got there, Willie was already on the train and I breathlessly interviewed him as he stood in the carriage doorway. Just as I finished the guard blew his whistle. I slammed the door shut. The train moved off. And so did I; the Uher's carrying strap was caught in the door, the other was around my neck, and the train, tape deck and reporter were accelerating gently but smoothly out of the station.

There was a huge kerfuffle with Willie and me, both of us convinced I was about to be dragged to my death as he struggled to reopen the door while I sprinted down the platform. Finally, I managed to get the strap off my neck as Willie simultaneously unjammed the other end. The Uher smashed to the ground in pieces, and my last sighting of our former Home Secretary was a hand waving helplessly from the window.

Most of my new colleagues were married. We'd have a few drinks after work and then they'd go home. The social scene in Carlisle was surprisingly busy, but I didn't know anyone so I wasn't involved. Work was settling down and during the day I was happy, but the evenings were lonely in my bedsit. Then I met the 'girl downstairs'. She was called Lynda Hooley and we first came face to face when she came out of her flat into the hall. I was twenty and she was twenty-seven, and we liked each other straight away. She had a very upbeat style, and when we went out for a drink I began to cheer up for the first evening in months.

Lynda worked as manageress in the Chelsea Girl boutique in Carlisle. We began meeting up in our lunch break, when I got one, and because I lived above her it was easy to build a relationship. And that was exactly what I needed – a relationship. Inside a few weeks we were living together and by the autumn we'd rented a bungalow out in the Cumbria countryside, and set up home together. Within a few weeks of moving in, I asked her to marry me, and she said, 'Yes.'

By 31 July 1977 we were walking up the aisle of a tiny

country church at the foot of the Caldbeck Fells, our slightly astonished parents the only witnesses to our marriage. Yet already there had been ominous signs: huge and exhausting arguments over nothing; rows neither of us had experienced in previous relationships.

It's only in recent years that I've been able to work out why I moved so quickly in my relationship with Lynda. I'd had plenty of girlfriends in London, but I'd never lived with anyone before. Looking back after more than a quarter-century, I think I was the problem. I was superficially mature with my journalistic experience, but emotionally I was hardly out of the egg. I was much too young to make important decisions such as who to pledge to spend the rest of my life with, but my need for love and affection and stability in my new environment simply overwhelmed me. This turned out to be very unfair on Lynda. She took me at face value and I was too relieved to have found an anchor in my life to question what I was doing. Idiot.

If my parents thought that I was making a mistake, they certainly didn't say so. My London friends were surprised that I married so quickly, but assumed that I knew what I was up to. Well, I didn't and five stormy years later the marriage collapsed. More on that later. Anyway, we had our wedding reception at a pretty hotel in Cockermouth, and spent our wedding night at the Elizabethan Feathers Hotel in Ludlow, Shropshire. We were both happy and it all felt properly romantic and honeymoony. We had very little money, so we drove to Brentwood and spent a few days at home. Only Mum was there; Dad was away all week on a business trip; but he came back on the Saturday and we all had dinner together. Then Lynda and I drove to Somerset for a few days. We'd be back from there much sooner than expected.

We were staying on a caravan site at Wookey Hole. On our second day – a Monday – we got back from the beach to find a message for me to ring home. Apparently it was 'very urgent'.

I knew straight away that something was wrong. As I walked quickly to the public call box, I couldn't think of one good reason for my parents to ring me.

The phone at home had barely begun to ring when my mother picked it up. She was very calm.

'Your father died at one o'clock this afternoon. He was in my arms. He had a massive heart attack.'

I can't remember much about the rest of the conversation. I think I stuttered that we would be home as soon as possible and, quite literally, I reeled out of the phone booth. My ears were ringing and I couldn't keep my balance.

It was a sunny August afternoon. I was on honeymoon. It all seemed utterly unreal. I flopped down on a low wall alongside the phone box. You don't expect your legs to literally give way when you get a shock but, believe me, they do. I lit a cigarette and just sat there, paralysed. When I tried to stand up, to walk back and tell Lynda what had happened, I couldn't. I remember people walking along the village path from the campsite to the shops, and I had an intense desire to stop them, to tell them my father had just died. God knows why. But, anyway, I couldn't even speak. My tongue was pressed rigidly against the roof of my mouth. After a very long time I managed to stand up, and walked very slowly back to Lynda.

She'd become extremely fond of my father. I can still remember her screams of horror when I told her the news. We packed and left for London.

My father's death was a brutal shock for all of us. He had no history of heart problems at all, although his father had had a coronary a few years earlier, and recovered. But Dad must have had an inkling the day he'd died. He'd gone to work, and afterwards his colleagues told us they'd heard him on the phone talking about his business trip the week before. He'd had to hump a lot of video equipment around which, in the late 1970s, was heavy, bulky stuff. They heard him say,

'Thanks for the loan of the VCR, but it was bloody heavy. I'm really sore today. I think I've pulled a muscle in my chest.'

The next thing they knew, he'd vanished. I believe he must have realized what was happening to him. Many heart-attack victims who survive say they were overtaken by a desperate urge to get home as the attack began. And that's what Dad did. He only lived a mile away from his office, and he lunched at home.

My mother, who always liked to look pretty for him, was upstairs in the bedroom putting on fresh make-up, when she heard a lot of fumbling by the front door. It was too early, she thought, for it to be my father and she went downstairs to investigate. Finally Dad managed to get his key in the lock and staggered in, looking terrible. His car was slewed diagonally across the drive. The driver's door was open and papers and stuff had fallen out on to the ground. Dad looked straight at Mum and said, 'I think I'm having a heart attack.'

She helped him on to a sofa in the front room, loosened his tie and tried to help. The pain was coming in waves and Dad was very distressed. Mum called the doctor, and rang for an ambulance. But by now my father, although still conscious, was in a bad way. The journalist in him was still there, though. All reporters have a special relationship with their expenses, and Dad was no exception. He managed to tell Mum that he'd left his expenses from the week before under the seat of his car! Then it all happened very fast. He drew in a final deep breath, and simply died there in her arms.

Mum wasn't trained in resuscitation, but she did her best to revive him, as did the doctor when he arrived, but it was a massive attack. Dad, at least, had made it home to die with his wife holding him, and not at some office desk. It gave us all a tiny crumb of comfort.

He was just forty-nine. We were totally unprepared. My sister, who had herself only been married a couple of months, arrived with her husband and we tried to rally round each other. But that first day was horrible. Eventually everyone went to bed, but the sound of my mother's tortured sobbing all through the night still haunts me. Her own heart was broken.

———

Lynda and I were happy for a time, but the cracks appeared pretty soon. Whatever might have happened in that marriage – and I am not making any excuses – there's no doubt that my father's abrupt death was not a good beginning. The honeymoon, quite literally, was over. My grieving affected our relationship during the first year, and perhaps for longer. Lynda tried to be there for me, but I was very low. It took me ages to get over Dad's death. My focus should have been on our marriage, but it wasn't.

Nothing particularly shattering happened between Lynda and me over the following months, but the dreadful wearing rows returned. I remember my mother coming to stay, four months after my father died. Lynda and I were going at it hammer and tongs about something or other, and we ended up going out to our woodshed for the ferocious conclusion. When I came back in, absolutely drained, my mother said, 'Good God, Richard, what are the two of you doing to each other? Why are you rowing like this?'

I couldn't answer. I hardly knew myself what the rows were really about. We did have happy times – days when we enjoyed each other's company – but the rows were so damaging, so draining. After a colossal one, towards the end of our first year, feeling very unhappy and knowing our marriage was not working, I was unfaithful.

I've thought very hard about how to describe this bad time. Years later when *This Morning* had made Judy and me well known in Britain, a lot of what happened in my first marriage came back to haunt me in lurid tabloid 'monsterings'. Friends and family urged me to tell my side of the story.

I actually did write it all down for this book – corrected all the slurs and daft exaggerations and, of course, in doing so, made my own criticisms of Lynda.

When I read it back, though, it was singularly unedifying and frankly looked as cheap as the kiss 'n' tells I've had to put up with. There may be two sides to the story of a failed marriage, but my instincts have always been to avoid nasty games of post-marital ping-pong. Of course, Lynda has to take responsibility for her part in our marriage mistakes – although I don't believe she was ever unfaithful to me – but it was all so long ago. We were both extremely young, and I just don't have the heart for a set-the-record-straight chapter on what was, after all, a private marriage. I let it all go a long time ago and I don't think my reputation is important enough to warrant some belated counter-attack. That aside, I don't want to say anything unpleasant at all about Lynda. She formed another relationship, had a child, and, I believe, found happiness. I wish her nothing but the best.

We sometimes talked about whether we should have children but Lynda, to her credit, always said, 'I don't think we should. We don't get on well enough to risk it.' It was a shrewd opinion and significant, too. I remember her adding: 'Let's wait and see whether we are going to stay together.' I really do think that at some level we both knew that one day the game would be up for our marriage, but neither of us wanted to admit it. No one likes to fail.

————

I needed a couple of weeks off to get over the first shock of Dad's death. Then I went back to Radio Carlisle and, almost straight away, was made a producer working on the *Breakfast Show* – the news-talk programme. This is the flagship slot of any radio station, and it meant me getting in at about half past four in the mornings. I detested the early starts, but I loved the job.

Output producing can be nerve-racking. You're making fine-call judgements every minute about when to chop out of an interview, take a phone call or break a story. We ran national and local news side by side, on the American model; and the presenter, Chris Rogers, was a fluent and confident role model for me. I learned a lot from him and eventually began hosting the Saturday morning magazine and filling in for Chris on some weekdays.

This was my first real taste of presenting and it simultaneously terrified and excited me. I made some terrible cock-ups: I once turned two pages of script at once and found myself babbling thanks to the newsreader for giving us the headlines before he'd even started. My time-checks were slightly less reliable than a broken watch – at least that's right twice a day – and under pressure I still tended to speed up and mispronounce words. Some mornings I'd sign off air at nine o'clock damp with sweat and hot with shame.

But things progressed and one day I was having a drink with a reporter from Border Television, Tony Baker. A job was coming up there because Jeremy Hands – who later covered the Falklands War for ITN – was leaving.

'If you can just stop talking so fucking fast,' Tony said, 'I reckon you're in with a chance.'

I was twenty-two and thought I'd be too young, but I went for it and found myself opposite Derek Batey who, as well as hosting Border's one network show of *Mr and Mrs*, was also head of the station's programming. The interview went better than I'd expected and Derek told me he was seriously considering me for the job.

'But how will you be with the fame thing?' he asked.

I was so focused on the technical skills I would need to

learn as a TV reporter that the 'fame thing' had hardly occurred to me.

'How do you mean?' I replied.

'If you do this job,' Derek replied, 'you will quickly become very well known in the region. Think of what's happened to the other reporters, think of Jeremy. Your face, like theirs, will become instantly recognizable. People will come up to you. I'm not saying this either to frighten or excite you but, within three months of being on the box most nights, everything you do will come under scrutiny. You will feel watched in the streets. And if you make it to a network TV show any skeletons in your closet will come tumbling out.

'At this stage, you will just be a reporter for little Border Television, but you need to think about all this carefully. A career on camera can bring unexpected problems and tensions and pressures. Up to now you have been a newsman but, like it or not, you will soon also be a "personality". Take stock. Think hard. It will have an impact on your life. And we – and you – need to know that you can handle that.'

'Oh, I'll be fine,' I said, not taking him very seriously.

Derek sighed. 'No, you're not listening to me.'

He then explained in a very self-deprecatory way how *Mr and Mrs* had transformed his life.

'For God's sake,' he said, 'that's just a little quiz show. But it changed my life in ways I could never have imagined, not all of them pleasant. The same could happen to you. The company can give you a few guidelines on how to deal with it, but take it seriously, and don't decide until the morning.'

Still thinking he was over-exaggerating or being self-aggrandizing – actually he wasn't and he was spot-on – I pretended to mull it over. I phoned up the next morning and flannelled away about having weighed everything up very carefully, and said I felt I could handle the 'fame thing'. An older and wiser me would have taken a lot longer than one night to think things through. But that was me. Over-confident, and prone to rush into things.

Later that same day I had a hand-delivered letter telling me I'd got the job.

I cut my teeth at Border. It was a very small company; the only smaller one in those days was Channel Television. A lot of people began their careers at Border, among them, as I said, Jeremy Hands and Liz Howell (who went on to launch GMTV). It was a good starting point and, because it was small, it was a very friendly place to work.

Behind a radio mike, nobody can see you shaking. My first night on screen was terrifying. I had to present a short news item for Border's *News and Look Around*. I went into make-up and got a real confidence boost straight away when the woman in there told me bluntly that I had 'a very bent nose'.

'Oh, dear!' she said, looking worried. 'We'll have to do something about this nose of yours, won't we?'

So, I sat there having a dark line drawn down the centre of my nose and what looked like Tipp-Ex painted on one side of it.

'Hmm,' she said. 'It still looks really bent – almost corkscrew-shaped.'

I tottered into the studio feeling like something out of a freak show. Why had no one ever told me about my deformity before? As usual when I was nervous I began perspiring freely and the dark crayon on my nose began to run down on to my top lip. I caught my reflection in a camera lens and thought I looked like Hitler.

I can't remember what the first report was about. My main sensation was of being very exposed. This seems odd now because I'm so used to being on camera. But then, to be seen as well as heard felt like walking into a party stark-naked. I sat behind the desk, my left knee trembling so violently the microphone on the table vibrated in sympathy. Of course, it's the same for most live TV virgins. Brand-new newsreaders all sit there with their hands clasped tightly in front of them – a great mountain of fingers with white knuckles – because it gives an illusion that they have a grip on the situation. I wonder more of us don't pass out the first time we go on air.

Somehow I survived my first studio appearance. Then I managed to break the camera on my first location story. I'd gone out with a film crew to do a report on the RAC Lombard Rally, which was going through a section of the Kielder Forest. All we really needed to do was get a few shots of cars belting round the track to back up the interviews with a couple of drivers. But I wanted something special for my first-ever report. The world-weary cameraman looked at me. 'Well, go on, you're the reporter. What do you want?'

'Well,' I said, thinking fast, 'how about when the next car comes into the checkpoint, you put the camera just behind his back wheel. Then we'll get a great shot of the tyres spinning as he pulls away.'

The cameraman's face was expressionless. 'Fine,' he said. 'You're the boss.'

A whole screed of gravel went straight into the lens of the camera and shattered it.

I didn't get the story, didn't get the shot. Our only camera was broken and we were miles from base. It was a disaster. We knocked off for an early lunch and then went back to the studio.

So my first week ended with a broken camera and, apparently, according to the make-up girl, a broken nose. Not the best of starts.

During those days, I soon learned how delicate the relationship could be between reporter and camera crew. At that time television was very much a closed shop. Tensions could quickly arise between reporters and highly trade-unionized technicians. You had to be extremely careful about observing all the rules and not stepping into the minefield of demarcation. Our news crews were quietly flexible and helpful, most of the time, but sometimes you would find an industrial dispute spilling into your relationship with them.

Jeremy Hands really screwed up big-time once. He was out on a job and he'd rubbed his crew up the wrong way. I think he'd worked them through a lunch break, and there'd been a lot of stand-offs and general ill-tempered muttering during the day, and this was obvious to the interviewee Jeremy had just spoken to. As the crew were sullenly packing up, Jeremy took his man aside.

'Sorry about all the hold-ups and tension,' he said. 'Those fuckers are in a right strop. Useless cunts.'

And he then added more of the same.

When he went back to the news wagon, Jeremy turned on the charm.

'Thanks for today, boys. Sorry we didn't get on too well. Let's all go and have a drink.'

'Just listen to this tape, Jeremy,' the soundman said. 'You're still miked up and I didn't know if you wanted me to keep recording, mate. Good to know how highly you regard all of us.'

And they played the tape back to him.

It was a very silent journey back to base.

In those days it was the electricians who could be really difficult. Everything had to be 'lit', and if it wasn't necessary to use lights a notional payment was made to the electricians anyway. When I was at Granada, we were planning to transmit some wartime footage of the Manchester blitz, recorded by the old Co-op Wartime Film Unit. A furious shop steward from the electricians' union gatecrashed the editorial planning meeting.

'You can't show this film tonight,' he said bossily. 'Who lit it, anyway?'

The producer stared at him. 'The fucking Luftwaffe,' he said.

That got a laugh; but the film was pulled.

One Christmas we sent our cameras to a local school to record a carol to close our news programme in the five days before Christmas. The musicians' union threatened industrial action, saying we were 'using non-union musicians to fill airtime'.

You couldn't make it up back then.

————————

I spent two years with Border. Then a film editor, Paddy McCreanor, buttonholed me.

'Psst. Want a job?' he asked.

'I've got one, thanks,' I said.

But Paddy told me that a producer he knew at Yorkshire TV wanted to see me. YTV was a much bigger company than Border, so down to Leeds I went and was eventually offered a job as a reporter/presenter on the nightly news show, *Calendar*.

Not long before this, Lynda and I had bought our first house – a Victorian terrace – in Eden Place, Carlisle, but she told me to go for it anyway. We didn't want to sell up straight away, so I drove down to Yorkshire on Sunday night and came back on Friday evenings. We were perfectly happy with this arrangement for quite a while; I think we both appreciated the breathing space, and the rows lessened. Significant, looking back.

During my first appearance on *Calendar* there was another cock-up in store for me. I'd been there for three days getting to know how the teatime regional news programme was put together. Then I was allowed to present my first studio item about the Penistone railway line, which was about to be axed, and very much a local *cause célèbre*. We filmed at Penistone, I interviewed a few people and put the whole piece together as a mixture of location and live studio commentary to camera. I don't remember anyone that day actually saying the word 'Penistone'. They just referred to it as 'the town' or 'the station'. So, throughout my piece, I said it the way it was spelled, 'Penis-tone'.

The programme's director, David St David, had a wild sense of humour and during rehearsals had managed to stifle his laughter and send out the message not to correct me. So, it was 'Penis-tone' this and 'Penis-tone' that for three glorious minutes live on air. Afterwards, in the YTV bar, David performed a brilliant impersonation of my debut performance to howls of laughter. He closed with a flourish: 'And remember, folks – use Penis Tone, guaranteed to give you bigger, better cock-ups.'

David became a tremendous support and encouragement to me at Yorkshire as well as a good friend. He was, we all knew, headed for directorial glory. Just three years later he was killed in a helicopter crash while filming over the Humber estuary.

The first big star I interviewed for Yorkshire Television was Gloria Swanson, who had just written her autobiography. Usually there's never time to read someone's book before the interview, but for once I got an advance copy, and read her life story from cover to cover. She was in her eighties, but when she arrived at the studios everyone was knocked out by her looks: piercing blue eyes, clear skin and a sharp intellect.

David St David was blown away. 'First time I've ever wanted to snog a granny,' he said over my earpiece.

Gloria was very frank in the interview and flirted with the crew. But I was over-prepared and the whole thing was a bit stiff; it didn't have the freewheeling style that Judy and I later developed together.

One piece of research did pay off. Gloria Swanson had said somewhere that she hated 'air kisses on the cheeks' – you know, that luvvie thing – and that she preferred a man, on introduction, to kiss her hand but never to raise it to his lips. He had to bend down to her hand. So, I thought, What the hell, and I did – and definitely picked up some Brownie points.

After the thirty-minute interview aired, *Calendar*'s editor, Graham Ironside, characteristically direct, said, 'Not bad. But you won't improve on that for quite a while. You need a lot more miles on the clock.'

So I was given the weekly sports programme to present, and more studio spots on the nightly news show – anchored, incidentally, by Richard Whiteley – and something called 'Calendar Goes Pop' where I was so truly awful that I've wiped my brain's memory-bank clean. It was the series where Shakin' Stevens tried to beat me up. Looking back, I don't blame him.

Many months into my new job Lynda and I sold up in Carlisle and we moved into a pretty cottage in the village of Aberford, between Leeds and York. We'd barely settled in when Granada TV entered the frame. Some of my news reports had been 'lifted' by ITN and in one of them I ended up with a throwaway piece to camera – something quirky about a Rubik's cube. It went out on *News at Ten*, and next morning there was a message on my desk: 'Rod Caird at Granada Television wants you to call him.'

I thought this was to do with a huge on-going row I was having with Granada Television Rentals about our set at home which kept breaking down. They'd been avoiding my angry and increasingly frustrated calls, and now that I had a name and number, I went for the kill.

I was put through.

'Right,' I said, 'it's Richard Madeley. And it's about bloody time. What are you clowns playing at?'

There was a distinct pause.

'Er, hello, Richard. I don't quite follow.'

'It's Mr Madeley to you, Caird,' I snapped.

'Well, I know we haven't met,' he said, 'but do we have to be that formal?'

'Don't get cute with me, mate. I've had a month of you guys screwing up and . . .'

And on I went. Finally I paused for breath.

'You think I'm with Granada Television Rentals, don't you?' he said, laughing.

'Aren't you?'

'No,' he said. 'This is Granada Television, Manchester. I want to offer you a job.'

Rod ran Granada's big regional programmes department, including the nightly *Granada Reports*. He and Mike Scott, the presenter and Programme Controller, had seen the ITN piece the night before and thought I'd be right for the three-presenter line-up on the show.

This was a terrific break for me. Granada had real clout at ITV and made a huge amount of programmes for the network. And it was a staff job – no more short-term contracts.

The other male presenter was Tony Wilson, well-known to everyone in Manchester and the north-west for running Factory Records, a really hot label in the late 1970s and 1980s. He also owned and ran the Hacienda, *the* Manchester nightclub. Tony was very hip, very cool, very opinionated and hard to control. I think Granada wanted a straighter, less wayward presenter to help counterbalance him.

The female presenter was Judy Finnigan.

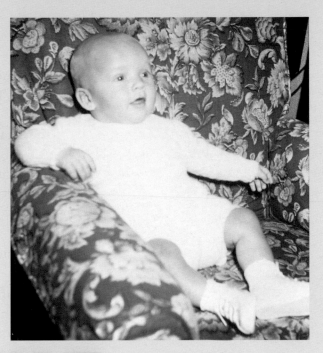

'Thanks for joining us. Coming up on today's show . . .' Getting some practice in early, in my grandad's armchair.

An early visit to London Zoo and Pet's Corner. The goats later ate my cap.

Sheer British grit in the face of a freezing, rain-lashed summer holiday in Morecambe. Mum subsequently went down with a mild case of pneumonia.

Our first new car – a Ford Popular. Three gears, no heater and 0 to 60 in a snappy three days.

Above: 113, Dagenham Road, Rush Green. I was born in the downstairs front room (behind the lilac trees here).

Right: My sister's skipping rope was no match for my bike over the distance, but Liz never learned. Actually, I think this is my fourth birthday – the laburnum's out. (See p.16)

Left: Dad and me in my grandma's vegetable patch at Shawbury. We were on holiday but Dad still wore a suit and tie – even when gardening.

Right: Not catching anything again in my grandad's river.

Below: Epping Forest and chocolate cake. It must be my birthday.

The Madeleys pull off the difficult trick of not quite looking
at the camera simultaneously. Christmas 1966.

The terror of the first XV. Look at the
awesome power in those thighs.

In my beloved woods opposite our new
home in Brentwood.

Fifteen and never been blessed. Just before my confirmation, 1971. Liz now had great hair and, as you can see, so did I.

Coming second in a music talent contest at The Three Rabbits, Manor Park, 1976. I forget who won, but Brian Poole from the *Tremeloes* came third.

The East London Advertiser newsroom five-a-side squad celebrate stuffing Stepney Fire Brigade in the still-talked-about 1975 grudge match. God knows how our side won – we were so unfit we all threw up at least twice during the game.

Left: The Queen visiting Carlisle during her 1977 Silver Jubilee. The keen radio reporter (*behind, left*) had no idea he was about to be bounced by Special Branch for getting in front of the police cordon. Transmission abruptly terminated.

Right: My first-ever publicity shot, for Border Television. Yes, I know. You don't have to tell me.

Below: Being allowed to anchor the nightly news at Border Television for the first time. Only the cameraman behind me could see my knees shaking.

Government Minister Kenneth Baker visits a Carlisle factory after I joined Border Television. I'm trying to write a piece-to-camera short enough to remember.

Yorkshire Television's 'Calendar' new team, 1981. One of the most professional outfits I ever worked with. Richard Whiteley (front) was yet to become a legend on *Countdown* and Robert Moore (back row, far left) would become a familiar face on BBC network news.

Lynda at my niece Charlotte's christening, 1982.

Getting ready for 27 hours' live programming on ITV's *Telethon* – in a way the conception of *This Morning*. (See p.107)

4: JUDY

The first time I set eyes on Richard in the Granada studio corridor, I'm not sure what I thought. He was obviously very attractive, and charming, but perhaps a little too confident for my taste. Anyway, although my marriage wasn't going well, I was trying to make a go of it. And I was a mother, and that made me feel older than I was, and certainly not particularly attractive.

I discovered almost immediately that I really liked working with Richard on *Granada Reports*, which in the world of TV presenters is surprising. The men, and I must admit some women, too, can be very edgy, territorial and 'me-me-me', and often do not take kindly to their co-presenters. But, from the very beginning, Richard and I had a strong mutual professional respect for each other. There was none of the backbiting and bitching, which sexists may expect to be more common among women while in fact it's much more so among men. The older and more established guys can be very condescending to a young woman. Richard was never like that. We got on at once, found that we laughed at the same things, talked naturally and discovered that, in some special way, we were in sync. Long before Richard and I became more than colleagues, a psychiatrist who came into the studio for a 'No Smoking Day' programme said, 'You two have an incredible professional bond, haven't you? There's a real chemistry between you.'

There was.

Outside his studio work, Richard was a very private man. I knew he was married, but I never met his wife. At the time, she was still living in Yorkshire and because Richard was driving back there every evening he never took part in any of the social trips to the pub after the programme. We didn't really know each other for ages, except at a work level. But he was always good fun and, as neither of us was experiencing any of the usual professional grief with the other, we became less and less wary and more and more talkative. So a close professional friendship developed quite quickly. He joined in May 1982 and in the late autumn we had to do a promo: 'This is what's going to be happening on the forthcoming run of *Granada Reports*.' Along with the camera crew, we went to Blackpool. After we'd had a great laugh shooting the promo, we decided to have dinner together and then get a cab back to the studio.

That evening was the first time we had been alone together socially and we never stopped laughing. On the way back in the taxi, we chatted all the way. We talked about my kids, childbirth and our marriages. It was then, although he was very loyal and didn't tell me much, that I realized he was not happily married. At the end of the journey, he said, 'Thank you for talking to me,' and gave me a peck on the cheek. But, no doubt about it, something had happened that evening. Some months later, when we were lovers, I told him that being together in the taxi had reminded me of that wonderful quote from *Brideshead Revisited*: 'the first faint bat-squeak of sexuality'. And that, I now know, was what it was. On that occasion we both realized we were very attracted to each other. We didn't talk about it then, but the way I looked at him and felt about him changed that night.

Within a few months, side by side on screen, Richard and I had become what people called the 'lead presenters' of *Granada Reports*, and I remember feeling very pleased when our colleague Tony Wilson described us 'as the ultimate TV pros; the kind of people who enjoy it when everything starts falling apart because that's when they're at their very best. They love it when a film breaks down because it means they can ad lib their way out of it and smooth everything over.'

At Granada, we always had a big staff party at Christmas in the newsroom where a band, formed from within the company, played. The same guy always headed this, and the musicians performed pop songs to an impressively high standard. As Richard played the guitar well, he was recruited and started rehearsing with the band for the big day. During this time, I remember hearing that he wasn't living at home any more and, because of the rehearsals, was staying in Manchester. Then somebody else told me that he was going out with one of the secretaries at work and was lodging at her house. Ridiculously, I was really shocked and disapproving. I knew he wasn't happy, but . . . Of course, I never spoke to him directly about this. I remember going to the Christmas party, and watching him in the band, knowing that feeling was far from right. Then I thought, What you are experiencing will not do either you or Richard any good, so back off. And that, for the time being, was that.

Then, one day at work when, for once, I wasn't out filming, I decided to go to a local bookshop during my lunch break to get a book about Cheshire walks. On my way from Granada to the shop, I heard footsteps behind me and Richard's voice saying, 'Can I join you? Where are you going?'

'To the bookshop,' I replied.

'Oh, good, so am I,' he said.

So we carried on walking together.

'What are you going to buy?' I asked.

'A handbook on do-it-yourself divorce,' he answered.

'Oh, really?' I said, almost stopping in my tracks. 'So it's true, you are getting divorced?'

'Yes,' he replied, 'we're not happy. We have decided to call it a day, and have agreed to do it ourselves rather than go to a solicitor. It's all fairly amicable.'

Having arrived at the bookshop, he got his handbook on divorce and I bought mine on Cheshire walks. That was that. Nothing more. But, again, it was like a step towards each other. And I certainly realized that I had an unhealthy interest in what was going on in his life. I was still trying to resist this at that stage, telling myself it was nonsensical; that I had two children, and he was eight years younger than me. Above all, I felt I had a huge responsibility towards the kids, and, however unhappy I was, I didn't want to drift into an affair. It never works out, it happens all the time in TV. Besides which, my own unhappiness needed a much more radical solution than a light-hearted fling with no strings attached.

Soon after our lunchtime meeting, Richard ended his relationship with the secretary, and moved temporarily into another colleague's house. This time it was a girl from the newsroom who had just split up with her husband. When she had a party, we all went there, then off to a restaurant. At the end of the evening, Richard and I once again found ourselves sharing a taxi. I know that sounds naïvely accidental, but these things often are. Nevertheless it became obvious during that drive that there was something unspoken between us that was refusing to go away. After we had kissed each other goodnight, I was scared, excited and worried. Then, during the next few weeks when Richard sent me notes, saying, 'Can we meet? Can we have dinner again? Can we do something?' I eventually agreed. David was away working again and it was just one of those inevitable moments. I went to Richard's flat for dinner and he cooked a tuna fish casserole for me. Nothing physical happened, but we both acknowledged that there was a very strong attraction between us. I knew the way I felt was going to be big trouble.

We became lovers soon after that. However hard I tried,

it was too late, I could not resist him. I broke the affair off almost immediately and, God knows, how many times after that during the next year. Three, four times? It was terrible. I felt awful. But Richard was amazing. He didn't put me under any pressure whatsoever. I knew he was in love with me and would wait for me as long as I needed, but it was all very traumatic and horrendous for both of us. It was dreadful for him knowing I was married to somebody else and going off on family holidays. Very early on, I said, 'If anything does happen to David and me, you do know that I come in a three-pack. There's absolutely no way I'm going to leave my children behind. They mean everything to me.'

Richard was very mature for a twenty-six-year-old, but I kept thinking, Surely a young man, who has no children of his own, wouldn't want that kind of burden, and I could not risk my boys going to somebody who wouldn't love them as much as I did. I just could not have forgiven myself for doing that to them. Apart from that neither Richard nor I ever gave a thought to the eight-year difference in our ages. Some people have deemed this worthy of comment, but the days when such things seemed to matter are long gone. Times have changed. Women can now marry men who are younger than they are because they no longer need the traditional dependent–spouse relationship. They have their own careers and money and can marry whoever they love, regardless of age. Joan Collins, for example, recently married a man thirty-two years younger than her, and Madonna's husband, Guy Ritchie, is ten years younger than she is.

The misery we were going through was because I was a married woman who was forever getting upset about being in love with another man and calling it off. Then we'd start seeing each other again and I'd end it once more. It was hell. Then I went away on a kind of make-or-break holiday with David, which was just utterly wretched. I had never been so unhappy in my entire life. When we came back, Richard and I didn't get back together again, but David and I started to have some serious discussions about our marriage, about things not working out for us. It wasn't just me, it was David, too. We had just drifted totally apart and now had very little in common. We didn't seek any marriage guidance counselling because there didn't seem to be any point. In the end, we agreed to part. It wasn't easy, these things never are, but we did eventually separate in the early summer of that year.

In the autumn, I realized my father, who had cancer, was going to die. He didn't want to go back into hospital, he wanted to be nursed at home. Granada was great and gave me lots of time off. I used to go into the studio, do my bits, then go to help my mother who was exhausted. It was an absolute nightmare, a ghastly time. I didn't take any of these events lightly; I was terrified, and feeling very guilty about everything and everybody. The marriage breaking up was not David's fault; he was a good husband, never hit me, didn't drink to excess, so how could any of it be his fault? No, it was mine. That's how I felt and, what's more, I had two little boys. I was now living alone with Dan and Tom in the marital home, crippled with self-blame.

When my father was dying, my brother Cal, who was living in London, used to come up every weekend to give my mother a rest; and Roger, who was working in Yorkshire, would come down when he could. But I was the closest, in Manchester, and so much more able to help Mum. Then, as time went on, I had to be with her in the evenings, too. That's when Richard was fantastic. He just stepped in, looked after the twins, and took a huge weight off my shoulders. From the beginning, he got on superbly well with Dan and Tom. He took them out to the pictures, read them stories, stayed with them until I got home and sometimes stayed the night. I'd known right from the beginning he wanted to marry me. I wrote to David and was absolutely straight: 'Richard has asked me to marry him and I have accepted. I'd like a divorce.'

David agreed.

My father died on 25 November 1984. I was very upset, of course, and, just before that, I had a miscarriage. Crazy, perhaps, but Richard and I had decided early on in our relationship that we wanted to have children. Then, sadly, at the end of October, when I was six weeks' pregnant, I lost our first baby. The distress was heightened all the more because I was already feeling emotional about my dad dying. But, even though our divorces were not yet through and we couldn't get married, we decided to try for another child. In February, by which time Richard and I were living together, I became pregnant again.

It was a strange pregnancy. Although I was terribly happy, I was also depressed. There was just too much going on. I remember setting off alone for great long walks, thinking, I'm not sure I can cope with all this. Then, unbelievably, when I went for my first routine scan at sixteen weeks, in May, I was told there was no heartbeat and the baby had died. Reeling from this shock, I was also told that they had found a huge cyst on one of my ovaries, and that this had possibly caused the loss of the baby. It was wretched.

Richard was with me at the scan and I was kept in overnight so that, to be absolutely certain, they could repeat the procedure first thing in the morning. When they did, it confirmed that there was definitely no heartbeat. It was particularly heart-rending because, at four months' pregnant, I had to give birth to the baby anyway. The labour had to be induced and proved to be very painful. It was also complicated because, as I had had a Caesarean with Tom and Dan, the medical staff had to be careful that the scar in my uterus didn't rupture. Then the induction didn't work and I was in fruitless labour for thirty-six hours. Richard remained with me throughout, and was incredibly supportive but, in the end, I said, 'I can't go through another night of this, I just cannot cope with the pain.' And, as my cervix was still not fully dilated, I was prepared for theatre and given a pre-med for a D&C. Just as I was feeling woozy, my waters broke, but they whipped me into theatre. When I came round, I was just relieved it was all over. It was a horrible experience. We were supposed to be going on holiday to the south of France the following day and had assumed that this was off, but the consultant said, 'Go. Why not? You could do with a holiday.'

Above all, I remember Richard bringing the boys in to pick me up from hospital. I was so glad to see them. Thank God, I thought, that there are two I've managed to hold on to. We then went to the south of France but this, despite the blue skies, the smell of sun-ripened melons and drifts of lavender, was a miserable experience. Everywhere we looked we saw pregnant women and mothers breastfeeding. I spent most of the time in tears, but was tremendously glad to be with Richard again.

We talked through what had happened. After two disastrous pregnancies, I was now worried that I wouldn't be able to have another baby and I so wanted this for Richard. I knew, in logical moments, that I had had twins and was capable of successfully carrying a child, but . . . Something had gone wrong twice. When we returned home, I went to the hospital for a check-up, but all they told me was that the baby we had lost was a little boy; that there was absolutely nothing wrong with him, no abnormalities, no infections. It was just one of those things; and it might have been something to do with the ovarian cyst.

The big decision then was what to do about the cyst?

'I know you desperately want a baby,' the obstetrician said, 'but if we operate on the cyst this might delay or compromise that. I'm inclined to give it a few months and keep an eye on you while you try to get pregnant again.'

I agreed. This was in May and, three months later, in August, I was pregnant. All through this pregnancy I was terrified that the same thing would happen. The medical staff were great, especially Cath Lambert, the radiologist, who tragically died in a car accident shortly afterwards. I used to panic like mad if I couldn't feel the baby moving, and would be on the phone to Cath who'd say, 'Come in.' Even on New Year's Day I did this, had a scan and she said, 'It's fine. Look, it's moving.' When Dr Donnai, the obstetrician who had done the induction for the baby we lost, caught sight of me that day, he hid.

'When I saw you come in,' he said later, 'I stayed under cover until I heard that everything was all right. I just couldn't face breaking bad news to you again.'

But all was well. The pregnancy proceeded normally and I gave birth to our son, Jack, by Caesarean. This time, even the epidural worked, so I actually saw him born. He came out like a starfish, with great long legs like Richard's, screaming his head off. When they gave him to me in the recovery room, he immediately began to crawl up my abdomen, using his elbows to propel himself on to my breast. He was extraordinarily strong. Richard was over the moon, a completely besotted father, and he had a week off work; Tom and Dan loved Jack. And we had all had a lovely bonding few days together – what we called our baby-moon.

Richard and I have always been very close, but we were especially so then. For us, from the beginning, it wasn't just a physical attraction, powerful though that was. We wanted the same things, shared the same ideal of a family life, wanted to spend as much time as we could together. We had a passionate relationship, made each other laugh, found each other interesting and stimulating. We were then, and are now, incredibly happy in each other's company. This didn't mean we didn't have blazing rows but, when we did, they did not dent the strength of our relationship. He has always wanted what I wanted. I had always dreamed of having a big family; had seen marriage as a partnership in which two people could be exceptionally close. I didn't want a marriage in which one person is away for weeks on end while the other is at home with the children. I was never interested in that. Neither was Richard. He is a fantastic father, a marvellous stepfather, and is totally involved in family life. He really enjoys being with the children. I am very lucky.

———

After Jack's birth, the next big thing on our agenda was to get married. Richard was already divorced, but mine was taking for ever to come through. I thought it was never going to happen. In the meantime, I was on maternity leave from Granada, and this time successfully breastfeeding. Then, when Jack was nearly five months old, my decree absolute did come through.

Much as I had wanted this, it was distressing, especially when the time came for us to move out of my old marital home. Richard had gone off with the kids to our new house and, after the removal van had left, I took a last long wander around the home. I then went and sat in my car just opposite and, as all the memories came back, gazed at it through floods of tears. Whatever people say about divorce being easy, it is not. Divorce and bereavement are the worst things in the world to cope with, and they are officially listed as two of life's highest stress factors. I had experienced several bereavements and divorce, and moving house while Jack was still so small. So much had happened in such a short time, I was over-emotional, up and down. But Richard was great throughout, a very steadying influence.

My decree nisi came through in early November while I was still on maternity leave and just as we were about to go on a two-week holiday with Jack, Tom and Dan to the

Canaries, which used to be one of our favourite places. The islands are volcanic in origin, rugged in contour, have some fertile valleys, a really pleasant mild climate, Mediterranean and African plants, and wonderful fresh bananas, oranges, lemons, vegetables and wines.

'Let's have our honeymoon/holiday first and get married as soon as we get back,' Richard said.

So we went to the Manchester Registry Office and booked our marriage for the week after we returned from the Canaries, and told our families it would be a very quiet wedding on 21 November 1986. We then went off with the kids to the Canaries where, don't ask me how, Richard managed to tip Jack out of his pushchair a couple of times and also dropped him once during a power cut! The poor child spent the holiday with his face covered in cuts and bruises, and we had to endure people giving us very strange looks. That aside, it was a very happy holiday and a wonderful pre-wedding honeymoon.

When we returned, we finalized the arrangements for our marriage. This went off wonderfully well with just thirty of us present, and we then took everyone out to a lovely pub-restaurant in Cheshire. Afterwards, Richard and I went off for another two-day honeymoon in our favourite hotel in Wiltshire. Jack was six months old.

I was due to go back to work the following Tuesday. I should have gone back when my maternity leave ended, but Granada had allowed me to postpone my return for a few days. In the hotel, we were both ecstatically happy.

'How do you feel about being married?' Richard asked me. 'Do you feel any different?'

'As a matter of fact I do,' I replied. 'I feel really odd. I can't quite put my finger on it, but I feel different, spaced out in my head.'

When we arrived home, I had a couple of days left for Christmas shopping before I went back to work. On one occasion when I had planned to go into town to meet Richard for lunch, I suddenly started to feel really queasy. From then on, I felt nauseous at exactly the same time every day: for some reason, ten o'clock in the morning.

'I do feel odd,' I said to Richard.

'You know that first period you had,' he replied. 'It wasn't really a proper one, was it?'

'No,' I said, 'but that's not unusual when you've been breastfeeding.'

'I think you should take a pregnancy test,' he added.

I was totally dismissive. This was the last thing I had expected him to say. I was still breastfeeding Jack and, anyway, we had been using contraception, even if it was only the rhythm method. But Richard, ever practical, bought a pregnancy test. It was a Saturday morning and I remember it vividly. I did the pregnancy test, put it on top of a chest of drawers and, while waiting for the result, was sitting up in bed reading the *Guardian*. When Richard came in, he said, 'Right, I'll check it.'

'Honestly, Richard,' I said, 'I'm *not* pregnant.'

Having gone across to the chest of drawers, he queried, 'What did you say was supposed to appear if you are pregnant?'

'A little blue line, I think,' I replied.

'You *are* pregnant,' he said.

'Oh, yeah? Very funny, ha ha,' I muttered.

'No,' he said, serious. 'You really are pregnant.'

I got up and looked. And I was.

Our first reaction was to laugh and we did. Then, becoming all rational, we said, 'Well, we always planned to have another baby. There's a nine-year age gap between the twins and Jack, and we didn't want him to feel lonely. We did want another. True, not this soon, but . . .'

So, on my first day back at work after my maternity leave,

I had to take a deep breath and tell Granada I was pregnant. I was so embarrassed. It felt as if I couldn't control my life.

This pregnancy was easier, I think because I had had enough of the whole thing. Since falling in love with Richard, I'd been pregnant three times, and this was my fourth. Jack was only six months old and I was now facing another Caesarean. I was thirty-nine, exhausted, back at work, and not looking forward to the birth. The good thing was, I was so fed up I wasn't as worried about the baby.

The hospital suggested I should have an amniocentesis test. Richard and I talked about this, asking each other, 'What would we do if we were told there was something wrong with the baby?' We honestly didn't know. But we both decided that 'knowledge is power' and that at least we would be prepared. I had the test and, about three weeks later, the obstetrician's secretary telephoned me. Results are not usually given over the phone, but I pleaded, 'Go on, *please.*'

'The baby's fine,' she said, giving in. 'There's nothing wrong at all.'

'Wonderful,' I replied.

'And,' she whispered, 'it's a girl.'

She knew that was what I wanted to know; that I would think this was fantastic. I had conceived four boys in a row; I thought I was destined to have only boys, and the knowledge I was carrying a girl really cheered me up. I rushed upstairs to Richard, yelling, 'It's a girl. It's a girl.' We were both so chuffed.

Everything should have been wonderful, but it wasn't. When Chloe was born on 13 July 1987, she was lovely, an incredibly sweet, smiley baby, and so different from Jack, who was wiry, all over the place, very demanding and, if he didn't get what he wanted, very wilful. Chloe was a tiny baby, and was fast asleep when she was born. I was absolutely besotted with her. But then, about eight weeks later, possibly even earlier, I suddenly started to feel dreadful. I was weepy, everything was too much for me, I didn't want to do anything, and I went completely to pieces. I was on maternity leave again and, when Richard went to work in the mornings, I would have terrible panic attacks. I had a part-time nanny to help with Jack while I dealt with Chloe but, even so, everything was too much of an effort. I couldn't face the day and I got worse and worse. Even when I took sleeping pills I still found it difficult to sleep. I couldn't make out what was happening to me. I thought I was over-tired and fazed by traumatic pregnancies, Caesareans and babies, and told myself that when I got back to work, this would focus me and I would feel better. But when I did return to Granada, things were even tougher. All that had changed was that I was doing more and, when I got home in the evening at about seven, I would hear Jack screaming, and sometimes hear Chloe wailing, too. I would sit in my car in the drive, not wanting to go into the house, thinking, I can't face it. I can't cope.

Somehow I managed to cover up reasonably well at work. But, one day after I had returned to Granada, I had a panic attack, hyperventilated and was terribly frightened and upset. When I told Richard about this, he took me to the doctor who immediately referred me to a woman psychiatrist.

'Just tell me how you feel,' she said. 'Tell me about your day.'

I described how the sky above my head felt as black as midnight and that there was nothing good, nothing to look forward to, no light or sweetness.

'It sounds as if you no longer have any pleasure in life at all,' she said.

'I've forgotten what pleasure is,' I agreed. 'I just don't know—'

'Look,' she interrupted. 'It's an absolutely classic case of clinical depression. You're suffering from postnatal depression.

And we can treat it with anti-depressants.'

I know it sounds incredible, but it had never occurred to me or Richard that this was what it was. Of course, given our jobs, we knew about postnatal depression but, like so many people, we thought this only happened to others.

Three weeks after I started on the anti-depressants, it was as if the clouds had parted and a shaft of sunlight had broken through. It felt like a physical sensation in my head. This is why I am always so enthusiastic about advising any woman who rings in, saying, 'I've had this baby and I feel terrible and can't cope,' to seek medical help. These pills work and are not addictive like Valium or sleeping pills. They just give you a vital lift so that you can cope again. I took them for about six months and, when I returned to see my GP, Chris Steele who became *This Morning*'s doctor, he said, 'Just consider what you've been through in the last few years of your life, and you will not feel ashamed or surprised.'

Richard knew throughout that something was wrong, but he couldn't figure out what. Clinical depression is very hard on your partner because you are always sitting there unhappy, and there's a certain amount of resentment and blaming that goes on. 'It's all right for you. But I'm here with the kids, and I'm too tired.'

And, of course, I wanted to escape into sleep all the time. It was very tough on Richard and, although he didn't understand what was the matter, he was good to me. But I wouldn't wish living with a depressed partner on anyone. It is awful.

Perhaps I inherited my father's depressive gene without realizing it. Knowing more about depression would certainly have helped. One trait in clinically depressed people is that they are completely un-amenable to a partner's persuasion or sentences like, 'Don't worry. Everything will be all right.' Every moment is seen as black, hideous and pointless. There's no future because you're thinking, What's the point? We're all going to die.

Another characteristic is guilt. There I was, regardless of what I had been through, tremendously happily married to a man I loved so much. I'd got four beautiful healthy children. But . . . I couldn't explain and I couldn't justify how I felt to anyone. Postnatal depression hits you like a truck, flattens you and distorts everything.

When I told Chloe recently that I had had postnatal depression after she was born, she said, 'Oh! Does that mean you didn't love me, didn't want to look after me?'

'No!' I replied. 'I absolutely adored you. That was never the problem. I just couldn't cope with the rest of the day.'

That was true. I never felt resentful towards the kids, not even when Jack was incredibly jealous of Chloe. Who could blame him? He was just six days short of fourteen months when Chloe was born. Still a baby himself, there was his mum with another baby and he was no longer getting my undivided attention. If they both woke in the night, I would go to Chloe because I was breastfeeding her and Richard would see to Jack. Suddenly his mum's priority was somewhere else. He was extremely difficult in those days. The first time Richard brought him into the hospital to see me after the birth, I'd got him toys and thought I'd done all the right things. But when I put my arm around him to give him a big kiss, he kicked me right in my stomach where I had had the Caesarean, and burst into tears. I had been away from home, had abandoned him, now there was another baby in a cot, and it was all very confusing.

It was also very difficult for me, of course, as I was the one who had to cope with his behaviour. The twins, though, were smashing. They were great with Jack and adored Chloe because she seemed like a little doll to them. As she grew up, they teased her a lot, called her 'Beanz', because, they said, she was very round like a baked bean. She used to be furious about this, but now gets upset if they don't call her Beanz. She's very much the adored baby of the family.

————————

In the spring of 1988, by which time I was fully recovered from the postnatal depression, Richard and I were thrilled to bits when Granada asked us to co-present its first *Telethon*. A twenty-seven-hour, non-stop, good-cause marathon: we couldn't wait to start. It was really smashing to be working as a double act again; and I remember that, along with Michael Aspel and lots of regional producers, we went to London for a lecture by the producer of the *Jerry Lewis Telethon*. It was a very American, fascinating lecture.

'Your programme will be pointless,' he said, 'if you do it for political correctness reasons, or to simply give a voice to the disabled. The *Telethon* is about raising money to help the needy and the deprived. Don't patronize them by turning it into a political vehicle. Your job is to make the viewers, whatever their physical condition, disabled or not, pick up the phone and pledge money. And here's how you do it. You must pluck at their heart-strings; engage their feelings; make it easy for people to make a pledge. And you do this through what you say and the kind of back-up films you make. But whatever you do, do *not* make political films.'

Richard and I absorbed this message right down to the pit of our stomachs, went back to Granada and spread the word. A production team was set up and, as my current show *Scramble*, which was a mixture of community action and consumer affairs, was only a weekly programme, I had time to start making films for the *Telethon*. My films were about children and babies: a beautiful little boy with brittle-bone disease; a struggling special-care baby unit which had saved the lives of hundreds of premature babies. I was enormously moved by some of their stories, and I really put everything I had into those films. I was so pleased when they turned out to be good, and were considered so communicative, heart-warming and effective that, about halfway through the actual day of the *Telethon*, they were picked up by network television and given repeated showings. This, of course, moved even more people to give money.

In addition to the films, Richard and I co-presented the programme in the studio. For us this was a celebration of being back on screen, working together. We had a wonderful time and it was one of the highlights of our careers. We went on air at five o'clock on the Friday evening, continued all through the night on screen for ten minutes every twenty minutes, and finished at eight o'clock on Saturday evening. By about five in the morning we felt absolutely exhausted, couldn't think straight. During one short break, I sprayed deodorant on my hair when I was freshening up and hairspray under my arms. We didn't dare take a ten-minute nap because we were frightened we'd never wake up again. We felt really rough but, by eight in the morning, we had a bacon butty, got our second wind and were on the home-straight. It was a huge fun experience. The entire population of the north-west seemed to come into the studio with donations, people did sponsored walks, and all the stars joined us to give their support. Granada raised a huge amount of money and it was a tremendously satisfying event for all of us.

———

After Chloe's birth and the postnatal depression, Richard and I decided that our family was complete. Richard then volunteered to have a vasectomy. It's a funny story, but it was horrible for him at the time. We sat in this clinic, wives alongside their husbands. All the men went in and, about fifteen minutes later, came out saying, 'All's fine. Yes, everything's fine,' and off they toddled. But when Richard came out, he was white, absolutely ashen and limping in agony. Driving home, I was so short and impatient with him because all the other guys had coped so well. He'll explain why it was so awful for him!

Our operation days were not over. After Chloe, when I was obviously not yet menopausal, my hormones were never quite in sync again and I started having horrendous menstruation problems, terrible mood swings and had to take so much time off work. All this eventually necessitated a hysterectomy. Despite the fact you hear so many negative stories about this procedure, it proved to be one of the best things I've ever done. Every time I went for a gynaecological check-up, the nurses would say, 'It's your decision. We won't do anything until you feel it's the right time.'

'I can't, I can't,' I kept replying.

Then, when I did, it was a huge relief and freed me from so many worries both on and off the screen. It is, perhaps, only other women who have been through such problems, while trying to work, who will understand this. Since the hysterectomy, HRT – hormone replacement therapy – has completely transformed my life for the better; I feel a much more stable person, too. It's such a pity that so many of the books I read were so downbeat and off-putting. I felt a new person, full of energy, really well in myself.

During my not-so-good days, though, the press had a field day whenever I was missing from a programme, and rumours began to fly that I was mentally and physically drained and ready to throw in the sponge.

Yes, there had been some *very* difficult times in the past; but I had pulled through all those: the break-up of my first marriage, the death of my father, divorce, a miscarriage, a stillborn baby, giving birth to Jack by Caesarean section, moving house, another pregnancy, Chloe by Caesarean section, postnatal depression, returning to work.

It was just as well that by the time the press caught up on all this, I was no longer physically and mentally drained and certainly had not hit the bottle. Why? Because, thanks to our success on the *Telethon*, Richard and I were about to start the biggest challenge of our career as co-presenters on a new, live, network programme, *This Morning*.

5: RICHARD

I had already seen some editions of *Granada Reports* when I had to be over in Manchester. In those days – 1982 – it had a distinctive, 'hip' feel. Tony Wilson was the epitome of laid-back, slightly arrogant cool. Judy Finnigan really stood out. She had an open, accessible style of presentation I hadn't seen before, and her interviews crackled with an understated intelligence. She never flaunted her brightness – Tony did that (and he won't mind me saying so) – but you knew she had plenty of IQ in reserve if it was needed. Like a lot of men watching her, I found Judy intriguing, and I fancied her, too, although Rod Caird's suggestion that I should quit Yorkshire TV and join Judy and Tony on the nightly news show meant I had to push that last thought right to the back of my mind. This was about weighing up a purely career option.

I said yes.

On day one at Granada, I was sorting my desk out when I felt a hand on my shoulder, followed by a woman saying, '*Boo*, I'm your mummy' – an incident that has since entered our cuttings files as some sort of Oedipal moment. But, as Judy has explained, Granada operated what they called a parenting scheme. Anybody who joined the newsroom was assigned a 'mother' if a man, or a 'father' if a woman. The parent's job was pretty functional: to show you where the toilets and editing suites were, explain the in-house jargon and how everything worked, and tell you who was who. So yeah, Judy *was* my 'mummy', and the seeds of much quasi-psychoanalysis of our relationship were irrevocably sown.

I was often asked, 'Was it love at first sight?' Well, it wasn't quite like that. What I did think in that first moment was that Judy was even more beautiful in the flesh than on screen. Once we started working together, I discovered she was a kindred spirit. After we became good friends I also realized that for much longer than I'd been prepared to admit, I was very drawn to her. Not just attracted – *drawn*. It was a slow-burn relationship in the sense that nothing improper happened for a long time. I thought she was beautiful, sexy and very bright. But I was not yet divorced. And she was married and the mother of twins.

Granada was quick to notice that we had hit it off. They saw how comfortable we were in the studio with each other, and that we usually shared the same judgement of a story's newsworthiness. We rarely did joint interviews then in the way we did later on *This Morning*, but we acknowledged each other's style. Everyone has seen on-screen pairings founder on the rocks of professional jealousy or personal incompatibility, but Judy and I, to our growing pleasure, genuinely hit it off. It was fun being together in studio. We were able to tease each other about our mistakes and there was no upstaging. We both loved Tony Wilson's mad, unique style and within a few weeks, a terrific camaraderie and loyalty existed between the three of us. As for me I was having, yet again, a ball. I couldn't believe my luck.

After one season of *Granada Reports*, the format changed and Tony moved on to do other programmes. The presenting line was down to two, and Rod decided to try that for a while. Judy and I began to operate as a double act for the first time.

The moment I realized I was falling in love with her was about six months after we met. We went to Blackpool to record promotions for the next series of *Granada Reports*. When we finished filming we had dinner alone, and then grabbed a taxi back to Manchester. During the journey the conversation became almost confessional. For the first time we exchanged secrets, fears, desires and disappointments. It was dark and the taxi was noisy. The driver couldn't hear us. Then suddenly the brakes were squealing and we'd arrived back at Granada. It was about eleven o'clock at night. If Judy had told me she'd left her bag back at the restaurant I would have turned the cab around with both of us in it. I didn't want our conversation to end. But of course, we said goodnight, kissed chastely on the cheek, and went our separate ways. Much later, we would admit to each other that we'd said goodnight in a turmoil of confusion, suppressed desire and longing.

In the late spring of the following year, when my divorce proceedings were under way, I invited Judy to my flat for dinner. Recently there had been far too many unfinished sentences, mute glances in the newsroom, tangled and protracted goodbyes at the end of the day. It was time to meet alone and talk honestly.

In many ways, our conversation after we had finished my appalling tuna fish casserole had almost Victorian, even courtly qualities. Judy was still married. I knew there were difficulties there. I said I was more than prepared to wait and see how things would turn out. She thanked me. It was like something out of *The Forsyte Saga*! But at last some kind of statement of intent had been made, and we both felt hugely relieved. I think now that, in the best sense, our romantic relationship began that evening.

The inevitable eventually happened – Judy and I became lovers. This lasted a few months and was then followed by a self-denying ordnance. Judy was in anguish. She was desperately worried about the twins, and wanted to be absolutely sure that her marriage was really over. So she called off our relationship. I was completely floored by this, but I knew it was pointless trying to persuade her to change her mind. She had to find her own way and make her own decisions. So I backed right off. We stopped seeing each other in private or phoning each other. I still have bad dreams about this time.

It was incredibly difficult. We were still presenting *Granada Reports* and constantly in each other's company. We'd been so open and engaged with each other for months, but that was no longer allowed. I knew I couldn't make Judy love me or do something against her better judgement. It was Christmas, so I went away to my sister's. She and the rest of my family couldn't work out what was wrong with me.

Winter crept by and I waited for Judy's decision. I was prepared for her to tell me she'd made a mistake with me, but I really didn't know where I'd go from there. Find another job? Forget her? It didn't seem possible. But it might have to be. More bad dreams. Suddenly, in a fogged, confused, nerve-jangled phone call Judy was telling me she and David had called it a day. But she repeated, again and again, 'You must accept that I come in a three-pack.'

I had already met the twins before Judy and I fell for each other. I was actually pleased she came in a pack of three. Tom and Dan were seven and utterly adorable – blond, sweet-faced and with lovely natures – good enough to eat. They were even-tempered little boys, with distinctive personalities. Becoming their stepfather – it had been decided whatever happened the boys would live with Judy – would be no burden. I honestly looked forward to it and felt sure I would grow to love them.

Early in the spring of that year, 1984, Judy's father was diagnosed with cancer. He died in November. He was cared for at home and Judy spent a lot of time at her parents' house. I would babysit the boys who, by now, had come to know me pretty well. Indirectly their granddad's illness drew us all closer. In August we drove down to Cornwall with the boys for a holiday. It was a turning point for me.

The boys were fantastic. I was by now genuinely fond of them, found them very entertaining, sweet and funny. I made sure I didn't present myself as an alternative father. They had an excellent dad in David. As far as father figures were concerned, it was important that their primary relationship was with him. There was no question of me replacing anybody. I just saw myself as an additional presence in their lives, but hopefully one that would enhance them. And both boys seemed very relaxed about it all. Compared to many step-parents I had it easy, believe me.

We had a blissful time in our rented Cornish cottage. The weather was glorious, and by the time we came back a good deal of bonding had gone on all round. Judy was now far more relaxed about the future as far as the boys and I were concerned, which made me, in turn, more confident and at ease. In fact she allowed me the freedom actively to express what has since become my strong personal view on step-parenting.

The received wisdom is that a step-parent should never aspire to go beyond a warm friendship with the children; that somehow it's presumptuous actually to dare to love them. It's certainly much more fraught for everyone when teenagers are suddenly confronted with a new parent figure, but young children need to be loved, have a great capacity to be loved, and a stepfather or stepmother shouldn't hold back. They need to take time and tread carefully, but what's wrong with loving a child that isn't biologically yours? It must surely increase children's sense of stability. In our newly configured family unit Judy never said or implied to the boys, 'You must think this way about Richard,' or 'Behave this way towards Richard.' That would have been self-defeating. I just loved the boys from the beginning in the way I do now.

At work when Judy and I broke cover and everyone knew for certain what they'd long suspected, that we were 'an item', there was a reaction. A lot of people at Granada – and this is quite common when two people in a workplace form a relationship – were worried, thought it destabilized things, and even felt threatened by it. It was not that they made any particular moral judgements – television would implode if affairs were a sacking offence – but some thought we might become an awkward alliance. We were presenting *Granada Reports* together, and most producers like to have control over their presenters. We soon became conscious of a certain *froideur* coming from some quarters of the newsroom. And by the summer of 1984 the on-screen double act was split up.

The programme was going to be moved from Manchester to Liverpool to become a kind of American-style rolling news bulletin, quite different from its previous magazine format. Judy and I hated the idea and said so. So she was moved to other factual programmes, and I came under pretty heavy pressure to decamp to Liverpool. I had nothing against Liverpool – we would both spend many happy years there in the future working on *This Morning* – but I thought the new format sounded as dull as ditch-water, so I held out. My friend and protector Rod had been promoted and the new boss put me in detention as a back-up news reporter on the occasional 'soft' story around Manchester. I often spent days on end sitting on my arse in the now tiny Manchester newsroom waiting for orders to cover the 'and finally' story. My career had suddenly found itself in a cul-de-sac, but to my surprise I didn't care. I was with Judy and that's all that mattered.

———

I asked Judy to marry me ridiculously soon. It was only a few days after our first kiss, and I found myself proposing and simultaneously thinking, You stupid bugger – she'll think you're mad! But as ever Judy surprised me. 'I'd love to,' she said quietly. 'But there's a long road before we get there.'

I babbled something about thorny valleys leading to sunlit uplands, and that I'd make the journey if she would.

'I will if I can,' she replied.

When it looked as if we could finally marry I set a treasure-hunt of riddles on tiny notes for her to follow round my flat. Yes, I know it's cornball, but I don't care. I had fun writing and hiding them, and as the trail progressed we were both in tears of laughter. The hunt eventually led her to a box holding an emerald engagement ring. I was virtually broke and it was a very small ring, but Judy wears it to this day.

We decided to have children about eighteen months before we got married and when we were living together. We found ourselves discussing the subject one day in a pretty country pub, the Bells of Peover, Cheshire (where one day we would hold our wedding reception). We were having a coffee after lunch when we suddenly began talking about whether to have children. I suppose at the back of our minds we had always known we would, but our priority had been to get Tom and Dan settled, and . . . well, then see. Now that we knew the twins were fine, we found ourselves talking about extra children, and I suddenly realized I did actually want to have a child, wanted to create life, see a baby born and bring him or her up with Judy. She'd always said that she wanted more children one day. The moment had come.

We stopped all birth-control stuff and of course nothing happened. Judy couldn't understand why. She'd always thought of herself as being extremely fertile so I rushed off to have a sperm count. Result normal. Still nothing. I doused my balls every evening in freezing water to maximize the sperm count and the next month Judy got pregnant. She miscarried after six weeks.

Worse was to come when Judy became pregnant again. This time everything seemed to start out well, but when we went for the first ultrasound scan at sixteen weeks the radiologist called me in, white-faced. Something was obviously wrong. Judy, who was still lying on the examination couch, turned to me, her eyes wet with tears.

'It's died, Richard. Our baby has died,' she said.

It was a dreadful moment for me but indescribably awful for her. There had been no gentle lead-up. One moment she was eagerly anticipating her scan, the next she felt she had failed her unborn child, herself and me. She was overcome with grief.

There then followed the long, painful process of labour and birth, while knowing all the time that the outcome would be a dead child. It was heartbreaking. I just felt a raw emptiness and a very real sense of having lost a person. It wasn't until this happened to Judy and me that I fully understood why people who lose babies within the womb are so grief-stricken. I know, in my heart of hearts, that it isn't as bad as losing a baby when you've had a chance to bond over hours, days, or weeks, but it still engenders a more powerful sense of grief than many people can imagine. Our baby was a little boy, half me and half Judy, and he had been alive. When he died all our hopes for him died with him. There was no warning, no time to prepare ourselves and we were in deep shock. We'd never heard him talk or laugh, or seen him play; we didn't know what he would have looked like, or what kind of person he would have become, but he had existed and his absence was a great personal loss and we mourned for him.

When Judy came out of hospital, her mother looked after the boys and we flew to the south of France. Everywhere we looked there seemed to be newborn babies. Seventy-two hours after feeling healthily fecund, Judy was now experiencing the aching emptiness of suddenly being without child. It was extremely hard for her. But gradually during that week we forced ourselves to focus on the future. We knew that early miscarriages are very common. There was clearly no fertility problem. Obviously Judy could carry babies: she had the twins. So we just kept going over the realities: that this was a tragedy which we would get over in time, one that was unlikely to be repeated, and we could try again once we'd said our inner goodbyes for the tiny boy that we had lost.

A few weeks later, though, Judy was plunged into remorse and depression again. It was a cycle that had to be broken.

'Look,' I said at last, 'these things don't happen without a reason. There must have been something wrong. Nature took care of it – that's the reality. So we mourn our child, but understand that what happened was somehow automatic; meant to be. It wasn't anybody's fault, let alone yours. How can you have anything to reproach yourself with?'

I suppose that's the standard male line: try and analyse your way out of a problem or difficulty. I was grieving, too, but I couldn't stand seeing Judy beat herself up any more.

Anyway, somehow we both hauled each other out of that particular dark well and, sure enough, Judy became pregnant again. We were very happy but that pregnancy was a nightmare. You can imagine how tense Judy was throughout, and how secretly worried I was. I tried to act confidently, but Judy was incredibly jumpy, particularly in the fifteen-to-sixteen-week period. Even later into the pregnancy, a few hours of stillness in her womb sent her into a blind panic and down to the ever-patient ultrasound department at St Mary's, Manchester. They were wonderful and always sent her home reassured. Me too.

The day of her Caesarean, Judy was prepared for the epidural anaesthetic. Watching your wife have a six-inch needle rammed into her backbone is – well, not as bad as having it rammed into *your* back. It wouldn't go in properly and she almost fainted with pain. Finally, lower-half numbed, she was taken to the delivery room and I was allowed in, scrubbed, masked and gowned. I stood holding Judy's hand, but because I'm tall I could see over the little fence they put across her tummy and the view was spectacular. With amazing speed she was opened, clamped and cauterized. Then the womb was deftly cut, and *voilà* – there was our baby fast asleep.

You imagine that a Caesarean is a delicate operation, but it's not. It's almost violent. The obstetrician really has to get his hands in there and tug. The delivery table rocks from side to side, the mother's body jerks up and down, then – whoosh – out comes baby. Our Jack looked like a parachutist jumping out of a plane, his arms straight out in one direction, his legs in another. He was like a big X, a sky-diver in free-fall. But his mouth opened and he let out a tremendous bellow, an extraordinary noise for someone who up until then had been completely silent. He was *furious* we'd woken him up. (As a matter of fact, he still is in the mornings.)

When he was brought back to us, Judy was still being stitched up, so I got to hold him first. Up until that moment it had all been a very fast-moving technicolour experience. The months leading up to it had been overshadowed by just getting through the pregnancy. I hadn't really thought how I would feel holding my son for the very first time, and it came as a real shock. Suddenly there was this beautiful brand-new human being in my arms – mine, ours, what Judy and I had made together. An instant miracle. I was absolutely swamped; couldn't speak (for me, exceptional). In fact, I burst into tears. Then Judy was able to hold him, and we then held him together. I was indescribably happy. There he was: Jack, our son.

It was an amazing day. I spent the next eight hours at the hospital. St Mary's was opposite a big tyre- and exhaust-fitters. The weather was very hot. The garage's sliding doors were open and a boom-box was pumping out hip-hop so loud that it would have drowned out Concorde on take-off. All the women in the maternity ward were getting distressed. So I went across, and there were these big Manchester mechanics, all torque-wrenches and tattoos.

'Er, would you mind turning it down a bit please?' (Pure Richard Briers in *The Good Life*.)

'Fuck off. What's it got to do with you?'

'Well, my wife's just had a baby over there, and a lot of other blokes' wives are still having theirs, and they'd quite like you guys to fuck off yourselves, actually.'

I wish I could say that they gave me cheery grins and thumbs-up as the stereo was unplugged, but that didn't happen. So I went back to the hospital's phone booth, called the garage manager and he got the music switched off. Not as macho, but the same result.

I spent all that evening with Judy in the hospital. I had no trouble recognizing Jack in the nursery and no worries of him getting mixed up with another newborn. He looked frighteningly like me. I spent half an hour just gazing at him. I couldn't believe what we had created and kept leaving the hospital only to sneak back for another look. Then at midnight I left a sleeping Judy and went home to wake up Tom and Dan. Of course I'd phoned them hours earlier, but they hopped out of bed and we all sat around the kitchen table drinking tea while they studied the Polaroids I'd taken at St Mary's. They were fascinated and proud as Punch.

––––––––

Five months after Jack's birth and three weeks after Judy's divorce came through, we got married. Judy wore all white: white dress and coat, white high-heeled boots. She looked fantastic. It was a full three and a half years since I'd actually asked her to marry me, and it was wonderful to have finally arrived at that moment. Talk about sunlit uplands – I was in heaven.

The wedding took place in the same room, in the same Registry Office, Jackson's Row, Manchester, where Judy was married to David all those years before. We were both okay about that, but there was one unfortunate gaffe, and guess who by?

Judy's brother Roger was taking photos as we pretended to sign the register again and again, and Judy was getting increasingly self-conscious and impatient. Then, as now, she hated being photographed.

'It's okay, Jude,' I said, squeezing her shoulder, 'we'll be through in a minute and anyway you've done this before.'

I meant that we'd been photographed together before – loads of times when we did publicity shots for *Granada Reports*. But Judy and everyone else in the room thought I was talking about her first wedding, at which everyone in the room, except my family, had been present. *Shit.*

'No, no, *no*,' I said. 'I mean you've had your picture taken with me before.'

But it was too late. The *frisson* between Judy and me chilled the room.

'I can't believe you said that,' she kept repeating in the car to the reception. 'Whatever you say now, they'll still all think you meant . . .'

So, at our wedding breakfast in the Bells of Peover, I had to go round to everyone saying, 'Look, when I said . . . what I *meant* was . . .' It was like something out of *Frasier*.

On the day we married we drove down to Wiltshire to our favourite hotel, an Elizabethan manor house in the Cotswolds. We didn't have much money so we could only afford a long weekend there. Next morning, we were sitting in the lounge after breakfast having coffee and I said to Judy, 'We've been living together for two years; do you feel any different now we're actually married?'

I didn't. I felt just the same.

'Yes,' said Judy. 'In fact, I do feel physically different – like I felt when I was pregnant with Jack.'

With hindsight this wasn't surprising. Judy *was* pregnant, with Chloe.

She didn't believe it until I went out and bought a pregnancy test-kit. We'd been using the rhythm method and Judy had been breastfeeding (nature's natural birth control). Anyway, I brought the kit in from the bathroom.

'You're only pregnant again,' I said.

Judy was in bed with the paper. It didn't even rustle.

'If you're joking and I get out of this bed and walk across the room to look at it, I'll—'

'Judy, tell me what colour the line goes if you're pregnant?'

'Blue.'

'It *is* blue. You're having a baby.'

Judy looked at me suspiciously as I held the test results up again and again to the window. Then she came over and looked at it. There was a long silence.

'Oh, well,' she said philosophically, 'at least this time we're married.'

A few months later the phone rang and, moments later, Judy came running up the stairs shouting, 'It's the hospital. It's a girl. I'm going to have a girl.'

So Chloe began her relationship with us as a surprise. Which is more or less what she remains today – an unexpected treat.

Jack was a big baby (about 8lb 8oz) and for the first few months he looked almost prehistoric. We called him our little dinosaur! Something about his nose and mouth. He's evolved very well, but his sister arrived looking, in utter contrast, like a porcelain doll. She was beautiful the moment she entered the world. When, a few minutes later, I held her in my arms, I was looking at a rosebud mouth; and later when she opened her eyes, they were the deepest of deep blue. In the small hours of the morning, when I left the hospital to go home, Judy was fast asleep and Chloe in her cot. But I did the same as I had with Jack: compulsive returns to the new baby just to stare and stare and stare.

―――――――――

When Judy began to feel unwell after Chloe was born, I had no idea what was happening to her. Looking back, I can see that the symptoms were obvious and I'm amazed that we failed to identify the problem. She got more and more morose and incredibly bad-tempered; and I thought it was a hormonal imbalance that would settle down. That, of course, is exactly what postnatal depression is – a hormonal imbalance – and I could kick myself now for not having recognized the condition earlier. It went on for quite a few months and Judy had all the classic hallmarks, including very disturbed sleep patterns.

If anyone reading this ever hears the words, 'I can't cope,' coming from the lips of their loved ones, listen up. It's the fingerprint of depression. Judy was saying, 'I can't cope,' more and more often. Nothing gave her pleasure any more, not the children and certainly not me. When she came back to work, she hated the job she had loved before. A sunny day wasn't a good day. A hot day was too hot. There was almost nothing we could do together – or as a family – that could make her happy.

At the time I found it almost impossible to accept that anybody could get that low. It's tempting to blame a person for being miserable all the time. Obviously I never said how I was increasingly feeling, but such emotions are very corrosive. Judy and I never came close to splitting up, but we weren't happy and I was becoming exasperated with her morose outlook. I thought she had lots of things to be happy about. I also started to take it all personally, and began to think, Why can't I make her happy any more? I've done this, tried that, and she's still wretched.

I was baffled. It felt as if our relationship was suffering from a mystery illness, and the arguments we did have during that time were defined by mutual frustration. Judy was frustrated because I couldn't understand why she was as she was, and I was frustrated because she was so negative. I can see now, of course, that that is how a person behaves when they're suffering from depression but, at the time, I just became increasingly bewildered, impatient and angry that this person whom I loved so much had changed and had become so bleak, inward-looking, unresponsive and unhappy. I also became increasingly hostile because I couldn't make her happy. We knew we still loved each other, but there were frequent periods of incomprehension and lack of communication that led to baffled silences.

Why we didn't seek help earlier, God knows. When we did, Chris Steele, our doctor, took about ten seconds to make his diagnosis.

'Judy, you've got postnatal depression and you need anti-depressants.'

It was such a huge relief to have the problem diagnosed; the whole landscape changed instantly because I no longer took any of it personally which, up until then, I had. To be truthful, I had thought Judy was going slightly mad – and so did she; and, engulfed by this huge cloud, I had thought that all our bright hopes and plans for our future were dashed. The moment postnatal depression was diagnosed, though, everything became much easier for both of us. Judy went on to anti-depressants which, contrary to all the rubbish you hear about them, had no side-effects and were not addictive. Inside three weeks there were glimpses of her old self.

'You look different,' I said one morning over breakfast.

'I feel it,' she replied. 'I hardly dared say anything in case I was wrong, but it feels exactly as if the sun is beginning to break through the clouds. The blackness hasn't all gone yet, but I think I'm going to be all right.'

It was a massive relief.

Thereafter it was two steps forward, one step back but, within a month or so, she was herself again. And because Judy is intelligent and very self-aware, she didn't suffer, as so many people do, from a sense of shame, of being stigmatized by the diagnosis. For her, it was like being told she had a heart condition, high blood pressure, or a tendency to migraine. Some people are depressed about the fact they're diagnosed as depressed! They shouldn't be. As Judy and I know, it's a completely involuntary condition which descends like the flu. It can be treated and people do get better.

That was probably the most difficult interlude in our marriage and it lasted for about a year. A very long year. But, even at its worst, it never split us too far apart; and we never doubted we loved each other.

We had Tom and Dan, Jack and Chloe – and Judy was now forty. With 'four in the cot', as the gynaecologist put it, we decided to call a halt. Neither of us was happy for Judy to be on the pill indefinitely. She wasn't happy about the coil and we both loathed condoms, so one of us would have to be sterilized. Because Judy had had quite enough operations with the Caesareans, I said, 'Fine, I'll have a vasectomy.'

I was completely relaxed about it because everything I had read made it sound like a simple, painless operation. Then we discovered we had to go to a Family Planning Clinic for counselling which, given our age and experience and with four children already, we thought was ludicrous. But they don't give you a choice, so off we went and it turned out to be really embarrassing. The woman doctor was surprisingly fierce and asked us ridiculous questions, such as, 'Why do you want to have a vasectomy?' I felt like answering, 'Because we want lots more children!'

She also asked questions as if we hadn't thought of them. 'What would happen if all four of your children were wiped out in a bus crash?'

How the hell do you answer that?

'I suppose I might try to get the vasectomy reversed, and, yes, we do know there's a chance that that would not work. But we can't make this decision based on remote hypotheticals. That's potty. We have to deal with the realities of our life.'

Then it was: 'What about your sex life? Do you have regular sex?'

I stared at her. 'What on earth has that got to do with my decision to have a vasectomy?'

'I'm asking the questions.'

'Well, yeah. We do – okay?'

'How often?'

We both glared at her. 'Regularly, thank you.'

'Is it enjoyable?'

Enough. 'Oh, no, we both hate it. That's why I want a vasectomy.'

She backed off then and that was the end of our 'counselling'.

To be fair, as she was reading the questions off a card, I don't think she was being prurient because we happened to be television presenters. And, in the end, I got my appointment.

Judy drove me to the clinic and we went into a waiting-room where there were about ten other guys. As usual, I was last on the list. I always am. There was no male bonding in that room. All the men looked pale, but their wives and girlfriends looked amused. One by one they were taken away. When they came back they all looked fine, and the rest of us waiting gradually cheered up.

I breezed in at last feeling fine. The local anaesthetic did its stuff and the scalpel went to work cutting through the sac holding the testes. Still fine. I was completely numb. Then the surgeon said, 'Right, I'm just going deeper into the tissue now to get to the vas deferens, which is the tube we cut.'

'No problem,' I replied.

But suddenly I started to feel something. It was like a very cold pinprick.

'Are you feeling that?' he asked.

'Yes, I am actually,' I said, 'but it's okay if it doesn't get any worse.'

'That's odd,' he muttered. 'Have you had a sporting injury here?'

'Not particularly,' I replied. 'I was probably kicked in the balls a few times when I played rugby at school.'

'Ah!' he said. 'You've got some old scar tissue around the tubes and that's blocked the anaesthetic. Sorry, but this might get a bit rough.'

I swallowed, and said, 'All right.'

'I'll be only a couple more minutes,' he added, and started to get properly stuck in.

Suddenly it was as if someone had taken a 240-volt cable, strapped it to my bollocks and pulled the switch. I knew in that instant that if I was ever captured in a police state and had the old electrode treatment I would tell them everything. Oh, yes. Everyone I knew would go straight down the Swanee. I let out a blood-curdling roar and virtually took off from the table. The nurse burst into tears. Black dots swam in front of my eyes.

The doctor sawed on. 'I'm ever so sorry, old chap,' he said, 'but I can't stop now. I've gone too far. Won't be much longer.'

Time is certainly relative. The next two minutes felt like a fortnight. Then he finished stitching me up and it was all over. Talk about post-operative shock – I was clammy with sweat and I could hardly speak. The surgeon was very uncomfortable.

'I'm really sorry,' he said again. 'It's only about one in five hundred men who experience that; and those only include the ones we do under local anaesthetics. There may be others done under generals who might have felt the same.'

'Great!' I said. 'No one told me there was a one in five hundred chance. If they had, I would have had a general.'

'Er, please don't mention any of this on your programme,' he said nervously. 'We don't want to put other chaps off.'

When I went back to Judy, I hadn't actually been gone any longer than the others. I tottered into the waiting-room and her jaw dropped.

'What have they done to you?' she asked. 'Cut it off?'

'That,' I said slowly, 'did *not* go well. Take me home. I need to get very drunk very quickly.'

It was a day before I managed to stop trembling.

––––––––––

About three months after Chloe's birth, Granada decided to put Judy and me back on screen together again. They needed a double act for ITV's *Telethon*. Concerns about our relationship had faded. We'd been married two years and we were now legitimate. Perhaps it had been a mistake to separate us. So, for twenty-seven hours, we co-presented the *Telethon* in Granadaland, and it felt as natural as ever.

The weekend the programme was transmitted was a busy one for two key Granada executives. A couple of floors up from the studio were David Liddiment, later ITV's boss, and Steve Morrison, who rose to become chief executive of Granada TV. They'd locked themselves in an office to work on a 'hot' treatment for a new show. As yet untitled, it was going to be a new ITV morning programme, modelled on American lines, to fill the yawning vacuum that was daytime ITV back then. Everything in daytime TV in those days was in disarray. There were no fixed schedules, just old game-shows, ancient

American soaps and creaking repeats. The ratings were grim. Now the big ITV companies – Granada, Central, Thames and Television South – were competing to win the commission to make a new live show that would break the mould and build an audience.

Liddiment and Morrison had more or less got the format worked out, but hadn't made the final decision about who should present it. In a corner of their office a television flickered, tuned to the *Telethon*. As Judy and I ground on towards the end of the marathon, Morrison later told us, a light went on in his head.

A few weeks later Judy and I were approached separately and asked if we would do a pilot. There was no guarantee, of course, that Granada would win the commission. In fact, Granada's reputation for making award-winning programmes, such as *World in Action*, *The Raj Quartet* and *The Jewel in the Crown*, almost counted against it. Within the other ITV companies, there was also a suspicion that even if Granada did produce a pilot it would be too serious and too high-minded for the kind of populist, slightly tabloidy show that was needed. Our bid was definitely seen as an outside choice.

Making the pilot for *This Morning* took eight days. Granada was determined to get it right and win the race. Every night we'd go home with the thirty-minute show 'in the can'. Every morning our long-suffering producer, Max Graesser, would ring up with the same message.

'They didn't like it. We've got to do it again. Granada is being really perfectionist on this one. It's doing my head in.'

The final pilot was accepted and the night before the ITV companies met to view everyone's tapes, ours was still being edited. On the day, Judy and I just sat at home with bated breath. It was a truly seminal moment for us both. We knew that if this thing really happened, it would mean huge changes to our lives and careers.

I remember so well the phone call at about half past six that evening. Max had been waiting outside the committee room in London, and had just been given the news.

'Richard,' he said, 'it's Max. They've decided.'

'Go on,' I said, trying to sound casual and unconcerned.

'Are you sitting down?'

'Do I need to?'

'I really think you should.'

Fuck, I thought, we haven't got it.

'We've fucking got it!' he shouted.

I sat down then all right, and Judy saw from my face that we'd won. It was a very good moment.

So Granada had 'walked it', had won the franchise for the most coveted prize in daytime television – and *This Morning* was born.

In Granadaland the viewers, of course, knew we were married but, oddly, that wasn't a factor in the decision to put us on *This Morning*. Judy Finnigan was Judy Finnigan and Richard Madeley was Richard Madeley. They just happened to present shows together. We were never really 'sold' as a married couple; but it was one of the factors that made Granada's pilot so distinctive.

For the first couple of years, Judy and I felt uncomfortable whenever we read reviews that made a great play on our being married. It was as if *This Morning*'s success – and our success – was only achieved because it was presented by a husband and wife.

'Hang on,' we wanted to say, 'we're not doing this because we're married, but because we've developed the experience journalistically and technically to do the job.'

I'd been working in daily TV for ten years and Judy for

longer than that, and it did feel a bit galling to be sneered at and have what we'd achieved dismissed as a gimmick. Later, though, we got some perspective and simply stopped worrying about it.

Once *This Morning* was commissioned, we went into rapid rehearsal. It was chaos! We had just a few weeks before the show was due to be transmitted from a Victorian warehouse in Liverpool's Albert Dock. The studio was still being built, and we had no offices, telephones or computers. Gangs of technicians and workmen worked 24/7 to get us installed by the launch date: 3 October. Apart from Judy and me, none of the other presenters had been appointed. But, slowly and surely, they were: Fred Talbot, the weatherman, who became famous for not falling into the water from *This Morning*'s weather map. Denise Robertson, our agony aunt, who had been through the mill herself when she was widowed with children and stony broke. That's when she turned herself into a successful novelist. Chris Steele, our family GP, a gentle Geordie, who had a wonderful ability to put people at their ease. Susan Brookes, our cook, who'd been thrown out of a cookery class at school for talking too much. Andrew and Liz Collinge, hair and make-up artists, who had their own family hairdressing business on Merseyside; and Charles Metcalfe, wine expert.

We were given a fantastic director, David McMahon, who was very experienced in live programmes, and our launch editor was Dianne Nelmes. Dianne was a good friend; she was our news editor on *Granada Reports*, and she'd gone on to *World in Action* and the BBC's *Brass Tacks*. She had the rare but vital ability to produce both serious current affairs and light entertainment, and was refreshingly unpompous in her approach. Not surprisingly, Dianne eventually went on to become a key player at ITV's network centre. We also had Max Graesser as deputy editor.

We'd all worked together for years on regional programmes and the four of us – Dianne, Max, Judy and me – made a tight unit. We trusted each other's judgement and enjoyed each other's company. I believe that's one of the main reasons why *This Morning* was a success from the word go. Dianne handled the creative aspects of the launch; Judy and I worked closely with her on the editorial policy; Max took care of the technical and financial aspects and was full of ideas, too. It's quite common in television for teams to pull in opposite directions. We were all singing from the same hymn sheet, were totally dedicated and very determined that between us we would make the programme a success.

But TV, like any profession, has its petty jealousies and rivalries. The buzz in ITV during our pre-launch days was that Granada would cock it up, that Judy and me – two unknown regional presenters – wouldn't be able to hack it; and that the show would be off the air by Christmas.

Even as we launched, one of our execs – our old friend Rod Caird – told us bluntly that if we hadn't built an audience by Christmas, we *would* be off the air. Knowing there were plenty of Jonases predicating that only gingered us up all the more to make it work. And I don't know why, but we were confident. I was thirty-three, Judy was forty, Dianne and Max were in their thirties. Between us, we had half a century of modern TV experience.

'Fuck it,' we told each other. 'We can do this.'

To their credit, David Liddiment and Steve Morrison trusted us and allowed us a very long rein. We more or less planned and did whatever we wanted to do, and only on rare occasions, when they felt we were going adrift, did they gently intervene.

––––––––––

With the full *This Morning* team in place, we went on air at 10.40 a.m. on 3 October 1988. Our opening lines were: 'Hello,

I'm Richard Madeley and this is my wife, Judy Finnigan.' Judy gave a little smile and said, 'Hello!'

The mad reasoning behind these words was that I had already done a couple of networked quiz shows and should introduce Judy, and also be explicit about the fact we were married. But it was a heroically naff introduction by any standards, and when we saw a tape of it a few years later we were open-mouthed. Still, it was very funny.

By the middle of November the ratings were building. *This Morning* was still virgin territory, a completely different approach to television, not just daytime television. There was no publicity, no trailers, no newspaper campaign, no press interviews, and yet, within six weeks, by word of mouth alone, its popularity was spreading.

But we were all knackered. One Friday we went out with Max and Dianne for dinner. Max seemed preoccupied. Then he said, 'Can I ask you all a personal question? Am I the only one not to have had sex since the beginning of October?'

It wasn't as bad as that for us, but we knew what he meant.

––––––––––

Perhaps surprisingly, given our location, we had no problem getting celebrities and other interviewees to appear on the show. Most of them were perfectly prepared to come up to Liverpool. In fact, they enjoyed coming. *This Morning* was one of very few live network shows coming from the regions; and Albert Dock was a beautiful spot, especially on a winter's morning when the view from the window behind our studio set looked just like a painting. Albert Dock's beautiful red columns and brickwork, the light on the water, and the diffuse image of the Liver Building, a quarter of a mile behind us, could be eye-catchingly lovely.

Also, at that time, Liverpool was going through a renaissance because the previous Tory government, thanks to Michael Heseltine, had invested a lot of money in it. Albert Dock's regeneration project had just been completed, and opening a television studio for ITV's country-wide network was a big step for Liverpool. It was part of a new beginning, a new era, and there was an optimistic spirit in the city which spread, by osmosis, to our programme. People began to sit down, take note and talk about it; students began to watch it, and by Christmas it was becoming what today we'd call a 'brand'. And, even though the programme constantly evolved, the essence remained the same: a live, adventurous magazine format with a very broad agenda.

The main problem we encountered was that sometimes overseas celebrities couldn't spare a whole day out of their tight agenda to come and be interviewed; and sometimes the logistics of getting people to the studio were insurmountable. In winter our main difficulty was fog either at London's airports or the ones in Manchester and Liverpool. Often we would start the programme with three of our main guests – say, a politician, an actor and a pop star – still in the air above us, waiting for the fog to lift. We could actually hear the planes circling. Then Judy and I would have to improvise, keep the show going until the guests landed and were rushed over by taxi.

In fact we loved it when things went wrong. It was a challenge. Whatever aspect of a show went adrift – unless it was a legal issue which everybody always hates – it always made for an enjoyable watch. We knew the viewers were with us, and Judy and I always took them into our confidence. We felt very strongly from the first moment that *This Morning* was *their* show. As David Liddiment once said, 'Programmes that are really popular, and have endurance and longevity, are the ones people feel that they own.'

We never forgot that, and we always used to say to our

viewers, 'This is *your* show. If you don't like it, ring in, and tell us what you'd like us to change and, if we can, we will.'

That was our credo then and it still is today.

Over the years on *This Morning* we had many similar heated internal debates about what the programme's editorial policy should be, what subjects should or should not be covered. Sometimes these discussions were concerned with internal politics: what would please certain people within the power hierarchy; and sometimes about individual members of the team. But, when these arguments were taking place, Judy and I always said, 'The only fucking thing that matters is what comes out of that box. If we forget that and start broadcasting to ourselves or to our peers, or to those we fear because they have power over us, we'll make the biggest mistake of our lives and we'll be finished.'

The viewers are our masters – and they hold the whip hand. There's no such thing as 'brand loyalty' any more in television. Nobody watches a programme because they have a special allegiance to BBC or ITV or Channel 4. They watch because they like certain programmes and then, quite rightly, they switch to another channel for their next choice.

———

Up until *This Morning* Judy and I had only been recognized in the regions where we worked as local news presenters. But suddenly it didn't matter where we went; our days of anonymity in large parts of the country were over.

It was unsettling at first, but a sign that the programme was catching on – a kind of thermometer that registered the temperature of public awareness about the show. That's all fame or celebrity is, of course. Some performers certainly bask in it, but I can't see why. It's simply a register of performance, a sign that your show's being watched.

I'm a gregarious sociable person, and I mostly enjoyed viewers coming up and chatting, and I still do. But the flip side of what Derek Batey had called 'the fame thing' was that the show – and Judy and me – began to be picked up on in the papers. There was a very pejorative view of daytime TV then, and there still is here and there. We couldn't understand it; we knew how hard everyone worked to make the show, and the intelligence and commitment it took to keep it fresh. But we had to get used to being sneered at, and gradually some diarists and columnists became self-appointed experts on our characters. I remember reading one piece that said I was obviously the kind of person who if he saw himself reflected in a shop window would stop and stare. Uh? I was 'conceited', I was 'arrogant', the piece went on.

I was clearly a first-class shit! I was mortified. My friends and family read these papers; I felt hot with embarrassment every time something like this was casually tossed off in a review or column. I could hardly send out a press statement denying that I was conceited, arrogant, or whatever – what a delicious own-goal that would be – and for a while I stayed at home more often at weekends and felt unhappy and self-conscious when I did go out in public. It was a ludicrous overreaction, and it was Lenny Henry who put me straight.

We'd just interviewed him and were chatting after the show. He looked super-fit and I said so.

'Yeah, I'm really into my jogging at the moment,' he said. 'I'm in the park every day.'

I was surprised, and I told him how I'd started to feel increasingly awkward in public. He's probably forgotten this, but Lenny Henry's face became serious.

'Let me give you some advice,' he said. 'I've had seven kinds of shit written about me and I've had to go on stage that night. And no one's read it or, if they have, they don't care, don't believe it, or they've forgotten it.

'Man, you've got to be yourself and let your audience judge you, not some hack. And you've got to do your normal stuff when you're not working or you'll go crazy.' He put on his 'mother' voice. 'Go out for a jog today, or I'll tan your behind.'

I laughed. 'I hate jogging.'

'Well, buy a bike, my friend. Ride around. Let 'em laugh – though they won't. Do everything you'd do if you weren't doing this stupid job.'

In real life we hardly ever 'snap out' of anything, but that short conversation with Lenny had an instant effect. I bought a bike that evening and threw off my anxieties about what people might think, based on our remorselessly growing cuttings file. I had a new mindset along with my old attitude. And this was to be of enormous value a few months later when I found myself in one of the most grotesque periods of my life: the long year when accusations of theft hung over me. I don't think I've ever thanked Lenny for his robust advice, but I am doing that now. It was to help keep me sane.

———

Of course, not all public interest is welcome. We were at a fête in Manchester and I was being followed by a husband and wife and a couple of teenage kids. Jack, still a baby then, needed a major nappy change so I took him back to the car. If you've had babies you'll know what I mean when I say it was not going to be an easy or quick clean-up job. I was at the messiest stinkiest stage when I felt myself almost hit in the back. It was the guy who'd been tracking me.

'Autograph, *autograph*,' he demanded. Just like that. Really classy behaviour.

'I don't want to be rude,' I said. 'But, as you can see, I'm under a bit of pressure. I'll just clean up my baby and then I'll be happy to sign.'

'No,' he said. 'We're in a hurry, got to go. I want your autograph now – one for each of us. It's us that pay your wages.'

'Fine,' I said. 'But I'll have to sign in shit, I'm afraid.'

I showed him my glistening hands.

The following abuse was, I have to say, in a class of its own. I felt fully entitled to respond in kind and did so.

He was astonished. But I've discovered that, on the rare occasions when I come across a guy who thinks he can take liberties or be foul-mouthed, the best thing to do if you can't ignore them or get away is to give as good as you get. They're usually astonished to hear the bloke off the telly calling them a cunt.

Everyone finds their own way of dealing with the phenomenon of becoming 'a face'. Judy, I think, would rather like to become invisible after a programme. But then she's always been shy, an irony that doesn't escape her when she considers how she earns her living. So becoming well known because of the sheer frequency of her TV appearances hasn't actually altered her personality, which has always had a slightly withdrawn quality anyway. And after my slight crisis, which Lenny Henry so crisply despatched, I'm pretty much the person I was when I was working in newspapers. At least I think I am.

Being on TV is a weird, very contemporary human experience. It's something that's only come into being in the last fifty years or so. Uncharted waters, and no proper maps. For the first time, television means that the audience doesn't go to the performer. The performer comes into the living-room or kitchen or bedroom. It's all very personal and strange, and if you end up doing a job like ours it's better, on the whole, not to over-analyse the process.

Anyway, it's all so fleeting. Very few in TV stay there for ever. That's why, as I wrote earlier, it's so important to regard fame as nothing more than a barometer of how widely your programme is viewed. The experience of being recognized in the street is, I suppose, a bit like picking up a returning sonar echo. That's all. It isn't really a validation of you as a person. So the day it stops shouldn't really change anything – you just carry on being the person you've always been.

Well, that's my plan and I'm sticking to it.

6: JUDY

The first time I realized *This Morning* was having a real impact was quite strange. We were at home in Manchester in the days when Terry Wogan had his half-hour chat show, *Wogan*, on telly at seven o'clock in the evening. I always enjoyed watching this and that night the TV was on in the sitting-room while Richard was in the kitchen. Terry was making a comment about 'live' television when he added: 'There's hardly anything live on television these days. There's only me in the evenings, Richard and Judy in the mornings, and that's about it.'

I nearly fell off my chair. Jumping up, I shouted, 'Richard!' And, as he came rushing in, I said, 'Terry Wogan's just mentioned our names on his programme. Terry Wogan knows who we are.'

Richard was as chuffed as I was. It was a defining moment. To me Terry Wogan was a megastar. I'd never met him, but greatly admired him. He was famous, and the fact that he knew who *we* were was just unbelievable.

But let me go back to the birth of *This Morning*.

When the programme was first getting off the ground, it was pretty odd. None of us really knew what we were doing. Unlike America, daytime TV in the UK usually consisted of 'repeats', but our specially commissioned, network programme was a new concept. Once Granada's Steve Morrison and David Liddiment had won the franchise, Richard and I were trying to get our heads around what would be needed. During the first discussion concerning editorial content, I remember one

141

of Granada's executives saying, 'Well, we'll include items like, well . . . ironing.'

'Ironing?' I said, aghast.

'Yes,' he replied. 'You know, tips on the best way to do it.'

I couldn't believe it but, lo and behold, that item was included in the pilot. Fortunately, it was so dire it was dropped from the finished show.

Richard and I always felt that kind of approach was rather misguided; that there were far more interesting and entertaining topics for a magazine-format programme to concentrate on. Steve Morrison used to call it our 'hidden agenda'. But what we had instinctively sussed out was that a lifestyle-concept show, which would, of course, include 'fluffy' bits around its edges, such as tips on cooking, beauty, gardening, and so on, could also deal with the more serious challenging aspects of people's everyday lives. That was – and remained – our approach. Neither of us is remotely domesticated; Richard is certainly not interested in 'how to knock up a tool shed' and I'm no whizz with a paint-brush. What decorating I have done has always been carried out from necessity, rather than a desire to try my hand at it. So, knowing this about ourselves, and realizing this would resonate with a great number of viewers, we were determined to make it a broad-based magazine programme.

Once we were on screen, *This Morning* got off to a very slow start ratings-wise. This was not surprising as we had not been given any advance publicity or fanfare. We just kind of crept into the homes of the few people who were watching TV at that time of day. But then, as these viewers began to appreciate that *This Morning* was offering something different, they told their friends and the ratings began to rise.

In the beginning, we often found ourselves up against the usual sexist approach in television. I was expected do the

142

'womanly' items, such as the flower-arrangement sequences, and Richard was expected to drive the phone-ins and 'manly' topics. I was expected to interview the male celebrities, Richard was expected to interview the female. It was such a bore, so stupid, and I used to get really incensed with this sexist division-of-labour approach.

One early slot called 'A Troubled Shared', which I was asked to present, was in my view particularly patronizing, and nobody was more pleased than me when it was dropped. While it lasted, the format was for people to come into the studio to discuss the problems they were experiencing in their lives or with their families, in the hope that other viewers who lived nearby would help by responding. For a network programme, it was all very local newspaper stuff. For example, there might be a couple with two disabled children who were finding it very difficult to cope and wanted to get a rota of neighbourhood help established. It was a well-meaning format, but too 'one note' for network TV and became, 'Oh, God, now it's the problem spot' of the show. I really didn't enjoy presenting this.

The programme became much better when Richard and I started skirting the sexist approach and doing more and more things together, regardless of whether the content was classified as essentially masculine or feminine. There was some resistance to this behind the scenes, but fortunately we had a very good relationship with our editor, Dianne Nelmes. Although our non-sexist approach was considered unorthodox in those days, both she and others began to realize that for Richard and me this was an organic approach that stemmed quite naturally from us being a married couple. From then on, quite rightly, we both became involved with all the topics, regardless of what sex they were supposed to appeal to, and that worked much better for the viewers, the ratings and for us.

The Albert Dock was a magnificent setting for a television programme. Even though we only had a makeshift studio, with the editorial office situated half a dock away, and didn't even have any toilets, we loved the location. The problem was that ITV had set *This Morning* up on a 'let's see how it goes' basis, and there was no way that Granada wanted to commit itself to a really expensive infrastructure until the programme proved itself. In fact, when we went on screen lots of people in the business kept saying, 'It'll be off the air by Christmas.'

First thing in the morning, we would go to the office, put on our presenting clothes, go to make-up, which was just next door to the office, I'd have my hair done and then we'd set out, often in a howling gale, to walk along the side of the dock to the studio. Huge waves would be sweeping along the Mersey; and, my God, was it windy. Having been blown almost off our feet, we'd arrive at the studio, which had a makeshift set and a props room, but nowhere to repair my wet and windswept hair or make-up. We would then be there from around nine thirty to midday, and that's a long time to be without a loo. What we had to do was go to the toilet in the pub next door. Fortunately, the Wharf, as it was called, was an all-day pub that also served food.

Whenever I wanted to go to the loo I would have to wait for the commercial breaks or a five- or six-minute VT – video tape – running, then dash out, with my microphone and earpiece still on so that I could hear the PA's count-down. I would tear outside the building, go across to the pub, and race upstairs to the loo. The trouble was, there were only two cubicles and, being a Ladies, there was *always* a queue. I used to stand there fretting but, thankfully, as the programme and my face got better known, the other ladies would recognize me and say, 'Oh, it's you from the telly. I never thought to see you here. What are you doing? Aren't you on air?'

'I'm supposed to be,' I'd reply, laughing nervously, 'but actually I need to go to the loo.'

Sometimes I was lucky, they'd let me go first.

In the cubicle, I would be listening to the PA's count-down on my earpiece; and she'd be saying things like, 'One minute thirty on VT . . . one minute on VT,' and I knew I had to hurry up and get back. It was a nightmare. I put up with this for years until my agent, Annie Sweetbaum, got really stroppy with Granada and said, 'Look, you are going to have to build a toilet – even if it is just a Ladies. It's not such a problem for men.'

So Granada caved in and arranged for a tiny toilet to be put in at the back of the studio. It was supposed to be a Ladies, but it never was just that. Everybody used it, and I was still in the same boat because all the team waited for the commercial break, and it was always occupied. I'd stand there hammering on the door, yelling, 'For God's sake! I'm needed back on screen.' Then, on one of her visits, Annie Sweetbaum would say to all the others, 'Go away. Campaign for your own loo. I campaigned for this one for Judy.' At one level, it was hilarious.

There were other problems. The Albert Dock was part of a large tourist complex that had been opened with a huge fanfare. The idea was to get visitors, who were wandering around the cafés and chichi gift shops, to come in and visit it. As a result we had no real security in our studio, just an ordinary door which led into one of the main arcades on the dock. Occasionally, when one of the security men could spare the time, he would stand in front of our door. But most of the time, anyone could walk in. One day, while Richard and I were live on the set, two old dears, dressed in macs and laden with shopping bags, did just this.

'Is this Habitat?' one of them asked, mystified.

Given that the set was all stripped pine and modern furniture, they could be forgiven for thinking it was!

One disadvantage was that our studio was on the ground floor and, when we were on telly, we sat on the set with our backs to a vast, floor-to-ceiling, plate-glass window. As the pavement was just outside, the constant throng of passers-by soon noticed the cameras and, realizing that somebody was making a TV programme in there, would stand outside the window, pulling faces and waving banners. It was mayhem, but I enjoyed all that. Somehow it made the programme seem very immediate and informal, but we did, of course, also attract our fair share of 'nutters' who made the most of being on camera. The most famous of these was a streaker.

What happened on that day concerned Fred Talbot, our weatherman, who did his report on an incredibly low-tech map of the British Isles floating on an island in the dock. This absurd creation became very much identified with *This Morning*, but the real reason for its existence was that Granada had used it for the pilot because it couldn't afford to spend the money on special weather-computed graphics. Weird though Fred's map was, it subsequently became a tourist attraction, a magnet for the thousands of visitors present at any one time to come and watch him doing his reports. This also meant that anybody who wanted to leap on the floating map could, because there was one tiny walkway which led from the side of the dock straight to it. This was terrifying because when anybody stepped on to it, the whole edifice swayed.

Anyway, on this memorable occasion, Fred, while doing his report, suddenly saw a streaker in the distance. Alarmed, his vocal delivery got slower and slower, almost grinding to a halt while he was obviously thinking, What in God's name do I do now? Inside the studio, we were wondering why he had begun to mumble and what was wrong, then suddenly, as the streaker arrived in front of the outside cameraman, we could see what Fred had seen, and the streaker's backside was now on screen. The crowd, of course, was going mad, absolutely loving it; and, as the streaker stepped on to the weather map, Fred, really panicking now, broke off his report and started to run away from him. On screen, we were then left with the streaker running around the weather map after Fred who, abruptly collecting himself, stopped and held his clipboard over the man's genitals. Fred did the best he could to save the viewers' blushes, but they still got the occasional glimpse of them. In the studio, watching these antics on the monitors, we were all in hysterics.

Afterwards there was the inevitable hoo-ha from on high, saying that we should have cut away or gone to black, then come back. The camera team, in fact, were on the verge of doing this when Richard said, 'No, no, carry on filming. We must see what happens.'

Television executives always had a bit of a thing about streakers grabbing the limelight on TV, but I can't really understand why. It's live television, it's only a human body, and it's great entertainment. The theory, though, was that if one person was allowed to get away with it, live TV would become a prime target for exhibitionists, and everybody would want to do it. But how many streakers do you know? Our chap proved to be a well-known local one and, having got a taste of stardom that day, he did subsequently do the same thing on the *Big Breakfast* the following week.

Poor old Fred, he didn't half get landed with that map, and not only on that occasion. Because it was so low-tech and the weather report only consisted of him starting off at John O'Groats and walking down it, stopping off at various imaginary cities, and giving a little commentary, the producers decided to spice it up. To make the reports less boring, they arranged for various stunts to take place on the map while Fred was doing his report. One bright person, for example, decided to book a belly-dancer to dance on the map. A voluptuous lady, she was scantily clad for her 'performance', while Fred, poor chap, was trying to do his report. I don't know how he got through it. She was getting closer and closer to him, shaking her breasts in his face and, although he was clearly overcome with embarrassment, he was doing his best to carry on. Meanwhile, Robert Khodadad, our director in the box, was absolutely loving all this and going berserk with laughter. We could hear him chortling away in the gallery, then heard his phone ringing and our editor, Dianne Nelmes, who was in the editorial office, saying, 'Rob, get off the weather. Cut – get off the bloody weather.'

'Yes, sure, all right,' Rob replied, putting the phone down very slowly.

Dianne still gets angry about this incident; but it was terribly funny. I understand her point of view, though. *This Morning* was very new in those days and there was a justifiable fear that the show hadn't yet earned the right to be so daring and possibly upset the network and its viewers.

Ken Russell, the film director, was involved in yet another weather-map 'event'. Having come on the show to do what proved to be a really good-value, great fun interview, he mentioned that what he would love to do was direct a sequence on Fred's floating weather map. Having got our agreement, he then appeared on the dock with a huge old-fashioned megaphone and, having organized all the extras and props, he directed a battle scene while Fred was doing his report. He had soldiers on one side pitching mock grenades at Fred, who then had to jump from one side to the other to avoid the mock explosions. It was mad, surreal, but a lot of fun.

Sometimes, because the dock was wired up for sound, Richard and I did items outside. But this wasn't much fun as we always had to plough through crowds of people to get to the locations in time. Then, as both the shopping precinct and the programme became better known, there were even larger crowds standing there watching it. We would be desperately struggling to get to the right place at the right time while tourists and shoppers were constantly stopping us and saying, 'Can I have your autograph?' It was funny and very nice, but not exactly easy to get to the next item on cue.

The dock itself was so beautiful at times. When it snowed at Christmas it was just the most perfect backcloth, and we felt so privileged to be working there. I agreed wholeheartedly with Dianne Nelmes when she said, 'It's a location to die for.' Sometimes it was so surreal. A director, for example, might be rehearsing a bridal fashion item, and we would look up and see a dozen brides in full bridal outfits walking down the dock. The brides, of course, were all models about to be filmed, but in that setting it was extraordinary, just something else. Everybody who worked there grew fond of the dock because the atmosphere was so full of vitality and such good fun.

––––––––

In the beginning, it was quite difficult to persuade top-notch celebrities to come on to the show. They had never heard of *This Morning*, which came out of a grotty studio in Liverpool, and were reluctant to travel up for interviews. My first interviewee was the very attractive comic actor, Paul Nicholas. I had, of course, interviewed celebrities before on other programmes: Billy Connolly, for example, who'd succeeded in reducing me to tears of laughter all the way through; and the incredibly talented and versatile Michael Crawford. But somehow that first *This Morning* interview was different. For a start, there was so much more time allowed for these items. When Paul Nicholas came on, I was quite awestruck, unsure at first about how to conduct such an in-depth interview. Paul, though, was a very sweet guy and I soon got into my stride.

Then, still within the first couple of weeks, Nicola Paget

came on to the programme. I didn't know then – I don't think anybody did – that she was a manic depressive, but I soon found out she had a problem. With hindsight, possibly in the throes of an attack, she was disconcertingly offhand throughout the interview and totally unforthcoming in any of her responses to my questions. This kind of behaviour is always a disaster on a live programme. Just after we came off air, she said to me in a haughty voice, 'So, is it only Liverpool then which gets this programme?'

'No,' I said, 'it's a network show.'

'What do you mean?' she said, shocked.

'It goes out all over the country,' I explained. 'Everybody watches it.'

It obviously then dawned on her that she had been pretty cavalier throughout the transmission, and had put on the attitude of 'I'm a big actress, a big star. What am I doing here on this little programme and *who* is this person interviewing me?'

I've met her several times since and she's been fine. She was obviously just having problems at that time.

Most of the celebrities we had on the show in those early days, people such as Barry Manilow, Cliff Richard, Kathleen Turner, Amanda Donahoe, Hugh Grant, were all absolutely charming. But interviews can be a bit of a hit-and-miss affair, and therefore nerve-racking. Sometimes you come face to face with somebody you are really nervous about meeting or not wholly at ease with: Peter Ustinov, for instance, although I'm not really sure why. He was a brilliantly funny raconteur, writer and a talented actor, a perfect *Wogan* or *Parkinson* type guest, but he was not quite right for our audience, not sufficiently appealing perhaps to the majority of our female viewers. I guess that that was what was worrying me. Our job on *This Morning* was to help well-known people to be appreciated by a wider audience, but I didn't feel I succeeded in his case. It was, as I wrote above, much better when Richard and I started interviewing guests together; then the whole thing became more of a friendly intimate chat and much less formal.

The first guest we interviewed as a twosome was the country and western singer, Barbara Dickson. Now on tour, she had recently had a miscarriage and was very into talking about that. As I had also lost a baby in the past, we drifted quite naturally into a woman-to-woman chat and then when she began talking about her husband and his reactions to it, Richard was able to relate his experience. So what subsequently became a working-in-tandem approach to interviews really stemmed from that programme, and became a hallmark for both us and *This Morning*.

The star I associate most with those Liverpool days, though, is Paul O'Grady alias Lily Savage. Although we knew who he/she was before his/her first appearance on *This Morning*, we didn't know quite what to expect. Paul had come down from London to do an item with Charles Metcalfe who, at that stage, was our wine expert, and Richard and I were also present on the dock tasting wine. God knows why this sequence was being filmed outside, but it was. Paul, who takes for ever to put on his Lily Savage 'slap', was late, and the director and the producer were panicking that he wouldn't make the dock in time. We, having managed to arrive on cue ourselves, were with Charles and his wine bottles on what we called 'the pontoon', next to Fred's floating weather map. Unsure if Paul would make it, we had started the item, watched by the usual masses, when a huge roar and applause sprang up in the crowd. This was for Lily, who had just made her appearance outside the studio, wearing incredibly high-heeled shoes, and who was now tottering her way down the metal steps to make her way to the pontoon. For the piece, she was simply meant to taste the wine and provide some back-up fun, but her antics were so hilarious she completely took it over. Pretending to be squiffy, then seriously drunk, she started to sing mad Liverpool drag-queen songs like 'Oh, Titania', pausing every now and then to drain another glass and chuck it over her shoulder. I have never laughed so much in my life. It remains my all-time favourite *This Morning* item, and a lot of the viewers rang in to say that it was theirs, too. It was also the start of a long-lasting friendship between us and Paul.

Whenever we interviewed him on the show, he was fantastic. Everybody used to worry that his Lily Savage act would be too near the knuckle, too *risqué* for pre-watershed daytime TV, but I knew instantly that we could trust him. He had a line that he skated very close to, but he never ever crossed it on our shows. He even did phone-ins with our viewers and always had the lucky participants in hysterics. They loved him. He also said that being on *This Morning* was great for him, too, because when he was touring in *Prisoner Cell Block 8*, his appearances on our programme in the morning would put on an extra ten thousand ticket sales. It was a smashing, mutually beneficial friendship, and we remain very fond of him to this day.

I really enjoyed the challenge of presenting *This Morning* and refining the art of putting guests at their ease. When celebrities came on to the show for the first time to talk about a film or play they were in, or a concert tour they were doing, or a book they'd written, they'd be very nervous of Richard and me. It was really weird. We had honestly not anticipated that! I knew I was sometimes awestruck and intimidated by them, but I had never thought they would feel the same about Richard or me. That was a bit of a bind to overcome. But, having met us, they'd be much more relaxed and forthcoming when they made return visits to the show.

We got to know some of our guests, people such as Martin Clunes and Neil Morrissey, really well on the screen and had a great time with them. I loved the jokes that Neil and Martin cracked, and the growing familiarity between them and us resulted in some jolly interviews. I also particularly remember Vic and Bob coming on the show for the first time. When they arrived on the set, I thought they were very odd, not at all as I had imagined them to be. I'd expected them to be 'off the wall', and was looking forward to that, but the interview just didn't gel. In the end, getting a bit fed up, I interrupted the interview and said, 'Okay. Well, I don't think this is working so we'd better go to a break.' Vic and Bob – especially Bob because he really loved *This Morning*, had often watched it, and was looking forward to coming on the show – were mortified.

'Judy, what happened?' Bob asked, shocked.

'I don't know,' I replied. 'It just didn't work. I guess, we didn't know where you were coming from, and you didn't know where we were coming from.'

They came back after the break and everything was absolutely fine. Subsequently, we got to know them well on screen and have interviewed them many times.

Curiously, as the programme, and Richard and me, became better known, putting people at their ease became even harder. Once on screen, though, their nervousness usually dissolved. Sitting alongside us, they started to relax, and felt we were a friendly couple who had no desire to stitch them up. They were right. We never had any intention of doing that. First and foremost, we are not like that; second, we know that if people feel vulnerable they don't give good interviews. They simply go on the defensive, become hostile and refuse to come back.

In general, it's very rare for celebrities to restrict the hosts of a show by insisting on 'no-go' areas in advance of a programme. But it does happen. When it does, nine times out of ten, it's not the celebrity, it's their agent. When, for example, Anthea Turner was booked on *This Morning* to talk about a new programme she was doing, we were told, 'She doesn't want to answer any questions about her relationship with Grant Bovey and the whole marriage thing.'

That's bloody ridiculous, we thought. It's been all over the papers and is already in the public domain. The viewers will be amazed if we don't mention it.

We didn't know Anthea well, and had just come across her and chatted to her at media events. Having made up our minds that we had to ask her some personal questions, we decided to ignore what her agent said, and trailed the interview with, 'Coming up next, Anthea Turner talks about her relationship and getting back with Grant Bovey.' As Anthea came on set, during a commercial break, she was looking a bit shocked, having heard the trail.

'We can't ignore it, Anthea,' we said. 'It's all over the papers. For us to say, "We've got Anthea Turner coming in, but we can't mention any of that relationship stuff," would make us all look absurd. Just trust us. We're not going to embarrass or upset you.'

Her reaction was very professional. 'Okay,' she said, 'I will trust you.'

The resulting interview, including all the personal questions, was absolutely fine.

'I was just very nervous,' she said afterwards, 'but you were right.'

Occasionally agents also threaten presenters like us by saying, 'If you so much as mention this, so-and-so will walk off the set.' I remember that when All Saints was breaking up, our entertainment bookings desk told us that *This Morning* had to sign an undertaking not to mention Liam Gallagher. If we did, the other members of the group would walk off. I'd never heard such nonsense and told our booking people that. In the event, the group couldn't have cared less; they wanted to do the interview and were perfectly happy to talk about Liam.

My dad, a hatter, at work in his factory in the 1970s.

Below: My glamorous mother Anne, looking alluring at her 21st birthday party. December, 1934.

Middle right: In my pram outside our house in Amos Avenue, looking puzzled and worried.

Right: My fifth birthday. Mum curled my hair every day.

Left: An early taste of future indiscretions as my right nipple popped out of its bathing suit! I used to be terribly embarrassed by this picture.

Above: Me and my little brother Roger, about to embark on the annual Whit's Walks, 1955.

Left: The whole family: Mum, Dad, my older brother Cal, me and Roger on holiday on the Isle of Man.

Birchfields Road, Manchester. Where I lived aged 11 to 18.

Specky four-eyes with frightening hair. Aged around 13 at Manchester High School for Girls.

Me in 1969 outside our student house in Bristol – now I think I look so much like Chloe.

Above: Not quite the serious graduate (1969) but we all wore skirts that short.

Left: Me, my brother Roger and a cousin, Susan, in the garden of our house in Manchester, 1968.

Left: Oh those 70s flares. Me and David in my parents' garden, 1973.

Below: My first wedding, to David, 23 March 1974, with my mum and dad and my mother-in-law, Kitty.

1977. Tom (left) and Dan at one day old, taken at the Norfolk and Norwich Hospital – before I went into shock. I thought Dan looked like a tiny Martian because of his pointy head.

Above: My father with Tom, aged 2, in our garden in Manchester.

Right: Mum and Dad after Dad had been diagnosed with cancer of the mouth.

Left: Weary at Manchester Airport in the early 80s. David and I were taking the boys to Italy on holiday – we were delayed six hours.

A carefree stroll down past our house in Manchester – me and David, and Tom (left) and Dan, in 1983.

My first networked show, *Reports Action*. No autocue – and live!

This 'gagging' is just one of the absurdities that people in our line of work have to watch out for. Personally, I would never deliberately set out to embarrass or put down a person on air, but neither will I go along with the kind of vested interest where celebrities are trying to manipulate publicity to promote an album, programme, film, whatever, while saying we can't talk about what is in the public domain. That's not on; no show should short-change its viewers with this 'plug-only' approach; and I have found almost without exception that, as long as the celebrities appreciate that you are basically a kind person who's not trying to make a reputation for yourself by doing a hatchet job at their expense, they're happy to trust you not to step over the line. That's the kind of fair play, I hope, that Richard and I built a reputation for on *This Morning*.

There are, of course, always exceptions to any rule. Much depends on how private anything is. For example, if somebody is publicly living with another person and having a baby by that person, I see no reason why this shouldn't be talked about. But if I happen to know through the grapevine that something scandalous is happening in a person's life that's not yet in the public domain, then I always check it out with the individuals concerned. If she or he then says, 'I'd really rather not talk about this at the moment,' that's fine with me. For instance, when Amanda Holden, who's married to Les Dennis of TV's *Family Fortunes* fame, had a fling with Neil Morrissey, Les behaved wonderfully well, even though he was very upset. I talked to both of them in private, but there was no way I would ever mention on air what they told me about their marital troubles unless they gave me permission to do so. When they eventually got back together, Amanda and Les did accept our invitation to come on to our new show, and talked bravely about their problems. But that was because they knew and trusted Richard and me as friends.

In instances where something is being hinted at by the press, but is not fully in the public domain, our approach was to allude to it by saying, 'Obviously, you are in the papers at the moment. So tell us, how are you?' This left the way open for them to say as much or as little as they wanted on a live show. But we never grilled them about it.

———

On programmes such as *This Morning* you are subjected to some pretty daft ideas for the show. One of these, thank God, never got as far as the air in Liverpool. One of the team wanted us to do a phone-in on miracles. The producer liked the idea and suggested we should go along with it.

'Why?' we said. 'Why do you want to do a phone-in on miracles?'

'Well,' she replied, 'I'm basing it on a magazine that's just been launched. They obviously want publicity, and can supply us with people who can work miracles.'

'Like what?' we said.

'Well, they can supply us with an African doctor who can cure AIDS.'

'Right,' we said. 'So you're suggesting this miracle-worker should be our phone-in guest and that people should ring in to ask how he cures AIDS.'

'Yes.'

'How do you know he can cure AIDS?'

'Well, the magazine people say so. They've got all these miracles attested by people in Uganda who say they've been cured by him.'

'And these people are all over here to take part in the programme?'

'Well, no, there's just him and the magazine person.'

'Right! Do we have any written evidence that these people were diagnosed with AIDS and that they are now cured?'

156

'Well, I think there are one or two photostats in the magazine which show that people have written in to say, "Thank you, you've saved my life."'

What was so frightening from our point of view was the low level of intelligence behind ideas like that. Most of our producers were lovely, exceptionally bright people, but many were also kids with no journalistic or investigative experience. They would look at something and think, Oh, that's a brilliant story! We, on the other hand, would have been taken off air if we had gone along with some of the lunacy.

On another occasion, we were not, perhaps, as quick on our feet as we should have been. While we'd been away for a couple of days, this particular item had been agreed and signed up by the time we returned to the studio, and it was too late to cancel it. But we should have cancelled it there and then. The item was about a black Labrador that was able, it was claimed, to hypnotize its owner and anyone else willing to be subjected to its unusual powers. Hypnodog we called it.

'It's wonderful therapy to be hypnotized by a dog,' its master said on air. 'It's a remarkable meeting of the canine and human mind.'

It was also absolute bull. When the guy had finished explaining his dog's mystical power, he then demonstrated the animal's 'talent' by going down on his knees, looking into the dog's eyes, and then keeling over on to the studio floor. The way he fell proved this to be one of the most embarrassing items included in our shows. 'Right!' I interjected, heading straight into the commercial break. Afterwards we laughed and winced at the same time.

One more canine item came about when one of our editors, who was bonkers about dogs, decided that she wanted to include a doggie make-over on the show. She wanted, she instructed, a really scruffy dog to be transformed into a perfect dog. We fought hard against this idea, but lost the battle, if not the war! The next morning the little white terrier with attitude that had been selected for the make-over turned up in the studio with its owners. The problem was it now looked absolutely beautiful. Somehow, the researcher, Sally-Anne, who had booked the dog, had failed to communicate to the owners that the dog should look 'filthy and scruffy' so that it could then be transformed into a perfect pooch on air; and its masters, so proud that it was to be on telly, had shampooed, brushed and groomed it to perfection, so that it would look lovely for the big occasion. The editor in question, who didn't actually last very long on *This Morning*, went berserk when she saw the terrier from the gallery.

'What is that thing doing there?' she screamed.

Sally-Anne, now a good friend of ours, but at the time a graduate doing work experience, replied meekly, 'I thought it was the perfect dog for the item.'

'I wanted it dirty – *filthy*,' the editor screamed back. 'Spray it with some artificial grime from the props department.'

Sally-Anne got the spray, knelt down by the terrier, which was now definitely displaying an attitude, and started to spray it. Meanwhile the by now distraught owners were looking more and more appalled at what was going on; and the editor was getting more and more wound up because time was running out.

Storming down on to the floor, she stood over Sally-Anne and the dog. 'More dirt. I want more dirt. I want it dirty, really filthy.'

The whole crew, including me and Richard, were frozen, transfixed by the surreal tableau that was going on before our eyes. Poor, poor dog, we were all thinking.

Then, at long last, a decision was made and the item was dropped. Off screen, though, we had to pay for the now filthy dog to have a make-over, which would clean it up before its return trip home.

There then followed a producer who wanted to include an item about a laughter clinic that had been set up in the Midlands. This set-up was supposed to be studying the science of laughter and how – what a surprise! – it was very good for our well-being. It was supposed to be a serious, academic, scientific study and the clinic had come up with various techniques to make – and teach – people how to laugh. Richard was in America at this time, and I was doing the show with Matthew Kelly of *Game for a Laugh* fame. Neither Matthew nor I thought it was a good idea and, having had a terrible argument about this with the producer, I was in tears when Richard phoned me that night from America.

One of the clinic's techniques that was to be demonstrated on the show was 'bottom writing'.

'What's "bottom writing"?' I said to the producer.

In answer, she stood up, turned around, put her bottom up in the air and started to wriggle it about.

'What's that meant to be?' I said, unamused.

'I'm writing a word with my bottom. And it makes people laugh.'

Well, it didn't make me laugh.

The next morning when she and the team came in, Matthew Kelly, because he truly is a funny man, was told that his particular function in the item was to read out some of the jokes supplied by the laughter clinic. They were absolutely dire. We were also asked to put on a false nose and a funny hat, while the laughter clinic people were wriggling their bottoms in the air. I don't think I've ever felt so naff in my life.

In the end, while on air, Matthew and I just looked at each other and said, 'Oh, God, this is just awful.'

The item lasted eight agonizing minutes and I could hardly believe it was being transmitted into our viewers' homes. It was a good example of what happens when the wrong ideas get through the net.

On the whole, Richard and I did manage to keep a kind of quality control on *This Morning*, but it was not always possible. Half the art of putting on a show like that is to know when to say, 'No.' Colleagues are naturally desperate to fill the available time on a five-day-a-week live programme, and have to come up with lots of ideas, so it's no surprise some of them are turkeys. I still cringe when I remember how many of these embarrassing moments made it on to *This Morning*, but at least some of the producers and researchers would have the good grace to come up to us afterwards and admit shamefacedly that it had not been a good idea. But, I have to say, naff items which didn't work provide some of our funniest memories.

One gaffe I particularly recall – one of mine this time – was when we were interviewing Keith Chegwin, who did a lot of children's TV and who was also at one time on *The Big Breakfast* and married to the *Tomorrow's World* reporter, Maggie Philbin. Keith, known in the past as a squeaky-clean nice guy, had started drinking too much and had lost it in quite a serious way. Following some press reports that he had been admitted to a rehab clinic, he was booked to come on to our show to talk about this. When we heard that he had once again blacked out at his home, our bookings person went to see him to ensure he was all right and, if so, to get him to the studio on time. She succeeded in getting him on the plane to Liverpool and decided to stay at the same hotel she had booked him into overnight. Keith, still in truth absolutely out of it, woke up the next morning with no idea of where he was.

'Hi, are you ready?' our colleague said as she arrived in his room.

'What?' Keith replied, obviously bewildered.

'You agreed to come on the *This Morning* show.'

'Did I?'

'Yes. You agreed to do an interview with Richard and Judy. And they're expecting you.'

'Did I? Oh, well, I'd better get ready.'

Keith somehow managed to get dressed, and came into the studio, looking on the surface professional. But, as he sat down, we noticed he was sweating and said, 'Are you all right, Keith? You don't look very well.'

'Yeah, I think so,' he replied dubiously.

He had met us before, but was so spaced out he wasn't for once even nervous.

'What's the matter?' we said on air. 'There's all this stuff in the papers about you and stress . . .'

There was a pause.

'No, what it is,' he said, 'is that I'm an alcoholic. I've got to admit that now.'

It was quite a moment. This was something he had never owned up to before, not even to himself.

Richard and I were initially taken aback. We hadn't realized that things were quite that far gone with him and certainly hadn't expected him to come on to the programme and say, Alcoholics Anonymous style, 'I'm an alcoholic.' We then did a harrowing interview with him. He was completely honest and, having told us a number of horrific stories, said he was really going to beat his drink problem now and have proper treatment.

All that was fine. But then, in a moment of what was meant to be an expression of sympathy, came my gaffe. At the close of the interview, I leaned over, patted him gently on the hand and said, 'Well, Keith, you've got a lot of bottle'!

I knew immediately how idiotic that sounded. I'm sure I turned instantly bright red. Nobody actually laughed, but a few tabloid journalists ticked me off the next day.

Later, though, when Keith wrote his autobiography, he referred to that interview as the moment that saved his life;

and when I read his book, I realized that his drink problem had been even more horrific than I'd thought at the time. He told his readers he had a sound-recording studio in the garden of his home and that he would be in there drinking bottles of whisky until he passed out. It was just too awful, potentially life-threatening, and I'm so glad our interview was instrumental in helping him to pull through.

I didn't, though, make as many gaffes on the programme as Richard. Sometimes he would say things he shouldn't and then would be genuinely surprised at other people's reaction, including mine. He'd just go too far, be too outspoken. But there were also times when the press exaggerated this. Each time a journalist went on about it, I wondered why they didn't take into account how many live broadcasts Richard actually made and how easy it is to slip up with all sorts of things. It's true I didn't like him going into too many personal details about our private life, but I did get used to that. Richard's a genuinely open person, with a brilliant sense of humour that sometimes leads him astray.

————

Sex is always risky on a pre-watershed show, but *This Morning* was the first programme to risk putting a male stripper troupe on British TV. On the first occasion, the Chippendales went down an absolute treat with our viewers. Having then received moons of phone calls from our fans asking us to put them on again, we did so about a month later. This time we hired a hall in the pub next to the studio and invited loads of Liverpool housewives to come and watch them live in action. Big mistake! It all went horribly out of control.

The Chippendales had promised us that they would tone down their routine for daytime TV, but they, too, got carried away. Two of them, by now stripped to loincloths and wearing cheeky naval caps, marched into the audience, grabbed what can only be described as a salivating woman, took her up on stage, placed her sandwich-like between them, and started to dance provocatively with her. It was terrifying television because, before they do their dance routines, some of them make quite sure they're looking – er – rampant, and we could see their excitement quite plainly on screen. You can imagine exactly where our cameramen zoomed in.

Meanwhile the women, as they often do on hen nights, got very over-stimulated, completely lost all their inhibitions and the entire sequence became incredibly licentious and gross.

The director, knowing the end of his career was nigh and unfolding on the screen before his very eyes, was so frozen with horror that he couldn't even give the order to cut. But, in any case, there wasn't anything less offensive to cut to. Everywhere the cameras were pointing there was something torrid and lecherous happening.

Richard and I, having done our last link, said goodbye to the viewers, and then the Chippendales as prearranged were given a five-minute dance routine to end the show. The guys, who were by now only wearing jock straps, continued to grab women out of the audience and the women continued to wrap their legs around the guys' unclad waists.

For Richard and me, it was a case of, 'Oh, my God . . .' because, even though it was only midday, and not a time when you expect such sexual excitement, the women were losing what remained of their inhibitions and dignity. We ended up backing off the set, trying to pretend it was nothing to do with us. Just to make matters worse, the next programme we had trailed on the show was *Rainbow*, with Zippy and Bungle and nice Geoffrey, so we knew all the kids were watching as well.

Normally when *This Morning* finished and we were off the air there would be an instant fizz of conversation both on the floor and in the gallery, but on that day you could have heard the proverbial pin drop. The dismayed silence was only broken by the director saying, 'My God, my God! My career's over.' A moment later, the phone rang in the gallery. When this happened immediately after a show everybody knew it meant big trouble.

'Oh, Lord,' a PA exclaimed, placing her hand over the mouthpiece. 'It's the executive producer.'

We did all survive the anticipated wigging that day, but *This Morning* had to issue an on-air apology and write to the hundreds of mothers who claimed that they had left little Johnny or Susan in front of the telly and, when they came back into the room, the kids had said, 'Mummy, what's that man doing to that lady?' We were all suitably contrite, but it was great television.

Obviously, given such events, *This Morning* had many complaints during its years on screen but, on the whole, most viewers watched it with their sense of humour intact. Managing the tone and taste aspects of the programme was always a vital consideration, but when things go wrong there's not much point in being too shocked and overreacting. When we were interviewing Anna Chancellor, for example, who played the character Duck Face in *Four Weddings and a Funeral*, Richard rather naïvely said to her, 'I've always wondered – because you're such an attractive actress – why your character in *Four Weddings* was called Duck Face.'

With great spontaneity, Anna replied, 'Well, I think, really, it was supposed to be Fuck Face, but obviously we couldn't say that in the film.'

'*Oh*,' Richard and I groaned.

Anna, sitting next to me, suddenly twigged that perhaps this was an absolutely no-go word on daytime TV. Taking my arm, she said, 'Wasn't I supposed to say that?'

Seeing my expression, she collapsed against my shoulder

and I had to put my arms around her and say comfortingly, 'It's all right. I'm sure you are very sorry.'

As anticipated, through my earpiece, I heard the phone ring immediately in the gallery, followed by somebody squawking to me, 'The ITC code demands that *she*, the actress, not you, the presenter, says sorry. You can't just say, "Sorry," or, "I'm sorry," the ITC code demands . . .'

It's quite true that we have to apologize, but poor Anna was already mortified enough and covered in embarrassment. We helped her to recover as best we could, and off she went. Meanwhile, down the phone came a panicky repeat message, 'She's got to say sorry. The ITC code demands . . .'

Unrepentant, in the next link I said to the viewers, 'I've just got to say that Anna Chancellor, as I am sure you all realize at home, is absolutely mortified about what slipped out just then. She's desperately sorry and hopes she hasn't embarrassed anybody. But, to be perfectly honest, I feel more sorry for her than anybody else.'

We did receive a couple of complaints after the programme, but most people rang in and said, 'Ah, tell the poor girl not to worry. It could happen to anyone.'

Overall, those early days on *This Morning* were sheer fun – fantastic. But when the BBC's *Good Morning*, presented by Anne Diamond and Nick Owen, followed us on to the screen in 1992, it all became a huge ratings war. For us, it was a bit like the student/finals/graduation scenario. When you're a student in your first year at university you can have a barrel of fun, but then come finals and graduation. That first year, 1988, on *This Morning* was like that. It was such a great laugh it never seemed like work. But the moment some bod at the BBC said, 'Excuse me, we can do what *This Morning* does on our channel,' Granada thought, Ah! We'd better take this into account, and make bloody sure we win.

From then on, we had to behave ourselves and watch our

step. We did see off Anne and Nick, we did stay at the top of the ratings and did win but, in the process, it all became much harder work and less fun. This was inevitable. When ratings become the primary factor, you always have to be on guard, can't take risks and do spontaneous things. Before that, Richard and I, and the team, used to believe that as long as the items were interesting, challenging, entertaining and the viewers enjoyed them, we could do anything: serious stuff, frivolous stuff, lifestyle stuff, mad stuff. We loved that kind of mix and freedom, and it worked. But when lifestyle pro-grammes started to take off in a really big way and suddenly everybody was doing cookery, make-overs, hair and DIY, it became much more difficult to be innovative. Our favourite part of the programme had always been interviewing ordinary and extraordinary people and celebrities, and discussing topi-cal subjects. We also loved the phone-ins, which sometimes became so relaxed for both us and the participants that we occasionally had to remind ourselves that we were doing a television programme.

———

I will now tell you why I love Richard. He's steadfast, emotion-ally strong and a very kind man. He has tremendous energy and vitality which I admire enormously, but it can be a bit wearing at times! He's very funny and we make each other laugh often. I know tabloid writers sometimes said he didn't go to university and that I'm the one with the education, but he's every bit as bright as I am and is extremely knowledgeable. I love his passion and sense of commitment, and his problem-solving abilities, even though these sometimes lead him into believing that everything can be solved when I know otherwise. That can be annoying, but in general I have absolute faith in him.

When we go down to Cornwall, he chops logs for the fires

and can, when he wants to, turn his hand to anything. If he decided to go into pig farming, I'm perfectly sure he'd just read up about it and do absolutely fine. The same would apply to anything he'd like to do. He's fantastically loyal and was brilliant with me during the dreadful days when I was deciding whether I could end my first marriage and felt so guilty and awful. It was his utter determination not to make me feel bad, while at the same time letting me know that he loved and wanted me, that made me realize he had extraordinary qualities. And time has proved that he does. I was right in entrusting Dan's and Tom's future to him. He has never failed the twins, or me or Jack and Chloe. He's sweet, devoted and very attractive.

By nature we are both jealous, and were even more so when we were younger. Handsome pop stars and beautiful models were forever coming into whatever studio we were working in. On one occasion on *This Morning*, I remember Richard being absolutely furious with me because he was convinced I was flirting with Marti Pellow of Wet Wet Wet, but I wasn't, I was just being friendly! And sometimes I would be quite certain that he was staring a bit too much at some of the models and we would have words about that afterwards. Where male celebrities are concerned, some female presenters may think, Oh, isn't he gorgeous. I'm certainly going to interview him, but it's not like that for me. I've discovered that most people, however gorgeous, are really pretty ordinary.

In the early days, on the way home after an interview, I was given to saying to Richard, 'Hmm! You liked her, didn't you?' Or he would say, 'Did you have to tell him he was that handsome?' But these reactions stemmed from insecurity. Once I accepted that an inherent part of a presenter's job is the ability to charm people and make them feel special, I didn't react to what Richard said, didn't take it personally. Now, after so many years of interviewing exceptionally beautiful, handsome, sexy individuals, we're much more at ease with each other on the jealousy front, can tease each other about flirting because we're no longer insecure and know each other inside out.

From the beginning, we've always had a passionate relationship, and trust and fidelity have always been essential to both of us. Neither of us has ever taken the liberal view that infidelity doesn't matter. It does to us. We hold each other more dear than anybody else in the world, and the fact that we put each other first is vitally important.

————

When we were on *This Morning*, because we presented the show together as a couple and were so recognizable as such, we were on display from the time we got out of the car at the studios in the morning and remained on view from then on. The moment we arrived in our workplace we also had microphones on and everybody in the control gallery could hear what we were saying. You do get used to this, but there were times when I found it very disconcerting. I couldn't be as spontaneous as I would have liked to be and say exactly what was on my mind because someone somewhere might be listening.

One of the stresses, then, when Richard and I first started out was that we never seemed to be alone, were always on show, aware that others were watching how we were behaving. That was not always easy to cope with. I also found it a bit wearing always having to keep a cheery smile on my face and keep my make-up touched up and all that stuff. But you learn. Good manners, I've found, are very useful aids for guiding me through any emotional haze.

What we didn't realize, though, and what nobody told us for a very long time, was that when we were sitting in the studio, about to go into the phone-in, with the participants waiting on line, those callers could hear us, too. I still have nightmares thinking back on this because, quite often, Richard and I would be sitting there discussing their cases. I remember only too well the day we received a call from a lady during a slimming item. She began by telling us she was very overweight and, even though she had stuck faithfully to a thousand calories a day diet for a year, she hadn't lost a pound. Dr Chris Steele and our guest, Rosemary Conley, were very sceptical about this and, as kind as they were on camera, off-air in the commercial break they were saying she was deluding herself, that there was no way that she could not lose weight on such a diet, and she must be scoffing chocolate on the side. Unaware that she was still on the line and could hear us, I joined in the scepticism. Afterwards, it was me who was singled out – it would be, wouldn't it? I received the following letter:

> *I don't know if you remember me, but I was the caller on your slimming phone-in and I have to tell you, because I don't know if anybody has told you, that we, the callers, can hear everything you say, including all the negative things during the commercial breaks. I certainly heard what everyone was saying about me and I was very, very upset. I hadn't expected it from you, Judy. I thought you would be on my side and I was very, very hurt. But I just thought that you should be aware that this is happening.*

I was shocked to the core, felt absolutely dreadful and wrote back to her at once.

The next day, when we were being miked up, I said to our sound guy, 'Excuse me. But shouldn't you have told us that our phone-in callers can hear us during the breaks?'

'Oh, yes!' he replied. 'That's right. They can.'

I couldn't believe it. By then we'd been on air for a couple of years. 'Thanks a lot, guys,' we said.

Most TV studios have what's called the MDF system, an internal ring circuit, where people from anywhere in the building can switch on to any of the studios that are recording or rehearsing and hear everything that's being said both on and off the air. And, because of the pressure we worked under on *This Morning*, because it was a live programme, we were often guilty of discussing things. Someone, for example, might come in and say, 'Oh, God, I've just been speaking to Shirley Bassey and she's in a terrible mood,' or 'Faye Dunaway is being awful, so demanding, will only have lemon-flavoured chewing-gum in her dressing-room and we haven't got any.' And everybody could hear this. Or people might have come in with a shifty look trying to alert us to the fact that the next interview could be legally contentious, and we were only too aware that anything we might query or say in response would be heard by our guest in the Green Room.

At a personal level, Richard and I also found this mike business a huge tension because, if ever we were sharp with each other about anything, we knew somebody somewhere would hear us. These days, despite the problems, we still prefer the 'full-talk-back' system to the 'switch-talk-back' system. The latter means that, although everyone can hear you, they can craftily switch off so you can't hear them. Now when Richard and I need to have a private conversation, we just strip our microphones off.

———

I've never been very comfortable about being recognized, but I have become less edgy about this as time has gone by. For the sake of sanity I've had to stop noticing people staring at us or whispering and pointing us out. If I lived my life feeling terribly self-conscious, going out would become impossible and I'd turn into a monster. When we go into a restaurant I am aware of people looking at us, but by the time we reach our table and are sitting down we focus on each other or whoever we are with.

We know from our websites that an extraordinary number of people feel at home with us, and some correspond on a regular basis. Many who come up for a chat say they've been watching us since they were eleven or twelve years old, and have grown up with us. The other day, a woman, who now works in the media, said, 'I can't believe I'm meeting you in the flesh. I used to watch you every morning when I was at university, and you were so important to me. I'm so thrilled to meet you.' That was really sweet.

I've discovered that on the whole people are pleasant, and when they do come up to say something it's usually very nice. The most irritating thing is when people whisper and point, but that goes with the territory. Teenagers sometimes follow us, which can be quite difficult but, having kids ourselves, we understand the motivation. I definitely have a lower toughness threshold than Richard, who simply says, 'I'm not going to make any compromises. I'm going to live my life exactly as I want. If I want to go for a cycle ride, I'll do it.' I haven't got his kind of armour-plating, and tend not to be an 'in your face' person publicly.

Nothing in the world had prepared me for the kind of press coverage we would get once *This Morning* was off the ground. As I said to Richard during the negative-comment times, 'It's like getting poison-pen letters delivered to your door every day.' What bothered me most was that so many of the reports bore hardly any relation to the truth. I found it difficult to understand such malice, particularly when it came from people who had never met me. It still shocks and upsets me today, not just when it's the press but when anybody expresses pettiness or jealousy about any aspect of my life.

When press intrusion first begins, and you've never experienced anything like that before, it's absolutely horrible. I now understand why people in primitive societies won't have their photographs taken because they feel somebody is stealing their soul. It is rather like that. You're presented with a word image of yourself in a newspaper, which carries your name, but it's got nothing to do with the way you are or the way you see yourself.

I was upset enough when all this first started, but I didn't know then that there was a ghastly event awaiting Richard and me in August 1990. This particular nightmare would generate huge publicity, knock us off our feet, gut us, and mean that the attitude I was learning to adopt would help to hold me in good stead when life, as we had known it until then, was threatened after a shopping trip to Tesco.

7: RICHARD

In her book *The Queens and the Hive*, a novel about Elizabeth I and Mary, Queen of Scots, Edith Sitwell writes: 'Doom speaks to us sometimes, with the hum of a gnat. We hardly feel the prick that is no sharper than that of a pin; but it ushers in Eternity.'

On Friday, 24 August 1990, the 'doom' that struck at my life did not result in my demise, but it came perilously close to damn-well finishing off me and my career. That day, twenty-two months after *This Morning* first hit the screens, began sunny side up and well. We had just come back from holiday and, as we were not due back on *This Morning* for another week and didn't want to kick our heels around in Manchester, we decided to go to a little cottagey hotel in Devon where we had stayed several times before. But, before we set off, there were a number of things to sort out. Most important was Jack's school uniform. He was due to start at his first school when term began and, as usual, there was only one shop in the whole of town where the uniform could be bought.

The plan was that I should first go to Tesco, about a mile down the road from where we lived, and stock up with some freezer stuff so that, when we came back and would be straight into work, we wouldn't need to go shopping again. We also needed some booze, washing powder, and so on. There was a lot to do before setting off to the south-west later in the day, but I'm a fast-moving person and figured I could fit it all in.

That summer was Roman-hot and as I drove to the super-market it was another sizzling, sultry day. Not surprisingly, because of the heat, Tesco was not at all busy. I did our shop, got the food for next week, then some tomatoes and fruit. I selected some wines and got the kids' bottles of Coke, and stood these and the own-brand champagne, wine and gin upright in the front section of the trolley, so they wouldn't fall over and crush the other stuff. I always did it that way. Then I went to the checkout.

As usual I focused on stacking the shopping as fast as I could on to the conveyor belt, so I wouldn't hold up people standing behind me. Out everything came; in everything went into carriers after it was scanned.

Soon the trolley was full again, all the shopping bagged up with a couple of spare carriers to scoop up the odds and sods that always rolled out in the back of the estate car on the way home. I've always moved pretty fast but that day, with so much on, I was going even quicker than usual and my mind kept jumping ahead. This weekly shop at Tesco was strictly routine; I'd done it most Saturdays for years and I was more or less on autopilot as I planned ahead for the rest of the day and the next one: getting Jack's uniform sorted (bet they wouldn't have everything he needed in his size); what route to take down to the south-west; what to pack. I paid the bill, exchanged a few words with the checkout girl and nodded to the supervisor whom I knew by sight and who'd been standing there most of the time. Situation absolutely-bloody-normal. Shopping done.

As I left I remembered that Jack and Chloe were always nagging me about coming with me to Tesco because they thought the little in-store café there would be fun. (They were very small!) I always said no, but today I stopped to check out the menu. Actually it wasn't bad and I made a mental note to bring them along the next Saturday I was there. But there would never be another Saturday at Tesco.

Then I strolled out through the exit.

I can't say I had a premonition that something was wrong, but I did have a slightly uncomfortable feeling that something was not quite right. Suddenly a woman, wearing a grey tailored suit and a grim expression, confronted me, a man on each side of her.

'We have reason to think you have left the shop without paying,' she said.

'What!' I replied, startled.

She pointed to the front section of the trolley, where I had stacked the bottles. For a second, I didn't know what she meant. As far as I was concerned, I had paid for them along with everything else. Standing there, I mentally replayed being at the till, then said, 'Haven't I paid for them?'

'No, you have not,' she replied stonily.

My mental tape finished replaying. Fuck, she was right.

'Christ!' I said. 'I'm really sorry. I'll go back and pay for them now.'

'That is not an option,' she said. 'We're going to the manager's office.'

And off I was marched, along the outside of the building, with one of the men pushing my trolley. The woman mumbled something.

'What did you just say?' I said, stopping in my tracks and looking at her.

She muttered it again: 'Bet this isn't the first time.'

'What are you talking about?'

She hesitated, and looked ahead. 'Come on,' she replied.

I had my first inkling then that this wasn't going to be over in five minutes after a cup of tea and a joke with the manager in his office.

But my instincts were still overwhelmingly telling me that everything would be all right, because although I'd obviously screwed up, big-time, I hadn't intended to do so. It was a mistake. Even so, I was in a vulnerable position. I could only try to explain that because it was my regular practice to put any bottles straight back into the front section of the trolley after they'd been scanned, the sight of them there when I left the shop hadn't looked odd.

In the manager's office the store detective who'd stopped me – she was called Angela Orme – told him what I hadn't paid for. This now included, apparently, a soap carton hanging from a little hook on the back of the trolley.

What? *Bloody hell.* Where had my brain *been?*

The manager called his head office, who told him to proceed according to standard routine.

Fair enough. Why should I get special treatment just because I was on TV? The police were called.

At this point I said, 'Look, I must ring my wife. She's expecting me home by now and we're supposed to be going shopping with the kids for my son's school uniform.'

'Fine,' said the manager.

I phoned Judy and told her what had happened. First, she was dumbfounded, then incandescent.

'They're being ridiculous,' she said. 'How can they possibly think you would do this on purpose?'

'I don't think it's a case of what they think,' I remember replying. 'At the moment, it's a case of what's happened, and the interpretation they might put on it. I think this is going to get very heavy.'

'I think you should just leave,' she said.

'I can't do that,' I said. 'It's gone way beyond that, but don't worry. I'll get this sorted and I'll call you later. I love you.'

A policewoman arrived with a uniformed colleague. They were polite, but things began to unravel very fast now. I was taken downstairs, out of a back exit of the supermarket, and walked towards a waiting police van. A camera flashed: I had been photographed by someone. Once in the van, with the doors shut, it was very dark. There were no windows, just a couple of heavy dark panes of glass in the back doors. We drove off through the streets of south Manchester. I was bounced around like a pea in a drum. There were no grab handles and I kept getting thrown off the benches that ran along both sides of the vehicle. I still don't know why we went so fast; maybe we were trying to outrun my former colleagues – the press pack.

It was utterly surreal. Twenty minutes earlier I'd been a husband and father, enjoying what was left of the sizzling hot summer holiday, going to do the family shop, but now I was in the back of a paddy wagon going to Platt Lane police station. As the van shot through the streets I knew that what was now happening to me was potentially a career-breaking and even a life-shattering event. It took a tremendous effort of will not to 'lose' it, to stay calm and focused. But panic was very close.

We arrived at the police station. I was taken into the main charge room, where I had to give up all my possessions: money, watch, even the laces in my trainers.

'Look, is this really necessary?' I remember asking as I knelt down to untie my shoes. 'I'm not going to string myself up.'

'Standard procedure.'

Looking back, I can see they were right. Being treated like a common criminal – fingerprinted and photographed – was a phenomenal shock, my first absolute humiliation and, if I'd been a different kind of person, I *could* have strung myself up.

Once the welcome ceremonies were over, I was put into a cell and the door thumped shut. Cell doors don't clang, bang or crash. They thump. Then it all went quiet. That was probably the worst moment. I just stood there in this grim, scruffy cell, with its stainless-steel, no-lid toilet in the corner, and the remains of the previous inmate's take-away curry in a plastic box stinking the place out.

What the fuck do I do now? I thought. I'm incommunicado. What happens next?

What I did know for sure was that the press, TV and radio would already be gathering; and that Granada executives in their offices in Quay Street would be stunned to have heard that their presenter had been arrested. God knows what Judy was doing. I was in shock, finding it almost impossible to assess where I was in this unfolding nightmare. I can remember sitting very still on the cell's bunk, my thoughts slowing down into a kind of sludge of despair. But gradually I forced myself back and started to think rationally.

At that stage, I didn't think it would be a good idea to call a solicitor. I felt it would only add to the plausibility of the drama and make it seem even more serious than it was. When I had been put in the cell, the PC had told me that the CID would be along to interview me in due course, and I was still hoping that my arrest could be dealt with in a conversation with a detective; would be sorted by the simple truth. He would nod and smile as I said, 'Look, I am not a thief. I didn't go into that shop with any intention of stealing; I shop there every week. Why would I do this? Why on earth would I, a well-paid, successful, happy, well-balanced, non-criminal individual, suddenly take it into my head to relieve Tesco of £70 worth of booze? It was simply an oversight.'

Because I knew I was completely innocent of any wrongdoing, though guilty of stupid forgetfulness, I genuinely thought that the CID would accept the truth at face value. So each time a policeman pulled open the little spy-hole in the cell door, just like on *The Bill*, and asked, 'Do you want anything? Do you want to call a solicitor?' I replied, 'No. I'll wait for the CID. I'll sort it out with them.'

But then, after I'd been in the cell for about an hour, something significant happened. The sergeant, a nice guy, opened the cell door, gave me a plastic cup of coffee and sat down.

'Look,' he said. 'I'm going to be absolutely straight with you. If I were you – or if you were my brother – I would advise you to call a solicitor. From what I'm hearing, I really don't think this thing is going to go away this afternoon. You may be charged. In fact, I think you'll be charged today. Get yourself a brief, Richard.'

I'm glad he was so straight because, up until then, I'd been in denial and thought I could sort it out on my own. His words made it clear that things were going to get much worse before they got better. I felt as if I had swallowed a ton of rock and my stomach tensed, but I said, 'Thanks. Obviously you're right. Can I make a call?'

I was taken to the desk where I'd signed in and placed a call to Michael Green, our very good friend and lawyer. He had acted for us both in our divorces and conveyancing matters. He couldn't be found and, of course, I was only allowed the one call. I left a garbled message and the sergeant said he'd try to track him down for me. Then it was back to the cells – but not before I noticed a *Manchester Evening News* with my photo on the front page being handed round. It had begun, then.

Michael Green was principally a criminal lawyer. He knew Platt Lane police station as well as his own office. He'd represented many a recidivist there. He told me later that when he'd got the message that Richard Madeley was at that station on a shoplifting charge he nearly fell off his chair.

When Michael eventually arrived at my cell door and was shown in, I was sitting dismally on the bench. I stood up and we stared at each other. I will never forget his first words.

'I would imagine,' he said carefully, taking off his glasses and polishing them, 'that this is the very worst day of your life so far.'

I nodded.

'What the fuck happened, Richard?'

I told him as calmly as I could.

He listened carefully until I'd finished.

'There's no doubt at all, Richard,' he said, 'that you have to fight this charge.'

'Well, of course I bloody well do!' I was surprised at his response.

'No, no, listen to me,' he interrupted. 'I know they are prepared to offer you a caution, and that they will let the matter drop if you accept a caution. Then you will be free to walk out and there will be no question of a charge or court appearance.'

It was a few years since I'd covered court cases as a reporter. I had a vague idea that a caution was a sort of wagging finger where the police said, 'You've been very forgetful. Don't do it again. Make sure you've paid for everything next time. Now run along and don't do it again.' This seemed to me an eminently sensible way to deal with the matter.

'What's the problem with a caution?' I asked, reading Michael's expression. 'Why shouldn't I accept that?'

He then explained to me what a caution is. 'In order to receive the caution,' he said, 'you, as the person being cautioned, have to admit that you've done what you are accused of doing. You would have to admit that you intended to go into Tesco and shoplift. Which is, of course, absolutely unacceptable. You can't accept that because that is not true.'

Lawyers, as far as I know, do not often lay themselves on the line in this way for clients, but Michael was a friend.

'Richard,' he said quietly, 'I know all this is bollocks. So I know, as your friend, that you must fight this. But I must tell you straight that it won't be a short road to walk, and it will be painful. I don't recommend that you opt to have this dealt with in a magistrates' court. You must elect for trial at crown court. That's a big deal. The coverage will be enormous, and you will get a lot of adverse publicity. Shoplifting is one of those stupid petty crimes where, more than most offences, people are assumed guilty before they are proven innocent. Don't ask my why, they just are. So expect flak. Having said that, you absolutely must fight to preserve and protect your good name.'

He was right, of course, but as I nodded agreement my last hopes that the situation would somehow be resolved over a mug of tea in the interview room quietly evaporated. Michael touched my shoulder. 'Look, keep your chin up. You cocked up the weekend shop. That's not a crime. We'll do all we can to sort this out.'

I was then interviewed by two CID men in Michael's presence. I did my best but, as the sergeant had predicted, I was charged. At about seven o'clock that night, ten hours after I had left Judy and the kids at home, I was released on police bail and emerged outside with Michael. A scrum of press photographers and reporters, TV crews and radio vans were outside the police station's car park. A few years earlier, under other circumstances, I would have been with them.

Looking back now, I sometimes wish I had made a personal statement that night, but at the time I was absolutely shattered and not at all sure I would make much sense. My life had turned upside down. Anyway, once you're charged, the matter is *sub judice* and there's a strict limit on what you can say. You can't start defending yourself before you appear in court. So, perhaps it was the right decision that Michael was the one who made a brief statement, explaining that I had been charged, that I completely denied the allegations and that I would fight them in court. We then left to a barrage of photographs, but any attempt at calmness was sabotaged by two huge wasps in Michael's Jaguar and there was much flapping of hands inside as we pulled away. The day ended as ignominiously as it began.

On the drive home, I threw my head back, thinking, What on earth is this going to do to Judy? Jack and Chloe are probably small enough for it all to go over their heads. But what about poor Tom and Dan? How will they manage at school?

Jack and Chloe were so young they didn't really need to know anything about it, but I thought it would be terrible for the twins who were teenagers at secondary school.

This was turning into a twenty-four-carat gold-plated, platinum-edged disaster. I thought my family would be sucked in, too, and it was all because of me.

I was experiencing an overwhelming wave of shame that, because of my inattention, I had put us all into this terrible predicament. In his *Diaries*, Alan Clark writes that, however much you may long to, you can't turn the clock back. Not even by one second. But, oh, how I wished I could turn the clock back to just one second before leaving the checkout that morning. But it was too late. The consequences of my mistake had to be faced up to. And not only by me.

When I went into the house, Judy and I just stood holding each other; then Jack, who was only four and had gone to bed, came downstairs.

'You've been gone a very long time, Daddy,' he said.

We cuddled him, then Chloe toddled down and we cuddled her. They didn't know anything was wrong and soon went back to bed. We then talked things through with Michael, who laid out for us how things would proceed: magistrates' court; remand; committal proceedings, and then the crown court. The Scotch bottle was steadily depleted and the room was full of cigarette smoke.

'What if it all goes horribly wrong?' Judy asked. 'What if Richard gets a stupid jury or a mad judge? What if they find him guilty? Will he go to jail?'

For the first time that day, Michael laughed. 'As a lawyer,' he replied, 'I rarely go out on a limb and offer guarantees. But I can absolutely guarantee that if any of that were to happen, Richard would not go to jail. Anyway, we know where the truth lies and we'll do everything possible to make sure that it doesn't go horribly wrong.'

Hmm. 'Everything possible.' No guarantees, then.

Dr Chris Steele was also a hero of our family that day. Hearing the news on the radio, he had immediately come over to the house to comfort Judy. He was fantastic; he was the first outsider to offer us what we needed. You see, when you are accused of something that isn't true, you need absolute and unqualified support from those around you. You don't want anybody looking at you askance; or ringing up and saying, 'How could you have forgotten . . .' You just want friends to come in and, metaphorically, put their arms around you and say, 'I know this is total crap and anybody who knows you will know that, too. Everything's going to be just fine. Don't worry about your good name. It's safe with those who know and love you. It's as good today as it was yesterday.'

That's the kind of comfort you need, and Chris was the first to give it, in spades. He also took my spare car keys, while I was fretting in my cell, and walked two miles to Tesco's car park to collect our car and drive it to our house.

The rest of that evening is a blur. I know Judy and I got through a lot of whisky and went to bed. I should have been pissed, but I spent hours staring open-eyed at the ceiling. Quite a day.

The next morning, Saturday, I remember waking up, knowing that something dreadful had happened, but not quite sure what it was. Then of course it all flooded back. I found it very hard to get out of bed and face the day. When I did, I discovered that the story was all over the newspapers, and I was dreading the conversations I knew I would now have to have with friends, colleagues and the press, and the letters I must now write.

The first call was from Judy's brother, Roger, who was

appalled at what had happened and desperately concerned for us. Listening to Judy explaining the events of the day before, the sheer humiliation of the charge rolled over me, momentarily depriving me of any sense of self-respect or honour. I'd been accused of such a grubby, petty crime. It wasn't even like the Peter Hain case years before. Hain, then a firebrand, now an eminent government minister, had been wrongly accused, but at least he'd been accused of robbing a post office!

I learned later, though, that just being accused of shoplifting – not convicted – can, for some, be a death sentence. Every year in this country about fifty people, unable to bear the shame, commit suicide while on a shoplifting charge. And sometimes it emerges afterwards that the charges were being withdrawn anyway.

The only time I actually broke down and cried was while Judy was describing to Roger what had happened. She had to hang up on Roger and calm me down. After a few minutes, I got myself under control. I realized that, although crying had been cathartic, that was it. I couldn't let go again. I went and locked myself in the bathroom and gave myself a good talking-to: 'Okay,' I said, 'that's the last time you shed salt tears for yourself because there are a lot of people more deserving of tears than you are. You got yourself into this stupid mess, you get yourself out of it. Get your act together and sort this out.'

That day actually finished in an almost complete inversion of how it had started. This was because, as it progressed, friends and colleagues who phoned up spoke all the right words and gave pledges of unconditional support. Among these were two very welcome calls from senior executives at Granada: 'The company,' I was told, 'is standing absolutely four-square behind you.'

I had been with Granada for eight years. Many of the people

who had been producers and researchers when I arrived as a reporter/presenter had risen through the ranks and were now quite senior. We were friends, as well as colleagues, and they knew me well. So the personal support I got from them was strong and I was deeply grateful to them.

That very day, Granada announced that the next season's launch of *This Morning* would go ahead as planned on 3 September and that, despite all the rumours and speculation, there was no question of my being suspended. Part of its press statement added: 'Richard has our full support and faith, along with the strongest hope that his innocence will soon be re-established as publicly as it is now being doubted.'

Granada's support meant I could focus on the coming court case; I wasn't facing a war on two fronts. It was a ray of comfort at the close of a ghastly day.

———————

Almost a year later the store's own video footage would show me behaving perfectly normally at the checkout. I wasn't acting in what store detectives describe as 'a suspicious manner'. I wasn't doing anything covert. So if I really was trying to steal I must have been displaying a kind of mad bravado, especially as most people around me knew me from TV. I wasn't exactly going to pass unnoticed. I'd never done anything remotely illegal in my life. Why would I suddenly go mad in Tesco one summer morning and risk everything – my family's happiness, my own reputation, my whole career? All this was discussed endlessly that first day and I was comforted by everyone else's disbelief and general incredulity.

I got a call from the presenter of *The Krypton Factor*, Gordon Burns. We hardly knew each other, but he phoned anyway.

'It must be a nightmare for you, Richard, but I just wanted

to tell you that I truly believe it'll all come out okay in the end. And I know you won't believe this, but it's not as bad as you think. You'll get through it and, when it's over, it will all sink into perspective. You'll see.'

He was very kind, but my perspective was very out of whack.

The week after my arrest, I remember saying to Judy and Michael Green, 'Fuck this! I'm not going to be shamed or bullied into not behaving normally. I'm going back to Tesco to do our usual weekly shop.'

'Shop whenever you like,' Michael replied evenly, 'but I strongly advise you not to go back to Tesco.'

'Why not?' I said. 'Why shouldn't I?'

'You just don't need to add that stress to the pressure you are already under. Don't go back there – not yet, anyway.'

'You can't go shopping in a supermarket again,' Judy said, distressed. 'You'll feel terrible. How will you cope with people pointing at you or whispering behind their hands?'

'The hell with that,' I replied. 'I've got to lead a normal life. The situation's bad enough without me letting this awful thing stop me from being who I am, or stopping us from doing what we've always done as a couple. You give the kids breakfast on Saturdays, I do the family shop. I won't give a toss if people point at me or whisper.'

But it was very stressful. I went to Kwik Save, which was round the corner in Rusholme. As I parked the car, I felt dry-mouthed, sweaty-palmed – really dreadful – as if I were having a heart attack. But I knew that if I chickened out and drove away again, we would never be able to function as a normal family, a big family that needed to do a big supermarket shop every week. Paying somebody to do the shopping for me would look awful, as if I'd been spooked or, worse, as if I felt guilty about something.

So in I barged, antennae bristling for trouble. There was

none. Everyone was absolutely fine. I certainly got some surprised, even astonished, looks, but people either said nothing, or smiled and gave me a thumbs-up, or came up, squeezed my arm and said, 'Good luck,' or, 'We know it's rubbish. You'll be all right.'

I don't think I'd ever felt so self-conscious as I did while I pushed my trolley around and filled it with our usual stuff. But I didn't buy any booze. In fact, I felt completely unable to buy this at a supermarket for a very long time. I simply couldn't go to the wine aisle and actually put bottles in a trolley. It was psychologically impossible.

That first shop since my arrest was finally over, and I must have been the slowest person at the checkout ever, while I double-checked everything was paid for. Then I had to push the trolley to the car park, with everyone looking. Head up, teeth gritted, and get on with it. I arrived home totally drained.

———

A week before Judy and I were due back on *This Morning*, ten days after all this had happened, our new company car arrived. It was our first company car – one of the new-shape, better-looking Volvos – which we had been looking forward to. But, when it arrived, I took absolutely no pleasure in it at all. It was very hard to take pleasure in anything.

On the same day, Liam Hamilton, *This Morning*'s editor, and Dianne Nelmes, our friend and executive producer, returned from their holidays and came to our house to hear from me what had actually happened. By then I was calmer and went through the whole sorry event, blow by blow. They were gratifyingly outraged on my behalf and appalled that a lapse of memory had led to such a trauma, and the traumas that lay ahead.

'It's not as if you've been wrongly accused of a drugs offence or some kind of weird sexual behaviour or abuse,' Dianne said. 'For heaven's sake, it's only shoplifting.'

A lot of people said that to me while I was waiting to come to trial, but although it was said to comfort me, it never did. 'It's only shoplifting . . .' Yes, but what kind of people shoplift? Sad people with psychological troubles. Petty thieves. Kleptomaniacs. Criminals who made a steady living by stealing from shops. If it all went wrong and I was convicted, I'd join that group. And I'd have a criminal record.

Granada's support notwithstanding, a conviction would terminate my career and explode my reputation. Whenever I considered this bleak possibility, the future beyond it was always in impenetrable darkness. I couldn't see ahead.

You can imagine what gearing ourselves up to go back to work on *This Morning* was really like for Judy and me. I thought the young researchers wouldn't know where to look, but they were fantastic. On that first day, almost all of them came up to us quietly, just to say, 'We know it's nonsense. Good luck.' They didn't have to do that, they were not crawlers, and it meant a lot to us.

I can't remember now how Judy and I opened the show, but we agonized over the script the night before. My natural impulse was to tell everybody exactly what had happened, and the anguish we were going through. But the matter was *sub judice* so that was out of the question. We simply acknowledged that the shoplifting charges had been made, that I would have my day in court, and that, as much as we wanted to discuss it with the viewers, that would have to wait. Meanwhile it was business as usual.

So *This Morning* went back on air for series three with one of its co-presenters there courtesy of police bail. It was truly surreal, but it was also good to be back at work and to discover we were still able to function fairly normally on air.

After the first show, David Liddiment, then Granada's

Controller of Programmes, phoned up and said, 'I don't know how you just did that but it was ... Well, apart from the opening and that "see you in court" bit, it was a normal show! Keep going!'

––––––––––

About a week or so later things got even worse.

I had to visit Platt Lane again for more questioning and, to my astonishment and fury, I was accused of doing it all once before – a week before, on 18 August. Details were unbelievably scant: the charge that I had left without paying for an unspecified amount of booze didn't seem to rest on much more than the fact I had been shopping in the same store, which was true. Why hadn't I been stopped? Why hadn't anyone said anything? Why had it taken weeks for this second accusation to emerge? Why was the detail so vague? What was going on?

'It's what's called a propping-up charge, Richard,' Michael told me calmly as we drove from the station. 'They've been doing some thinking. You wouldn't accept a caution, so they had to charge you that day three weeks ago. Now suddenly they've got themselves a high-profile case. No one likes losing one of those. And the case against you is weak.

'Anyone can forget to pay for shopping once. But twice, and it smells like a fish. Frankly they don't even have to win this new one: just getting it into court will be a big help to them on the first charge. I'm still confident, but the fight's just got a lot dirtier.'

This time I wasn't distressed. I was absolutely incandescent with rage. I released a brief statement to the press describing the new charge as 'preposterous'.

Michael called me the next morning. 'Careful,' he warned. 'You're not really supposed to say too much until we get to court. Wait until then.'

He was right but, all these years on, this is the one single event in the whole experience that I still get angry about. I'd tried so hard not to take what was happening personally; to take responsibility for my stupid mistake and for the fight to explain it. Now I felt someone had crept up and tied one hand behind my back.

Overall, though, I worked hard at keeping a philosophical attitude. I'd cocked up the shopping and now had to take the consequences. It wasn't a personal 'Let's get Madeley' campaign being waged by Tesco, or the police. The Crown Prosecution Service was hardly going to shrug and say, 'Let's give him the benefit of the doubt.' To be honest it felt as if I'd fallen into a huge impersonal machine. The inertia was unstoppable, and I had to go with the flow and hope to be spat out eventually, please God, unscathed. But there were times when I hated the lot of them.

———

As the year progressed, I went through the bizarre process of appearing in a magistrates' court one moment and being on the telly the next. I'd go along to the court, usually to hear that the proceedings were being adjourned yet again. But they were kind. They put me first on the list, so I could appear at ten o'clock in court, then jump into the car and race across to Liverpool, where *This Morning* started at ten forty. Usually by about eleven I'd be driving into the studio car park while listening to radio bulletin reports about my appearance in court.

It was utterly weird – almost like being two people. I'd walk straight in and pick up the show with Judy. Earlier she would have opened the programme by saying, 'Richard can't be here for the moment. He's in court this morning – he'll be here later.' As show openers go, you have to admit it's original. Then I'd tip up, breathless, saying, 'Morning, everyone. I'm sorry I'm late, but I had to be in court this morning.' I would then tell them what had happened, that I'd been remanded so many weeks, with another court appearance planned for February or whenever, and get on with the show.

It happened so regularly that we almost got used to it.

'How's it going?' I asked Judy one morning as I breezed in from court.

'We've missed you,' she replied.

Looking back, it was absolutely bizarre television, but our viewers obviously found it gripping. And for me, being able to integrate such a surreal experience with my daily life made it more bearable and, to some extent, normalized it. It also helped that, unlike most people who appear in court for the first time, I at least had been in court many times as a reporter, sitting on the press bench. I knew how it worked and wasn't intimidated by the process.

There were a few unpleasant public encounters. Once Judy and I were shopping in Marks and Spencer. As we chose our frozen TV dinners, a very odd-looking bloke marched briskly up and then stood to attention with his arms straight at his sides.

'I think you are a disgrace,' he said in a loud, high-pitched voice. 'I think it is an absolute disgrace that you should dare come in here when you've been found guilty of shoplifting. It's a *disgrace*.'

He was small and middle-aged, and buzzing with self-righteousness.

Other shoppers stopped and stared.

'Hey, hold on,' I said. 'I've not been found guilty of anything and—'

He began to shout again. Judy sized things up much more quickly than me. She stepped very close to him and hissed, 'You are a little wanker. Now fuck off.'

He looked very taken aback and there was a ripple of laughter and some applause, and, 'Nice one, Judy!'

What I think was the guy's mother hurried up and took him away.

'I must speak the truth,' he piped up as they disappeared behind the fruit and veg counter.

'I'll give him the truth,' said a still-furious Judy.

You can take the girl out of north Manchester, but you can't take north Manchester out of the girl.

The only other abuse I got was shopping in Manchester's Arndale Centre, which of course had its regulation complement of yobs. Bellows of 'Shoplifter', or 'Thief', or 'Bottle of wine', as I came up or down the escalators, or walked across the malls, cut me to the quick at first. Later I toughened up a lot. Those lads didn't know any better and they thought they were being incredibly witty. It was never really aggressive. It was just their way of getting a rise and a kick out of teasing me. But, then, you pay a high price for being absent-minded at the checkout.

The year before I finally came to crown court ground slowly on. There were endless meetings at our solicitor's office to construct my stupefyingly simple defence.

The hundreds of letters I was receiving showed what I'd done was, if not a universal experience, a very common one. One man said he had gone shopping with his son to buy the boy a bike in a big superstore. He lifted it out of the rack and wheeled it around buying all the accessories: bell, lights, pump, puncture repair kit, etc. Then, after paying, he had left the checkout and walked the bike to the bus stop to go home. As they were waiting for the bus, his kid suddenly said, 'Dad, I don't think you paid for the bike!'

'What?'

'You didn't pay for the bike. Everything else, but not the bike.'

They turned back to the shop to see two store detectives running after them. He somehow managed to persuade them that he was just about to come back and pay. In the end, they believed him.

That was only one of hundreds of obviously sincere letters I received from people who had had similar experiences to mine. Many were from people who had filled their car up with petrol, gone into the shop, bought some sweets and cigarettes, paid for those, but then driven off forgetting to pay for the petrol. Some were prosecuted, others not. It was a lottery.

And others, who had been wrongly accused many years before, wrote to me in despair. They had nothing to gain in contacting me, but it was clear from reading their letters that they had never recovered their self-confidence or self-respect after being found guilty. They meant well, but those letters always left me depressed.

Shit, I kept thinking as I filed them away. What if the jury doesn't believe me, either?

But usually that little question popped into my head at about 3 a.m., and kept me awake until it was time to go to work.

———

The year rolled on, Christmas came and went but, at least, we now had Stephen Solley QC to act for us, and the defence was prepared. Stephen was a lovely man. When I first went to see him one rainy spring evening in our solicitor's offices in Manchester, the first thing he said after we shook hands was, 'I can't imagine what a nightmare this must be for you. It must be just the worst thing, just awful.' Then he said something else and I really warmed to him.

'When I agreed to take your case,' he said. 'I went straight to my local Tesco and did what you did. Well, up to a point, ha ha! I went round, filling up the trolley, put the bottles in the front section, went to the checkout, unloaded all the goods, except the booze, and the cashier didn't notice the omission. In the end, of course, I took them out and paid for them, but the fact is, even though the bottles were plainly on view, she didn't notice them. Had your cashier done so,' he added, 'you doubtless would have said, "*Christ!*" and paid for them. But she didn't and your mind was elsewhere. It happens all the time. We are going to win this case for you. You cannot be allowed to go down on these charges, they're ludicrous. You cannot lose your good name or career for a mental aberration that can happen to anyone. But it's going to be a very rough trial, thanks to the propping-up charge. We have to try and get the judge to see that for what it is before he swears the jury in.'

Then he asked me how much I could remember about the two days in question.

'Everything on the 24th,' I said. 'Fuck-all on the earlier one. I remember shopping there as normal and that's about it.'

'Exactly,' said Stephen. 'Other than the fact that you were in the store that day and a bit of tittle-tattle since, there's no case against you. It's deeply unfair. Leave this to me.'

Stephen Solley was very upbeat that night and I was reassured by him but, my God, the costs were mounting! Judy and I, thanks to *This Morning*, had just started to get straight financially, but we were looking at bills that would dwarf our overdraft of two years ago.

By then, we had our defence and our character witnesses lined up, but what I really felt I needed was a neutral person in my corner, some kind of expert witness who could explain my mistake. Then the most fantastic thing happened. I received a letter from the Portia Trust, a charity that had campaigned for years on behalf of people who had been accused of shoplifting. The letter mentioned the work of Professor James Reason, a highly eminent academic, and a world expert on human error. He advised the American government, NASA and various British corporations. He lived in Cheshire, quite close to us, and had spent years studying human error. Repetitious behaviour was one key cause of mistakes, be they on planes, spacecraft, air-traffic control centres, banks or shops and super-markets. He'd also studied why, when every single possible safety precaution had been taken, industrial accidents still occurred. And what he had established went to the heart of my case. Routine, mundane actions if repeated often enough are far more prone to catastrophic failure than we might think.

We might believe that because we've done something on a routine basis day after day successfully, we can 'do it in our sleep', but that is the problem. Because it is routine, it is too easy to lose focus and not concentrate on the matter in hand. As a result, very simple repetitive events could lead to catastrophe. In the case of the sinking of the *Herald of Free Enterprise* ferry, for example, the unthinkable human error had happened and the bow doors had been left open. And the potential for this kind of disaster exists at every level of society. Suddenly, thanks to the Portia Trust's letter, I had a glimmer of how my personal catastrophe had come about. I shopped at the Didsbury Tesco most weekends. Hundreds of times. I had my routine; what I usually bought and the order I bought it in. I could do it 'in my sleep'.

When I contacted Professor Reason, he was very cautious. He had read about my case in the newspapers, he said, and, from what he had gleaned, felt my actions might have been due to the human error syndrome, but he didn't know me and, as far as he was concerned, I could be guilty. If he were to become involved in my case, he would need to conduct some fairly exhaustive separate questioning of both me and Judy, in order to establish the truth to his own satisfaction.

The evening he came to see us, my heart was in my mouth. Instinctively, I knew that this was my way of proving that (as far as it is possible to prove any negative), I really had not intended, even at a subconscious level, to commit a crime.

Professor Reason was very polite and formal. First, he took Judy into the living-room and interviewed her for an hour about me and my behaviour and, in particular, homed in on the kind of forgetfulness I was prone to displaying. What kind of person was I? What was my approach to life and everyday household jobs and chores? There were a lot of 'blind questions' designed to reveal if a person was exaggerating his or her responses. Having dealt with Judy, he then asked me a great number of what appeared to be completely disconnected questions for about an hour.

'Okay,' he said, when he had finished with both of us. 'I'm going to take all this away, analyse it, and will talk to you again in about a week's time.'

When he came back to see us, he was a different person, much more relaxed, smiling as he came into the room and sat down.

'I've rounded it all up and established that you've both given me a very honest, detailed account of the kind of person that you, Richard, are. And I can now tell you that there's not a shred of doubt in my mind that your behaviour in Tesco was an entirely predictable oversight that has been on the cards for years. In fact, given your habitual approach to things, you are bloody lucky this has not happened before. On the one hand, you are incredibly highly focused, on the other you are incredibly absent-minded.' He then added something that was subsequently pounced on by the press when it was quoted during my trial: 'In some respects, you have the mentality of a ninety-eight-year-old woman.' I must admit I would have gone with that headline, too.

As he finished speaking, I felt an enormous surge of relief. I knew that when the trial started the prosecution would not play softball, would come at me very hard because that is their job. But now, at least, I felt we had an impressive, honest, honourable spokesman in our armoury: a respected champion who would come to my defence.

Professor Reason then told us a lot more about the human error syndrome, how seemingly ludicrous mistakes can occur, and how he had applied the discipline of his findings to what had happened to me and come up with ticks in every box. Both Judy and me, and our entire legal team, were hugely fortified by his response and we set about gathering his evidence for the trial.

While I was still on remand, I remember an MP, now retired, coming up to me at a charity do, and saying, 'The road to hell is paved with good intentions.'

'Probably,' I replied, 'but what are you talking about?'

'I have so often been on the point of writing to you about your tribulations, but always funked it,' he answered.

'That's all right,' I said.

'No, no,' he interrupted, 'the reason being that it happened to me. I was arrested and charged with shoplifting just before my first election campaign. Can you imagine what that was like? I'd go out canvassing on the street, with the charges hanging over me, steeling myself for the catcalls. It was like acid in my heart. I was acquitted in the end, but I vividly remember what it was like. And I so wish I had written to you.'

'Well, you've spoken about it now. It means a lot to me, thank you,' I said.

After it was all over for me, he did write.

About a couple of weeks before the trial, Judy and I decided to go on a week's holiday to Tunisia to prepare mentally for the oncoming storm. We had a calm time there and, most days, I was more or less able to put it out of my mind. One slightly bizarre thought troubled me, though. All the court documents relating to my case would be labelled Regina v. Richard Madeley. I quite liked the Queen and it was extraordinary to think I'd be, albeit in an arcane ritualized way, her opponent!

———————

After months of adjournments and remands, the date of the trial was set for July 1991 in courtroom number five, Manchester Crown Court in Manchester's Crown Square. In the lobby three youths pushed their way in just as the doors were about to close and one of them muttered, 'Thief.' Obviously I was embarrassed, but I said nothing. By then I knew that this was how it was going to be in some quarters; and I was psychologically preparing myself for the trial to be just as harrowing and testing as I had suspected it would be. Jack and Chloe had been sent away, oblivious, to spend the week in Norfolk with my mother and new step-father, Eric – an instantly wonderful grandfather to them – but Tom and Dan, now 14, insisted on staying home and seeing it through with us.

The proceedings began, as expected, with the legal argument about the second charge. Stephen Solley made vigorous attempts to get that charge separated from the first – either slung out altogether or heard on another occasion – to avoid it fatally prejudicing the minds of the jury by implying a pattern of behaviour where no such pattern existed. But Judge Michael Sachs ruled that both should remain on the sheet.

'If anything goes wrong, that's our first bloody grounds for appeal,' Stephen told me angrily in an adjournment.

As anticipated, the actual evidence for the 'propping-up charge' proved to be virtually non-existent. We were supposed to see a video, because the security camera had certainly been in use in the store on the day of the so-called offence, but the footage had vanished! Stephen Solley was very intrigued by this and there was quite a sensation in court about its disappearance, but we were eventually told that it was not available because there had been a fault on the day in question.

We had, however, been given a copy of Tesco's security video relating to the main charge, and we all watched it closely, including the jury. No arguments there – it showed me calmly stacking, packing, paying and leaving – although I must admit I was silently bellowing at myself, What about all that stuff at the front? And get that bloody soap box off the hook, you cretin! Wake up for Christ's sake!

The judge said drily, 'That won't win any BAFTAs, will it?'

It was a discouraging beginning in relation to the unfair second charge, but I was heartened by the strength of the argument that Stephen Solley QC had launched. Watching him in action, I could see that he had a good, direct and fundamentally honest approach to the case. He wasn't side-tracked by any courtroom theatrics, was clear about the forces at play and, although he hadn't succeeded in persuading Judge Sachs to let the second charge drop, I felt a lot of confidence in him.

In the meantime, poor Judy was left outside the courtroom because, as a character witness, she couldn't be allowed in until she was due to give her evidence on my behalf. She sat with her sister-in-law, Ro, and suffered very much.

The prosecution, of course, gets the first go, and I soon realized something I had never appreciated as a reporter. That is, there are things that the counsel for the prosecution – Mr Anthony Gee QC in my case – can say to the court in his opening address which do not necessarily have to be repeated later.

Mr Gee suggested that I had carefully worked out the trajectory of view from the eye of the checkout girl to the trolley, and had calculated that the bottles would just be outside her range of vision.

This was complete balls. The image of me going around Tesco with a sextant or protractor – or whatever you use to make such calculations – then sitting at home at night with a compass and graph paper to work out the equations was so bizarre that I burst out laughing and received, in return, a warning frown from Stephen Solley. But I just couldn't help myself. It was such a ludicrous portrayal of premeditation and an obsessional desire to commit the perfect naff crime, and was the maddest thing I heard in the entire trial.

In the adjournment that followed, I said to Stephen Solley, as I'm sure so many defendants do to their barrister, 'How can he say this!'

'Forget it,' he replied. 'Prosecuting counsels can say things like that in their opening. Let's not get side-tracked by that kind of wild speculation, which is all it is. Stay calm and don't worry. If he says it again we'll go for him, promise.'

It was already turning into an odd trial: a nexus of the impersonal and personal. The CPS was obviously going for a kill – as in any trial – but there was clearly a trophy to be won, too, a scalp to be had. It was, as so many trials are, far more about winning and losing than about justice. And although the charges were 'petty' the stakes were very high. For me they were, anyway. If the Crown lost it would be a disappointment for its team, but they'd get over it. If they won, I'd be ruined. Simple as that.

'I've seen thicker prosecution files in murder trials, and I'm not joking,' Stephen told me when we broke for lunch on day two. 'But I've never seen such a mass of almost entirely trivial research, statements and speculations to back up such ostensibly trivial accusations. I'm genuinely surprised.' He bit into a sandwich. 'They don't half want to duff you up.'

Throughout the case the public gallery was filled to capacity and many of our *This Morning* fans were sitting there listening. There were some good moments for me as the prosecution unfolded its case, but these never seemed to appear in the newspapers. I can understand that; the press was only interested in copy pertaining directly to me, and was not 'fired' by stuff relating to store assistants or nervous checkout girls.

There was one glorious moment, for example, when a

young, seemingly under-trained Tesco security spokesman was called in to give evidence about the propping-up charge. First he wandered his way through what little he had been given to say, backed up by a checkout girl who, it turned out, couldn't be at all sure about what she had seen; and then there was that little matter of the video footage, which couldn't be found. The poor lad was under ferocious pressure but he had precious little ammunition. On a personal level, I genuinely felt really sorry for him – he looked terrified – but I could also see that the charge was, thank God, being unpicked before the court's eyes.

Then something significant happened. Angela Orme, the store detective, was called to give her evidence and, although she was only doing her job as somebody who was paid to stop and apprehend shoplifters, I was furious with her. I knew there was no point in me getting personal, but I couldn't help remembering that Stuart Hall, the former host of *It's a Knockout*, who was bizarrely accused of shoplifting that year, too, feelingly described his apprehender as 'Rosa Klebb', the Communist witch in the James Bond movie, *From Russia with Love*. I didn't quite feel that about the woman who had stopped me, but let's just say it was hard to feel warmth towards her. Anyway, as she was giving her evidence, she said, in answer to a question, that she had seen me moving quickly towards the door as I was leaving the store.

'But he didn't do that,' Stephen Solley interrupted her. 'We know he left slowly; we know that he spent some time examining the menu.'

The witness hesitated and mumbled a general assent.

'Then why didn't you say so? Why did you say he was hurrying when he wasn't? What impression were you trying to create?'

I felt a ripple pass along the jury. I could tell this part of her testimony had not gone down well with them.

Incidentally, several years later, when I was at Manchester airport, just about to get the shuttle to London, I was tapped on the shoulder while I was paying for a newspaper. When I turned round, it was Angela Orme. 'Hello,' she said, giving me a slightly awkward but friendly smile.

I knew that she represented something horrendous in my life, but couldn't instantly place her. Then it all came flooding back. To my amazement, I found myself smiling back.

'Good God, it's you. What are you doing now, then?'

'I'm working here at the airport.'

'Do you enjoy it?'

'Oh, yes,' she said. 'It's much better. What are you doing here?'

'I'm going to London for a conference.'

'Oh! Well, have a good trip.'

We looked at each other for a moment, and then walked away.

I think there was closure in that moment for both of us. I don't hold any grudges.

But, to return to the court proceedings, I think that moment when she had misdescribed my behaviour helped to demonstrate to the jury that there was something a bit too intense and overblown – personal – about the case. Or that's how it seemed to me. The nature of our legal system is adversarial and the prosecution's job is to prove intent on behalf of the defendant, but that does not justify getting a person convicted at the expense of truth.

When the defence case began and I took the stand, I was cross-examined by my own QC, Stephen Solley. This, at last, was my moment. I knew I'd be tense, but the long year of not being able to speak out had formed a lake of words in my mind. Now the dam holding them back was removed and out it all came. My plan to be calm, measured, dispassionate, fell apart. I babbled, got emotional; it must have been like watching a firework going off.

'Slow down, Mr Madeley,' Judge Sachs kept rebuking me

in a firm but pleasant way, 'I need to write these points down.'

That was actually helpful because his constant 'Slow down, we've got all the time in the world' did succeed in calming me. I began to settle, became more composed, and spoke more clearly in answer to the questions. Then the prosecution counsel rose to his feet. Oddly enough this was easier. I wasn't denying the facts of the matter. It was simply a question of what interpretation was placed on the events. He did, however, succeed in needling me, probably intentionally, by constantly implying in his questions that I had gone into Tesco with the intention of stealing. Eventually I became impatient – bad idea – and said something like, 'Look! Just explain to me, why on earth I would go into any supermarket to steal things? Why? I don't need to steal, and the damage to my reputation would be incalculable. Tell me why I would do that?'

I knew by the look on his face that I'd just trodden on my own stumps. Pouncing like a cat on a mouse, he said, 'Well, every question deserves an answer, Mr Madeley. Greed! As simple as that. It was an act of greed!'

I was furious with myself as well as him. I'm not a greedy person, but I'd just invited him to tell me so. I had to calm down.

But in my head as he looked smilingly at his notes I was asking him, Are you greedy? I'm certainly not, so how dare you say I am? Better left unsaid, I decided.

But it was the first time during my session in the witness box that I had become rattled, and Judge Sachs turned to me and said, 'Would you like to take a break?'

I needed one! But, because these were moments I had been waiting for, building towards, for a year, had thought, worried, dreamed and had nightmares about, the last thing I wanted to do was to prolong the experience. Also, I certainly didn't want the jury, sitting directly opposite me, to think I needed time to re-compose myself. I was all fired up, wanted to get on with it.

'No,' I said resolutely. 'I'm okay. I want to carry on.'

'Really?' Judge Sachs queried. 'If you want to take a five-minute break, that's absolutely fine with me and the court.'

'No,' I repeated. 'I'm okay. I want to carry on.'

It was then that I noticed a spasm of annoyance pass across the judge's face. I looked down at Stephen Solley, who gave me a look that said, 'Mistake, Richard. You should have said yes.' It was only later that I was told that Judge Sachs was a smoker and may have wanted a ciggy break. Bugger.

When I finally left the witness box, I felt I had not done as well as I had wanted to; hadn't said all the things I intended to say. I felt as some of our guests on *This Morning* did when after an interview they complained, 'I didn't say half what I wanted to! You didn't ask me the questions I was expecting.'

At one point, too, when the enormity of it all had suddenly crashed in on me, I'd had to work hard to hold back tears. Damn! The press said I'd broken down. In a nutshell, I was left feeling that, although I had achieved seventy per cent of what I had hoped, it was not enough. I had wanted for Judy's sake and mine to do a hundred and ten per cent and blow it all away in one ringing declamation.

Throughout the case, our friend and editor Liam Hamilton was in the press box every day, making copious notes. As I left the witness box and looked across at him, he gave me a huge grin, with both his thumbs up. I shook my head desolately, but he nodded his even more vigorously, put his thumbs up again and mouthed, 'Well done!'

Having given the only defence I could – the truth – I had to return to the dock. Although the case was really very simple, the trial ran on for four days. Obviously, there were people of good standing who believed in me and vouched for my honesty, but they could not comment directly on the charges.

That's not allowed. They could only say under oath what they thought of me as a person. Dr Chris Steele, a Geordie and a lovely honest man, knows all our family secrets and, standing in the witness box, he grinned at the jury and said, 'What can I tell you? He's just a regular guy!' Chris was very generous and drew a picture of someone totally incompatible with the kind of person who would plan a pathetic shop-lifting spree.

Then Judy took the witness stand. I was so anxious on her behalf that I can't actually remember much of her testimony, other than that she was incredibly loyal and honest. She was also very exasperated with what I had done and, at one point, said, 'The stupid idiot – fancy forgetting . . .' which made most of the jury smile.

Every night throughout the trial we would come home from the court drenched in emotional exhaustion, and would talk about that day's events. Then, before I put the lights out, I would telephone Cal, Judy's brother. Because he ran the *Guardian*'s parliamentary desk, he would have all the early editions of the next day's papers. A robust good-humoured guy, he would read out all the lurid headlines, like the *Sun*'s YOU'RE THE CHAMPAGNE SHOPLIFTER, and the juicy court copy. He invariably succeeded in making me laugh. MY LOVE FOR DOTTY DICK, the headline that followed Judy giving her evidence in court, had Cal and me in tears of laughter. These moments were good for me, and became a light relief at the end of each day when I could glimpse the refracting prism through which the tabloids were portraying the most important incident in my life. An overblown court case was being cut down to size with witty headlines and snappy captions. Judy could laugh, too. But it didn't seem so funny the next morning when we left for court.

Then came the moment for Professor Reason's evidence. He gave his qualifications, which were impressive, and outlined his findings on human error, repetitive behaviour, and how it could lead to disaster. He was quite sure, the jury heard, that I was a classic case-study.

The prosecutor asked him if he'd seen Tesco's video of me.

'No,' said Professor Reason.

'Well, I think you should see it,' he was told.

I had a sudden crisis of confidence. I felt – probably unfairly – that Professor Reason was being ambushed. The video was shown again and we all watched it from start to finish in silence.

'What did you see there, Professor Reason?' Mr Anthony Gee QC purred as soon as it ended.

'I saw a man doing the family shopping!' Professor Reason replied with breathtaking simplicity.

Then, looking at the jury, Professor Reason began to expound. He talked about the questions he had asked Judy and me, how he was satisfied they had shown we'd both answered honestly. He said he was quite convinced that what had happened in my case was an accident, a simple human error that happens every day in supermarkets all over the world. He talked about the way I carried out tasks, that there was a definite negligence of attention in the way I sometimes conducted myself.

At one level, it was embarrassing for me. Nobody likes to be described as dangerously forgetful. But it was true. And, as he was speaking, I couldn't help but remember that headline: MY LOVE FOR DOTTY DICK!

My trial was concluding. The prosecution went over its ground again. Stephen Solley's own summing-up was very straightforward. In effect he asked the jury if they really thought it was likely that I would put everything on the line by nicking stuff from Tesco, or whether it was infinitely more likely I'd made a simple mistake with huge consequences.

The judge summed up. Suddenly the trial was almost over. The jury withdrew. We all went outside into the corridor.

The tension was utterly indescribable. Judy and I held hands, but could hardly speak. I suddenly needed to pray but, as there was nowhere to go except the toilets, I locked myself in a cubicle for a couple of minutes and silently asked, for the thousandth time, for deliverance. Then I came outside again and the waiting dragged on.

I was now passing through the final moments of an experience that just over a year ago I would have dismissed out of hand as something that couldn't ever happen to me. These were the closing stages of a criminal trial with me – *me* – cast in the role of defendant. It was still unbelievable. Probably more than at any other time, I felt detached from reality. This intense, almost dreamlike scene – journalists talking quietly among themselves; court staff standing around whispering to each other; lawyers sitting deep in thought; the accused and his wife almost suffocating with tension – was straight from a film or TV drama. But it was real and it was terrifying and *this* moment, *this* deafening pause before doom or deliverance, was absolutely the very worst, and I'll never forget the sight and smell and sound of it.

Suddenly, the tension broke. The jury was coming back in, and we rushed inside the courtroom. The foreman stood up. He was saying something. There was a gasp all around me. The judge was saying something else and the jury was leaving. Stephen Solley leaned over and grinned at me.

'That went right over your head, didn't it?' he said. 'They've found you not guilty of the propping-up charge, but they haven't reached a unanimous verdict on the other one, the main one.'

I was right to be confused. 'But if the one I'm cleared on was supposed to strengthen the other one, which wouldn't have stood up by itself, how can they . . . Why?'

He nodded. 'Yeah, how can there be any doubt about your innocence on the first one? Exactly what I warned the judge at the start has happened: the case against you is tainted and it's confused the jury. His nibs will be hoping they acquit, otherwise this will not look good on appeal. But I think you can relax.'

As if. So more waiting. But it seemed a much shorter time before the jury was back in, and the judge was asking if they'd reached a verdict. No, they hadn't.

The judge looked depressed and thought for a while.

'Could you,' he then said, 'just answer the question I am about to ask you "Yes" or "No"? If I gave you further time, do you think there is any reasonable prospect of your reaching a second verdict on which at least ten of you will agree?'

'It depends on what you mean by reasonable time, Your Honour,' the foreman replied. He was a pleasant-looking bloke and sounded intelligent.

'Is the answer "Yes"?' Judge Sachs persisted.

At this moment a kind of telegraphed look, that I will never forget, passed between the foreman and other jurors, then, shaking his head at Judge Sachs, and smiling slightly, he replied, 'I would think not.'

Judge Sachs then asked if that was the view of all the jury. Each of them nodded.

Mr Anthony Gee QC, counsel for the prosecution, rose to his feet: 'Your Honour, the jury has been unable to reach a verdict on count two after a trial which has lasted four days. The prosecution in this, as in all cases, has to consider whether it would be in the public interest for there to be a retrial before another jury in the future. And, among the considerations of this case, the Crown has regard not only for the nature of this charge and the character of the defendant, and in particular whether a fair retrial on the remaining count would be possible given the press coverage this case has received. Having regard to all those circumstances of and surrounding this case, the Crown has come to the conclusion it would not be in the public interest for there to be a retrial.'

I held my breath, but Judge Sachs moved like greased lightning. He was acquitting me on the last charge, dismissing the jury, and talking about my costs.

It was all over. I could hardly believe it. It was like witnessing a terrible monster of my own making crumbling in on itself and blowing away like smoke. I crumpled down in the chair in the dock. Stephen Solley was now asking for costs, which were granted. In the space of minutes, the huge legal bill that I had accumulated had evaporated, too.

Stephen said later, 'A double acquittal, Richard. I know you wanted the jury to come in with this within ten seconds, so we could say, "It's over," but the prosecution threw up a lot of dust. You've now been acquitted by the jury on one charge, the CPS doesn't want to go for a retrial on the second, and the judge has thrown it out. It's all over. You *won*.'

What followed was like a series of slides clicking at speed through a projector. I remember leaving the court to a huge crush of people, mostly journalists struggling to get out to waylay me in the corridor. The crush was so huge that the catch on my wristwatch, which Judy had bought for me at Christmas, snapped, and the watch was trampled underfoot and never seen again. Somehow I managed to get out, but God knows how Judy managed to do this from her seat in the public gallery.

Stephen Solley, his arm around my shoulder, propelled me into the side room where we had had all our consultations during the trial. The next moment Judy was also ushered in by Stephen.

'I'll leave you for a bit,' he said, and shut the door, which unfortunately had a big glass window.

Although nobody was actually peering in, we could see a

crush of bodies against it, and hear the unbelievable tumult as journalists shouted into their mobile phones. Judy and I just clung to each other.

'It's all right. It's over,' I kept repeating to her.

And it was. The impersonal legal machine that had sucked me in on 24 August and damn near chewed me up had spat me out again. I was still in one piece.

Later, surrounded by the media scrum, we walked from the crown court to Granada Television about five minutes up the road. Once there, we said we would do a photocall in about forty-five minutes and then give a press conference straight after that.

Upstairs in the offices among our colleagues and friends the atmosphere was euphoric. There were constant phone calls from friends, who had just heard the news on the radio, and many of them were in tears. The decision, eleven months earlier, to reject a simple caution had been the right one. Actually, whatever the verdict, it would have been the right one. There was never really any option.

I began our press conference with a short statement that I'd answer all questions. Nothing was off limits.

'Go on, have a go at Tesco,' several reporters invited me.

'No, I'm not here to slag anyone off,' I said.

I did add, though, that I felt there was a responsibility on supermarkets to help their customers to avoid oversights at the checkout. I knew from my mailbag over the last year the crippling damage done to people's lives because of a simple oversight that led to criminal charges. Perhaps I should have organized some sort of campaign for change but, to be honest, Judy and I were knackered. We just wanted our lives back.

We eventually went home to the most phenomenal party. The first person to arrive was Rachel, the schoolgirl from next door. She leaped at me, threw her arms around my neck, and said, 'I knew it was going to be all right. I just knew it.' That set the tone for the night. Neighbours and colleagues packed the house. We cheered every TV news programme to the roof. The phone rang every two minutes. I, I am proud to say, went to bed completely and utterly hammered.

The next day *This Morning* was on air, but there was no way Judy and I could do the programme. We were just too excited, too wired. We agreed to do a few more pictures for the local press, then went in to look at all the bouquets of flowers that had been arriving every few minutes. The house was like a florist's shop. I felt terrific! I don't think I've ever known such relief.

Later, though, I found myself, post-traumatic stress style, looking back at what had happened in the court.

'What would have happened if it had gone wrong?' I asked Stephen Solley just before he left to get his train back to London.

'We would have appealed and won,' he said crisply. 'Don't ever doubt that, Richard. The evidence wasn't enough to convict a mouse. We dealt with the charges honestly and rigorously. It would have been a travesty of justice if the verdict had gone any other way. I believe permission to appeal would have been granted on the papers alone. And I promise, you would have won the appeal.'

———

When Judy and I returned to work, the aftermath, with a few unpleasant exceptions, wasn't too bad. Three weeks after I was cleared I awoke to a brief smear campaign. Posters proclaiming the 'RICHARD MADELEY SPONSORED TROLLEY DASH' were sent to neighbours. We were pretty sure of their source, but the libel laws must draw a veil on that. But these were isolated incidents. Phone-ins passed without incident, although a couple of years later, a woman calling herself 'Elizabeth from York' came on the line.

'Can I just say something, Richard?'

When I nodded, she added, 'I just wanted to ask whether you could steal me a bottle of wine from Safeway.'

She turned out to be a student doing it for a dare – at least that's what she said when she wrote to apologize. What the hell.

————

It all happened at the start of another decade in another century but, although I recovered my balance long ago, the experience brought permanent changes that will never fade. And that's fine, actually. I learned so much between August 1990 and July 1991. I think I found where my limits lie; where my failures spring from. I was a young man in my early thirties and I had a young man's over-confidence and hubris. I thought I could sweep through life, handling everything and anything, and forgot that the devil is in the detail. What a demon leaped out of my oversight! What humiliating consequences flowed from it. What agony Judy was put through.

Her love and belief in me was what got me through the worst times. The unstinting kindness and robust support of friends and family were always there, too, for us both. I'd had periods of unhappiness and sadness before, but I'd never really suffered. I think it was a cleansing, strengthening process, although I didn't think that at the time. But there's a Jewish proverb: something about taking your suffering and eating it in order to grow stronger.

I said that once to my brother-in-law, Peter.

'Yeah,' he said. 'And sometimes we all need a bloody great kick up the arse!'

8: JUDY

On 24 August 1990 life could not have been better for Richard and me. We had just come back from one holiday with the kids and, because we had another week or so before *This Morning* began and the kids went back to school, we decided to go down to Devon. To stock up for this trip and for our homecoming from Devon, Richard went off to our local Tesco, in Didsbury, Manchester, where he had been doing the family shop for years. Some time later, I remember thinking he had been gone a very long time, and I was just wondering, Where is he? What's going on? Has anything happened? when the phone rang. It was Richard.

'I just want to tell you,' he said very calmly, 'that I'm in the manager's office at Tesco's.'

'Why?' I said.

'They say I've taken some stuff and not paid for it,' he replied.

'What!'

'That's what they're saying. They've taken me into the manager's office and at the moment we're waiting for the police.'

'The police?' I repeated, bewildered, unable to take in what he was saying. 'Why?'

'It's all a huge, hideous, stupid mistake,' Richard explained. 'And I'm confident everything will be okay, but I don't know how long this is going to take. That's why I'm ringing you now.'

'Okay,' I said in shock. 'Will you ring me as soon as the police arrive?'

Although Richard had sounded calm, I realized that this was simply to reassure me. In truth, I was instantly distraught. I knew it was a ludicrous accusation, that shoplifting was completely alien to Richard's character, but I was only too aware of what the press would make of such a charge.

At the time of Richard's call, I didn't have any make-up on because I was at home looking after the kids. I paced around a little, felt myself getting tearful but then thought, Hang on. There's bound to be somebody at the door any moment. Go and put your make-up on. It was the last thing I felt like doing but, sure enough, within minutes there was a ring at the door and there stood a woman from a local press agency. This was not surprising: everybody knew where we lived and, as we discovered later that same day, somebody had snapped Richard on his way to the police van, and the press had already been tipped off about what had happened at the store. Within hours, there was a huge front-page picture in the *Manchester Evening News* showing Richard, dressed in jeans and shirt, being accompanied by two police officers across the Tesco car park. It was horrific.

When Tom and Dan arrived home from a friend's house, they were absolutely brilliant. In their mid-teens, and at a very vulnerable age, they realized immediately that something was wrong because I was pacing the floor in the living-room.

'What's the matter, Mum?' they asked.

I explained Richard's predicament as gently as I could.

'That's just ridiculous,' they both exploded. 'We've never heard anything so stupid.'

'I know,' I said. 'But just do me a favour, will you? Take Jack and Chloe to the park. The phone will start ringing any moment and the press may well arrive on our doorstep.'

They immediately responded and took the kids out. Then I got another phone call from Richard saying, unbelievably, that the police had arrested him and that he was being taken to our local police station to be charged. Until then, horrible though the situation was, I had thought it would get sorted. But even as he was speaking, I realized that once the press had been tipped off the incident had acquired such a momentum that the police simply had to get on with it. It was just awful.

After Richard's second call I didn't hear anything for hours. Eventually, I rang the police station and spoke to a very nice sympathetic policewoman who, realizing I was desperately upset, broke the rules and told me that Richard was okay, was with his solicitor, Michael Green, and that he should be home within an hour or so.

The next person who telephoned was Chris Steele, our family GP and *This Morning*'s GP. He lived about half a mile down the road from us, and had heard about the day's disaster because the whole of Didsbury, it seemed, had seen the *Manchester Evening News* and was now on full buzz.

'How's Richard?' Chris asked.

'I don't know,' I replied, obviously very shaken. 'They won't let me talk to him.'

'Are you on your own?' Chris asked.

'Yes,' I said. 'Tom and Dan are looking after Jack and Chloe.'

'I'm coming round,' he said instantly.

About half an hour after he had arrived to comfort me, he said, 'Judy, where's Richard's car?'

'I've no idea,' I replied. 'I assume it's still in Tesco's car park.'

'I'll go and get it,' he said.

Soon after that, I got another phone call from Richard who was now in Michael Green's car. He sounded hugely relieved to be out of the police station, but very shaken. He told me that there had been a load of press outside, that Michael Green had given them a statement, and that he was now on his way home. When he arrived a few minutes later, we fell into each other's arms, then I asked him where Michael Green was.

'Outside in the car,' Richard replied. 'I wanted to see you on my own first.'

I had never seen Richard in such a state. Normally, he's a coper and problem-solver who doesn't get defeated by anything. He's not a person who's prone to depression or fear, he's always full of energy and just gets on with things. But that day he was completely devastated. I can't remember much more about that evening. I know Michael Green came in and talked about what would happen next.

'It will obviously be a magistrates' trial,' he told us, 'unless Richard elects to go to crown court.'

But a crown court, he then added, was what Richard should opt for because, as he's such a famous person, everybody would make such a big deal of it all.

'This is a matter which is hugely important to your reputation, your career and your entire life,' he stressed.

That was as far as we got that night. God knows how we managed to get to sleep, but we did. When I woke up, there was an awful feeling churning in my guts. But we had to make a start and face up to the press because the story was already in all the papers. We contacted Granada's press office which, along with our immediate bosses and executive bosses, was absolutely fantastic. The executive producer of the programme, Dianne Nelmes, was wonderful.

'It's all utterly ridiculous,' Dianne said.

We also had calls from Steve Morrison, now chief executive of Granada but the then Programme Controller, and other senior figures in broadcasting, such as Paul Fox, saying, 'We just want to tell you that we know all this is complete crap, and we do not believe a word of it. We are totally standing by you, and it will make no difference whatsoever to your position with Granada. We still want both of you to present *This Morning*.'

That was great; but, during a phone call from my brother, Roger, Richard broke down and cried. I'd never seen him so distraught and had only ever seen him cry when our babies were born.

'It's the sheer humiliation of it,' he explained to me. 'I would rather have been accused of a more shocking crime than this horrible petty thing. Shoplifting is just so tacky, foul and nasty.'

Because we were so vulnerable to being doorstepped by the press, we thought the best thing we could do would be to continue with our plans and go away with the kids to a tiny hotel in Hope Cove, Devon, where we'd stayed many times before. Given that the hotel's staff would already have read the stuff in the papers, Richard thought it was going to be tough, but the owner, his wife and kids, and everybody we met while we were there, were so kind and lovely.

It was very important that people should express absolute faith in us because, no matter how certain we were of the truth and how proud we were, we couldn't help feeling as we were walking around with our heads held high that there were people out there, particularly those who didn't know us from Adam, who would think it was true. We were only too aware of the 'no smoke without fire' syndrome, and that is something that's very hard to deal with. Fortunately, we also had many extraordinarily supportive reactions and messages.

It was perfectly clear in my mind how the horrible misunder-standing had come about at Tesco's. Richard is always on the go. He's a Speedy Gonzalez character – moves fast, walks fast, talks fast – and he's not very rooted in the present. Once he's focused on something, he screens everything else out, forgets things. That's why he's so hopeless at remembering people's names. He goes at everything at such a lick that I can quite see that in Tesco's, when he was thinking about our planned trip, his mind was on that and not in the present. He was just standing at the checkout, a can of Coke, which he always drinks non-stop compulsively, in his hand, his mind somewhere else. Then the whole thing just became appalling, a complete bloody nightmare. Even now I can't help feeling incensed with the Tesco people, who would not accept that he had simply forgotten to unpack some of the goods in the front section of the trolley.

Going back to work after this fiasco was good for us. It kept us grounded and occupied. But how Richard survived it, I will never know. I'm not even sure how I got through it all. I was very concerned for Richard and the kids. The little ones, of course, were too young to take it in, but Tom's and Dan's school was right next to the supermarket concerned, and they obviously must have had to put up with comments from some of the other kids because school kids can be very cruel. I kept asking them if they were having a hard time, but they always replied, 'No, Mum. All our friends have known you and Richard for years, and they know exactly what you are both like, so there's no problem.'

Looking back, though, I can see that I remained so worried about the kids, I wasn't always as helpful to Richard as I could have been. Although I knew he was innocent, I still felt very angry from time to time that, because of his foolishness, he had put us through this terrible ordeal. I'm sure I concealed these feelings from him at the time, but I will always regret that I kept thinking, How could he let this happen?

I honestly don't know how we slept during the following eleven months. Eleven months! If you elect to go to crown court the procedures just drag on and on. It's absolute torture and I don't understand why it has to take so long. Throughout all that time, Richard had to put up with being in the public eye more than usual, and some gossip columnists, of course, couldn't resist having a dig.

So it went on, a hideous time that never seemed to go away.

While I was five months pregnant with Jack – terrified I'd lose him.

Father and son. Richard with Jack immediately after his birth in hospital.

Above: Exhausted but happy. With Jack at home in Manchester, in 1986.

Left: A glass of red wine for me, a bottle for Jack. Summer 1986, with Tom and Dan at home in Manchester.

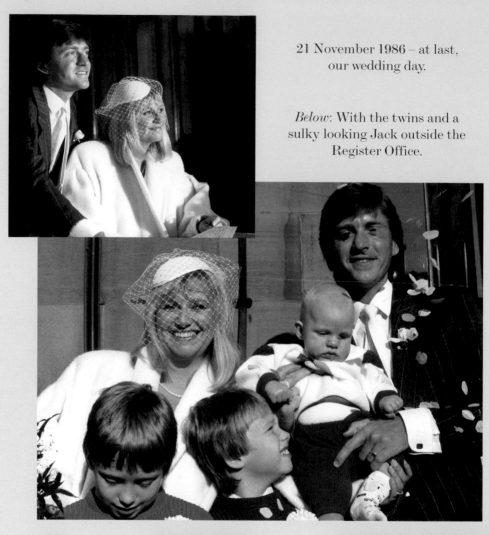

21 November 1986 – at last,
our wedding day.

Below: With the twins and a
sulky looking Jack outside the
Register Office.

Our wedding lunch in Cheshire.
(Not in a graveyard! But the Bells of
Peover Inn was next to a beautiful
church.) With my brother Roger.

Happy and relieved. A lovely day.
Jack was only six months old – little did
I know I was already pregnant
with Chloe!

Above: 1987. Chloe is held by her two big twin brothers, Tom and Dan, aged 10. They're still as protective towards her today.

Above: Me at our GP Dr Chris Steele's surgery in Manchester, filming Chloe having her MMR jab for the first *This Morning*.

Left: Richard filming at the Albert Dock in Liverpool for the pilot of *This Morning*, June 1988. The baby is Chloe.

1988 at home in Manchester just before we launched *This Morning*. Tom on the left, Dan on the right.

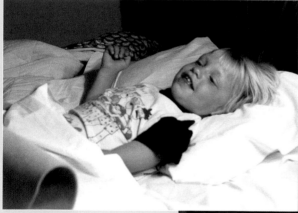

Left: Jack, aged 2, in Florida.

Right: Jack makes an early bid for the Rear-of-the-Year Award, 1989.

Above: All of us with Minnie and Mickey at Disneyworld in Florida.

Left: Disneyworld, Florida. Chloe had spilled juice all down her clothes, hence the nappy – much to one passer-by's disgust.

Left: A fancy dress party at our holiday hotel in Devon (I'm Snow White, Richard's a dwarf!). Just before our nightmare at Tesco's began.

Above: Minutes after my acquittal, July 1991.

Below: 1991 at the same Devon hotel soon after Richard was acquitted of shoplifting. As you can see, we all look very happy.

In a snowy Norfolk field near Richard's mum's house, with her dog Holly.

Three go mad in Norfolk – Jack and Chloe with Richard's mum.

Jack and Chloe with Judy's mum at the wedding of her younger brother, Roger, in the Lake District, 1994.

Fishing in Cornwall, Judy caught 12 mackerel more than anyone on the boat.

About to give my mum away, 1993. I lost a mother, but gained a father – a much-loved step-dad, Eric Matthews.

Me and Mum on holiday in Portugal, 1994.

However much we tried to enjoy other things it was always on the horizon of our minds.

Today, as I write this, I'm remembering all the people who wrote to us. We received so many letters from pillars of the establishment describing their own run-ins with the police regarding themselves or their children, and recounting how their view of justice, which they had always thought unshakable, had been turned inside out. The gist of their messages was: 'It's actually very difficult to continue to have faith in a justice system when you know how capable it is of getting things wrong. And you never trust it in quite the same way again.'

Sadly, although I still tried to ensure that our children knew the difference between right and wrong, I agreed with the correspondents, and no longer felt the same way about the police, or believed that our legal system was always just. Despite my total faith in Richard's innocence – and others' belief in him – I couldn't help worrying that, in the end, he might not be acquitted. That, for me, was the ghastly thought when I lay awake in the darkest hours of the morning. But Richard was magnificent. I know he had these times, too, and I suspect that there were even some terrible moments when he considered ending it all for the family's sake, but he was just fantastic.

One good thing during this period was that we fell in love with Florida. The case had been going on since August, and the two of us went to the Gulf of Mexico for a week in February. We stayed in a place right next to where we now own a little apartment. It was so calm, so beautiful there and, feeling very soothed, we sat night after night watching the sun go down. One evening as the sun was setting, I thought, It's going to be all right. I knew this just as clearly as I had known all those years ago that, despite all the pain our relationship was causing me, our lives were going to be joined together.

That night, the burden lifted a little and I knew that bit of the nightmare was over. Turning to Richard, I told him what I'd just experienced, that I was convinced everything was going to be all right. Even though this didn't alter the fact that we still had to get through some bad times in the very near future, it was a significant moment for both of us.

The court case lasted for four days, but I was not allowed in for most of the procedures because, when you are a character witness, you can't be present until you've given your evidence. That felt very strange. Richard and I would arrive at court together and would then have to kiss each other goodbye. Each day, I just couldn't believe the number of reporters, photographers and television crews that were present. 'I do not believe this,' I kept muttering to myself. Neither Richard nor I had ever thought we were that important.

People were very good to me. My sister-in-law, Ro, came to court with me every day; so did Dianne Nelmes, our executive producer on *This Morning*, who was also a character witness. Sitting outside the courtroom, I knew only too well what Richard was going through and how humiliated he would be feeling. I just sat there waiting until the day's proceedings ended and he'd come into the side room where we could spend a little time alone together before further discussions with our legal team and then home.

At the time, Liam Hamilton was our editor on the programme, and I remember holding his hand so tightly on occasions that he was left with fingernail indentations all across his palm. He never complained.

At one point we came up against the kind of human frailty you simply don't expect when you're in court. The judge, who we later learned was a smoker, seemed to be short-tempered during the session when I was giving my evidence about Richard's character. I know I was a bit tremulous, but I was doing okay. Then, as I was replying to a perfectly proper question by our counsel, the judge suddenly snapped, 'Yes, yes, yes, we've been through all this. We don't need to hear any more.'

But our counsel, Stephen Solley QC, said, 'Go on, Judy. Tell us more.'

I was furious. If I'd been able to jump out of the witness box and clock the judge one, I would certainly have done so. You don't know Richard from Adam, I thought.

When the jury was out, Stephen Solley came towards me, smiling. I thought, What does this mean?

'The judge,' he said, 'is going to abandon the trial.'

'Abandon it?' I replied, totally confused. 'What do you mean?'

'It's all right, it's good news,' he said. 'The jury hasn't reached a majority verdict, so Judge Sachs has discharged the jury, acquitted Richard, and Richard can leave the court without a stain on his character.'

My heart stood still.

Outside the court, in a private room, we fell into each other's arms and wept. Then we went out on to the steps of the court to face the photographers.

One thing that annoyed me then – and still annoys me now – although, at one level, it is completely trivial, is that when a wife goes to court with her husband the press immediately starts to comment on the clothes she wears. In my case, I had to contend with: 'This is what Judy wore on Monday. Will she wear this on Tuesday?' I was furious. How dare anybody suggest that I might choose a certain outfit as a sort of weapon in Richard's favour. How dare anybody imply that what I chose to wear might have a bearing on what would happen to my husband and my family. But, having said that, I do remember experiencing a wave of regret, when the case was over on the last day, that I'd forgotten to bring my hairspray with me. After Richard and I had embraced and wept in each other's arms, I certainly needed to repair my hair and make-up before facing the photographers.

After we left the court, we went to Granada who had laid on a press conference for us and, even more important, some food. Neither Richard nor I had been able to eat much during that week, and I hadn't eaten anything that day. It was a straightforward press conference, but almost impossible for us to tell people how deeply we had been affected by it all.

The next morning, I left Richard to sleep in. Journalists were hammering on the door and I went down in my dressing-gown and said through the letterbox: 'Please leave us alone. If you come back in an hour, I promise you will have some pictures and all the rest.'

I was so relieved that it was over, and so was Richard when he woke up. But there was no doubt, as others had said, that such an experience does poison your faith in institutions, and you never feel as safe as you did before. You realize that everybody's life hangs on a thread; that what you may think is an ordered, successful, happy existence can be overturned in a moment. Richard's only fault was (and is) that he's impatient, always in a rush, forgets things, and is not always as methodical as he should be. But we all have our faults and he was so disproportionately punished for his.

These days, I feel terribly sorry for any law-abiding citizen who gets into a mess, and when I read about these things I think, Do you realize how this guy's or woman's life is going to be ruined for a momentary lapse of attention? The kind of thing that Richard was put through is the equivalent of being put in the stocks in the Middle Ages. People do get over it and start functioning again, and we were obviously euphoric when it was all over, but it took us a very long time to recover and I felt quite bitter afterwards.

At such times, you learn a great deal about people. I remember being bombarded with letters from people in the press, whom we had thought to be our friends, but who were actually only interested in getting an interview. Their approach was always, 'Tell us your side of the story.' We always felt like saying, 'The only story is that Richard is innocent, and that's that.' Since then, I haven't spoken to a lot of these individuals because I saw a different side of them at that time. We were also offered a small fortune to sell our story, but we always refused. We both said that, one day, when we were sufficiently healed, we would write it ourselves.

Afterwards, I remember Terry Wogan saying to Richard on his chat-show: 'But why, when you are so well known, do you do your own shopping?'

But shopping's a basic function, and that's how we like to live. There can be tremendous losses in the achievement of so-called celebrity status, and you can, if you let it happen, lose the essential nature of everyday life. I don't actually like shopping in supermarkets, but Richard doesn't mind and that's a natural division of labour in our household.

I've always been a very private person; and, as I've mentioned before, my home's a kind of sanctuary, the place where I feel safe and the world can't get at me. I'm not as brave as Richard. I'm immensely proud of him. The shoplifting charge could have broken him, could have wrecked his self-confidence and fearlessness. He could have fallen into a black hole of despair, but he coped very well. We can now afford to look back and say, 'It was a hellish time for us, but it could have been worse.'

Recently, some friends of ours have been having an awful time financially and, when we were talking to them about their impending unemployment, the wife said to me, 'We have to keep looking at each other and saying, "Well, things may be bad, but we're still here. We've got our health, and the kids are fine."'

'That's just what Richard and I used to say to each other,'

I replied. 'We'd look at each other in the worst moments and say, "Nobody is dying here. The kids are well, are not in hospital, are not in intensive care on a life-support machine. We've got each other. Let's put this into perspective."'

You have to do that. It was ghastly, and I could never say I was glad it happened, but maybe we needed to find out, as so many people do, that life has lots of nasty little surprises in store. Maybe we all need to temper ourselves and become a bit tougher. I'm not saying that Richard and I became stronger for it but we are certainly wiser, even if this is not altogether in a good way. In one sense, you become much more cynical, start to see people for what they are, and develop an instinct for what they want of you. The main lessons we learned were to do with survival skills rather than any spiritual insights into who and what we are, or why this happened to us. Having got it into perspective, I suppose I could say it is useful for human beings to become aware of their own vulnerability and frailty, but on the whole it was a very negative experience.

The really good thing was that Richard and I stayed completely bonded together. It was a huge crisis for two people so much in the public eye. It wasn't as if I could be the 'little wife at home'; and I never for one moment felt that it was Richard's problem and nothing to do with me. I was in it with him, on trial with him, and we remained unquestionably together despite all the stress, the anxiety and the horror of it all.

Even now, as I put pen to paper, it's hard to relive the experience. It's rather like trying to remember childbirth: I can't quite get the feeling back, can't summon it up to order. The pain's there, but it all seems so long ago now. Perhaps that's how such times have to be. After all, if you remembered labour pains too clearly, you might never want to have another baby; if you dwell too long on the painful aspects of your life, you'd never move forward.

Richard has, I have. We may never again be quite as young

and carefree as we were before that time, but we have learned that, while events and stages of life are essentially transitory, the love we feel for each other is not.

We also have a very real understanding now of John Lennon's phrase: 'Life is what happens while you're making other plans.'

9: RICHARD

It was surprising how quickly we both settled down after the trial, and were able to move on from there. Even during the frozen year of my long appointment with the judge, the show had developed and put out fresh shoots. So, after a long summer break following my acquittal, we were back in the autumn of 1991 with a real appetite to move up a gear. I think the team felt the same and the September of that year kicked in with a determination to push the show forward. After all, if we'd all survived the previous year, we could really start operating freely and with confidence.

We did. *This Morning* began to freewheel in a way that would characterize the programme for the decade to come.

Paul O'Grady – aka Lily Savage – for example, had recently burst out of his Liverpool corral and was becoming established as the comedy drag act of the nineties. The very first time Paul came on *This Morning* we were, to be honest, a bit worried. We needn't have been. Paul knows exactly how to go right up to the line and teeter on it, without putting a toe over. We realized at once that we were dealing with a very intelligent funny man and booked him on the show as often as we could. His star performance, one that our viewers requested to see again and again, was when he pretended to get drunk on the floating pontoon in Liverpool's Albert Dock. Dressed in his leopard-skin tight mini-skirt and thigh boots, he burst in about halfway through Charles Metcalfe's wine-tasting item and completely took over. He knocked back the wine, tossed the glasses into the dock and personified a tart with a heart, getting drunk as fast as possible. The viewers loved it. Whenever Paul appeared on the show – as himself or Lily – the ratings went through the roof.

Paul is a complex man. His mind is razor-sharp; he has the warmest of hearts but the iciest of confrontational wit. He ferociously defends his privacy. Once some tabloid reporters were camped on his doorstep, chasing some story or other that didn't exist. Paul's partner, who wasn't very well at the time, was constantly disturbed by the ringing of the doorbell late at night. Paul went downstairs, opened the door and told the assembled hacks, 'I'll be with you in a minute.' He then went back in and returned, wielding a chip-pan.

'Now look,' he said, 'this chip pan is full of boiling oil. I admit it's medieval, but it's effective. Fuck off.'

They did.

From the beginning of *This Morning* we certainly had our fair share of brushes with the regulators: the British Broadcasting Standards Authority, the Independent Television Commission, Mary Whitehouse's National Viewers Association. And, although everybody in TV has to work with these people and take them seriously, it is always important to remember that most of them have never made a television programme in their life and don't necessarily understand what is involved. This was vividly brought home to Judy and me when a number of viewers complained about an interview we did with the feminist, Germaine Greer. For some reason we had got on to the subject of hormone replacement therapy which Germaine was dead against. She had tried HRT and said it didn't work.

'What went wrong?' Judy asked.

'It was the testosterone,' Germaine replied. 'I experimented with a higher dose of the male hormone and it made me incredibly aggressive. For the first time in my life, I found myself thinking and acting like a man. I was driving like a man, shouting and swearing in an incredibly aggressive hostile way, and when somebody cut me up I yelled, "Get off the fucking road."'

Germaine immediately bit her tongue, and said, 'Oh, my God, I'm so sorry.'

We did the quick formal 'sorry' routine that the regulator demands on such occasions, and steamed on. There were, of course, some complaints and the matter was referred to the authorities.

A few months later we were at a dinner party where one of the other guests happened to be a woman who was on one of the regulatory bodies. She was puffed-up, silly and arrogant. Halfway through the meal, by which time we had taken an intense dislike to her, she mentioned she was sitting on the committee that was adjudicating the 'Germaine Greer "fucking" incident on *This Morning*'.

'What have you decided?' Judy asked.

'We're just astonished that you allowed it to go out,' she replied, munching her way through spare ribs.

'How could we stop it?' I said, astonished.

'You should have edited it out; you should have cut it,' she answered.

I stared at her. 'What do you mean? *This Morning* is a live television programme.'

She looked flustered, but then said, 'Oh, surely you could do what they do on radio programmes – have that loop tape-thingy; then if somebody says something they shouldn't, you could press a mute button.'

'No, that's not possible,' I said. 'The technology to do that doesn't exist in television.'

'I'm sure it does,' she pressed.

'No, it doesn't. We haven't got the technology in TV to put a live show on using a video tape with a seven-second loop, and then re-transmit it. The only way you can edit as you go is to pre-record at least half an hour in advance of transmission. Anyway, you didn't even realize our show was live.'

To our fury she smiled with horrible complacency, picked up another spare rib and changed the subject. I somehow repressed the urge to pour my glass of iced water down the back of her silly neck. And another one. And one more. What an eye-opener, though.

———

When Judy was ill, recuperating after operations or simply away doing other things, there were times when the network had to experiment with other co-presenters for me on *This Morning*. I always found it very stimulating working with such a diverse range of talented women, and I got on extremely well with all of them. But nobody ever replaced Judy or superseded her particular blend of journalistic instincts, or the empathy that we have with each other. In fact, no other presenter ever expected to replicate that. All of them did a very competent job, but my personal favourites who stood in for Judy were Fern Britton and Caron Keating, with whom I share a very similar sense of humour.

Some of the gaffes I made on *This Morning* were, of course, avoidable. I have a tendency to go over the top sometimes and it's got me into trouble over the years. One day when Judy was off doing something else Caron Keating and I were presenting the show together. *This Morning* had been sent a preview of one of the hottest-ever editions of *Friends*. It was the one where Ross married his English rose, Emily, while still holding a candle for his ex, Rachel, who was in the congregation. Everyone knew something would go spectacularly wrong but no one knew exactly what. We did, and couldn't believe we'd been given permission to show Ross saying to Emily, 'I take thee, Rachel . . .' It was one of the classic moments from *Friends*, and we had the sneak preview at least a month ahead of the date it was due to be shown.

I must admit that the producer and I had lurking doubts that someone at Sky Television had blundered, but no one looks a gift scoop in the . . . well, whatever. As far as we were concerned the clip was legit and we used it to the max.

It was a beautiful morning and that's always bad news for daytime TV. The audience want to go out and you have to fight hard to hold on to them. So we used the *Friends* trailer as a teaser to keep them watching.

'You are not going to believe this,' I said, 'but Sky has sent us that Ross/Emily wedding and we'll be showing it at twelve o'clock today. It's a corker, a great scene.'

Before and after each commercial break, Caron and I plugged this midday scoop.

'Don't go out. We know it's a lovely day, but stay in. You've got to see this clip. It's fantastic, wonderful. We've seen it, it's hilarious, shocking . . .' Blah-blah-blah.

And as the ratings showed when we looked at them on the computer the next day, it did the trick. Despite the sunshine, people were staying in and watching. The show rolled on and we reached the commercial break leading up to twelve o'clock.

'Right,' I said, 'sorry to have strung you along, but this is it. We will shortly show the whole of that final scene from the final episode of the current series of *Friends*. It'll blow your socks off. So, see you after the commercials.'

The next moment I heard the phone ringing in the gallery, followed by a panicky conversation. It didn't sound good and I went in.

It was bad. 'The editor's having a massive row with Warner Brothers,' the director told me. 'Apparently Warner owns the rights to *Friends*, and the people there are going spare. One of them tuned into *This Morning* and saw the trail, and it's all been kicking off since then.'

'Warner says it's embargoed and if we show it they'll sue. It's all been a huge cock-up.'

Apparently, this ferocious argument had been going on for thirty minutes while the editor insisted on our right to show a clip that we'd been sent in good faith and had been promising to show our audience all morning.

'No. This is a terrible mistake,' Warner was understandably saying. 'You were sent the wrong tape. You must not show it. We forbid it.'

By then the matter had reached the lawyers, and there had been transatlantic calls whizzing backwards and forwards from Burbank, Warner's headquarters in California, and Granada in London. Actually we had no case and the clip was pulled.

'But I've promised two million people,' I protested. 'I've strung them along all morning. We've got to show it.'

The editor, the gloriously stroppy Nick Bullen, now at Carlton Television, came on the phone seconds before the commercial break ended.

'It's a complete arse, Richard,' he said, still out of breath from his final exchange with an even more (justifiably) furious executive. 'But tell 'em Warner pulled it, not us!'

'Right!' I said.

While all this drama was going on, the final part of the show had started without me. Caron had got it off the ground with our resident chef, Brian Turner. Incandescent with anger, I marched down on to the set and into shot.

'What's happened?' Caron said, as she and Brian looked up, startled.

'Hold the show for a minute,' I replied, then, turning to the camera, I said to the viewers, 'Look, I don't know how to tell you this. I know lots of you have waited in all morning for the *Friends* clip we've been promising you, but I'm terribly sorry, we can't show it. And the reason we can't is that the people who own the rights won't let us.' Looking straight into camera, I added, 'I hate you, Warner. I really, really hate you.' Then, returning to the viewers, I said, 'I'm *so* sorry everybody, really sorry to have strung you along,' and went on with the show.

Understandably, Warner went absolutely mental – berserk. Its Head of European Operations had already gone nuts with Nick during their bombastic slanging match and when I got back to the editorial office after the show, all hell had broken loose about my on-screen rant. Granada lawyers were on the phone, saying that I had to apologize on air for insulting Warner, and that Nick had to write an official letter of apology to them, too. Burbank were making terrible threats. Nick and I had followed our instincts to protect our programme and deliver to our viewers, but over a pint in the pub across the road, we realized we'd gone a tad too far. You don't hustle Hollywood. The kerfuffle raged on all weekend while my bosses at Granada handled the fall-out. Once I had cooled down, I admitted I had gone over the top and the following Monday I made an on-screen apology.

'I was,' I said, 'in the heat of the moment completely wrong to have blamed Warner. It was not its fault. It was a misunderstanding between us and another party. I'm very sorry.'

Nick meanwhile was penning a letter of heroic penitence to the corporate chief he'd insulted down the phone.

I wrote to my bosses at Granada apologizing for giving them a fractured weekend, and was summoned by reply to an executive's office. I expected six of the best or worse, but instead was forgiven, told that a prompt apology was worth a thousand inquests, and given lunch. The lesson was that if you fuck up, say 'sorry', mean it, and be prepared to take the consequences. It's surprising how understanding the world can be.

What was it about the rare days when Judy wasn't on the show? One day when she was off filming an archive special on

Coronation Street, I met Hercules the bear on *This Morning* and I was lucky to drive home with two hands, not one.

I'd been told about Hercules' appearance the day before.

'Fine,' I said, 'but he'll be chained up or in a cage, right?'

The producer laughed. 'It's Hercules, Richard. He's just a big teddy-bear.'

'He's an eight-foot grizzly and they rip people's heads off,' I replied. 'You interview him.'

But they insisted that the bear was as docile as a lamb, domesticated as a pussy-cat, and anyway would have his handler with him at all times.

'He's never been known to hurt anybody. He'll be on a chain all the time. It'll be a laugh and you'll have nothing to worry about.'

'You're sure about this?' I asked. 'We don't want people going home minus limbs.'

'No, don't worry. Honest, it'll be fine. Anyway, we're insured.'

On the day as we rehearsed camera moves and lighting changes, our floor-manager came in to say that the bear had arrived and was outside in his travel wagon with his owner. The floor-manager looked at the same time rattled and amused. He pointed at the big studio window that showed the Albert Dock behind the *This Morning* set. 'Can everyone listen up? I want everybody on the studio floor to line up against the window.'

'Why?' we all asked.

'Because,' he replied, beginning to laugh nervously, 'if Hercules sees water, he instinctively runs straight for it.'

Hercules had done this years before when he was living in the Scottish Highlands. He'd snapped his chain, run straight into the sea and swum to another island. The media-swamped bear-hunt had lasted weeks. And, according to his owner, if we did not block our picture window, Hercules would thunder across the studio, smash through the plate-glass, bound across the dock, leap straight into the water and swim off into the sunset. Incredulously we all stood obediently shoulder to shoulder, holding up jackets, cards, anything that would stop the bear from seeing the water.

The studio doors swung open and I was still expecting this great big, docile, cuddly bear to enter. In came a nightmare at the end of a chain. Grunting and growling, he was so massive he blocked out the light and threw us all into shadow. The owner and his wife were feeding him handfuls of raw meat to distract him. And every time Hercules had gobbled these he started thrashing around and demanding more. Boy, was he some cross bear, and he stank like an abattoir. They gradually enticed him across the studio, to a corner where there was a specially designed set ready for his interview. Hercules was clearly in no mood to be messed with. He'd never attacked anybody, and I'm not accusing the owners of any kind of irresponsibility, but I'm sorry – this was no teddy-bear. This was eight feet of rippling muscle, short temper and unceasing appetite for flesh. Hercules was a kind of horrible nexus of Mike Tyson and Hannibal Lecter. I began to sweat.

The show started and, playing it cool, I interviewed Hercules' owners first. I couldn't fail to notice that every time they were distracted from the raw-meat deliveries, Hercules would shake his massive head from side to side. After the interview, very sulky and angry, he was taken back to his travel wagon, ready for me to do the second interview with him later in the programme. I couldn't wait!

We reached our Hercules part-two moment and I climbed reluctantly into the travel wagon and sat down on a bench next to the owner who was sitting beside the bear. Hercules seemed calmer now he was back in his own space. During the interview I relaxed enough to ask about a big scar that Hercules had right across his nose and I casually pointed to it with my finger. Hercules obviously thought another light snack was on offer and lunged at me. Bears, despite their size, can move at lightning speed. But so, I discovered, can terrified telly presenters.

I snatched my hand away. But only in the nick of time. The next day, the still photographs published in the newspapers showed Hercules with his mouth gaping open, his fangs bared and my hand a mere breath away.

'But what if he'd bitten your hand off and swallowed it?' someone said to me afterwards.

'I'd have had the bugger knocked out, had his belly surgically opened and got my hand back out,' I said. 'And when they'd sewn it back on I'd have strangled the producer.'

Another of our none-too-happy guests was Shere Hite, the American feminist and author of the *Hite Report*. She gave a highly intelligent interview which was fascinating but, as you'd expect, delivered a fairly devastating judgement on men.

Judy – a lifelong feminist – was nevertheless amused and said teasingly as the interview wound up, 'You don't really like men very much, do you?'

Shere Hite gave Judy a withering look and said, 'I cannot believe you have just asked me such a dumb question. I thought we were having an intelligent exchange and then you come out with that. I just cannot believe it.'

'Now, look—' Judy began.

I should have kept quiet but said something like, 'Oh, come on, Shere, Judy was only—'

Big mistake. Hite was uncomfortable attacking a sister and her guns instantly swivelled on to me. Verbal tracer-rounds poured in and the studio was shaken by the crump of incoming anti-male mortar-fire.

Judy signalled a commercial break, and the bombardment stopped as we went to the ads.

Judy was now moving smoothly into the role of UN peace-maker: 'We're sorry about that. We had no intention of having a row with you. It was a very nice interview. Thank you.'

Shere ignored Judy completely and continued to eyeball me as I stood up to move to the next studio item. She fired a last burst: 'I suppose you'd have preferred me to pass on the interview and just give you a blow-job,' she spat.

Judy and I looked at each other and dissolved into laughter. Shere Hite swept out and we never saw her again.

Tony Blair was an occasional guest on the programme and the interviews usually generated headlines of one sort of another. For instance, we pressed him on the question of whether Glen Hoddle could continue as England coach after saying that handicapped people were paying for mistakes in previous lives. After a bit of prevarication Blair said, in effect, that Hoddle couldn't.

Other interviews we did with him before and after he became Prime Minister were followed up in the next day's papers, but Judy and I always had to put up with a very British type of media snobbery. This held that interviews with senior politicians were the province of political reporters and corre-spondents and that journalists like us – daytime presenters, for God's sake – strayed on to their turf at our peril. It was the same kind of ludicrous snobbery that poor old Jimmy Young had to put up with for decades before, grudgingly, he was allowed to interview prime ministers. Mad.

Once when Judy and I were on a train to Cornwall, the Prime Minister got on board at Exeter, headed for a showdown with farmers in Plymouth. We sent him a jokey note and a few minutes later were asked to pop down and join him for a coffee.

His carriage was stuffed with political journos and they were outraged when we sidled through and spent ten minutes chatting to the PM.

'What did he say? Why was he speaking to you? Tell us everything,' they hissed furiously when we went back to our seats.

Actually we talked about our kids, Cherie's pregnancy, Ulster and problems facing British farmers. Probably what the rest of the press pack would have talked about, too.

It was around this time that journalist Matthew Parris 'outed' Peter Mandelson on *Newsnight*. Mandelson's gayness was an open secret not only at Westminster, but in the media generally. However, these open secrets are sometimes canards and it's usually better to reserve judgement until you get the chance to reach your own decision.

Mandelson was due on our programme to talk about his plans for the as yet non-existent Millennium Dome. He arrived during a break for the news and I was busy rewriting scripts with Mel, our autocue operator. When I came back on to the studio floor, the Dome Führer was standing just outside the brightly lit central set and I knew instantly that Peter Mandelson was gay.

This Morning had always had a strong appeal to gays. They found aspects of it – our marriage, the general irreverence, the non-judgemental liberal tone – quite camp. Lots of gay people worked on the programme, both behind and in front of the cameras.

So when programme guests who happened to be gay arrived for an interview, they always had a trademark grin on their faces; they were getting a real kick out of appearing live on what was something of a gay icon. It was a very particular look of happy excitement we'd learned to recognize and, as I observed Peter Mandelson watching Judy preparing to go back on air, he had that look all over his face.

During the interview itself, Mandelson was relaxed and upbeat, and talked a good game. His grandfather, Herbert Morrison, had been responsible for the success of the Festival of Britain in the 1950s, and Mandelson was sure that the Dome would be a repeat success story. But the interview closed on a surprisingly coquettish note. As we were wrapping, he suddenly raised one finger and said, 'Before I go, I have a little something in my pocket for you. Can you guess what it is?'

Aye-aye, we thought, what's coming now?

Putting his hand in his jacket pocket, he shot another coy glance: 'Would you like to see it?'

'Yes, please, Peter,' we said patiently.

With a little flourish he pulled out a long white envelope, which turned out to hold a friendly letter from the Prime Minister congratulating us and the programme generally on its recent tenth anniversary. It was a nice gesture and engagingly delivered.

So, personally, we weren't surprised when Mandelson was outed on BBC 2. But it shouldn't have happened against his will. We all own the rights to our sexuality and it's deeply intrusive to have them snatched away. It's entirely up to a public figure to make his or her own decision whether to announce that they're gay. There was much criticism of the BBC's instruction to its broadcasters not to follow up the 'Mandelson outed' story but, although it was a case of locking stable doors on absent horses, I think the impulse was correct. Put it this way: if Mandelson wasn't completely out of the closet today I wouldn't have written a word of the above. And the actor Sir Ian McKellen, whom we've interviewed many times, has told us that he knows of almost no gay person whose life didn't improve after coming out, or even being outed. The relief and sudden freedom to be oneself, he says, is hugely liberating.

'Before I came out I lived in black and white,' he once told us. 'Afterwards, my life switched to glorious technicolour.'

Speaking of sudden bursts of colour, all of us on *This Morning* were dumbfounded by the explosion of publicity following a tiny sketch we did one morning. It had only been dreamed up the afternoon before, and quickly scripted by us before going home. But the Ali G impression had maximum publicity for minimum effort. It's a tiny bit frustrating, actually. Sometimes you can work for days or even weeks on what you think will make a cracking item, and when you proudly broadcast it no one pays a blind bit of notice, not even your old mum. A bit like that line in Robert Louis Stevenson's poem, 'Faster than Fairies': 'and ever again in the wink of an eye, painted stations whistle by'. Well, the train stopped at my Ali G all right and everyone got out to have a look.

It was meant to be completely throwaway. At the time Tom and Dan and most of their mates did excellent impressions of Ali G so I picked up a bit from them as well as from watching Sacha Baron Cohen's brilliant TV spoofs. Then the *Sun* ran an equally throwaway piece about it being time for me to have a different haircut. Their showbiz editor, Dominic Mohan, morphed photos of me with a 'Beckham', a 'Llewelyn-Bowen', a 'Clooney' (George, not Rosemary) and an Ali G. We asked our viewers which one they'd prefer and they overwhelmingly voted for Ali G. Then, as I said, Judy and I bashed out a quick script for the sketch. Our favourite line was: 'Why does you bother wid all them make-overs? Why don't you just get women who is fit to start wiv?'

The wardrobe department got the Ali G outfit in, down to the gold jewellery and yellow sunglasses, and our make-up man, Lee Din, drew a little beard on my face. Fifteen minutes before transmission I strode down the corridor into studio. I didn't even have to say anything: everyone dissolved into helpless laughter the moment they saw me. This was an encouraging start. Nothing like looking completely ridiculous to get a laugh.

We decided to pre-record the sketch just in case the impression 'slipped', and it was a good job we did. On take one, I sounded more like Richard Briers than Ali G. With five minutes to go we tried again and this time it was just about passable. Typically, I was tempted to gild the lily and do the whole show in character – it would have made for some interesting moments in that day's interviews – but brevity is the soul of wit, etc., so I changed back into my suit. The phone lines went into meltdown after the sketch went out, and we were made to show it again and again.

A few months later the clip coasted home to the number one slot in *Top One Hundred Worst TV Moments*. We toasted this solemn moment in champagne and went to bed trailing clouds of glory.

Later we heard that Sacha Baron Cohen had watched it during a scripting session with his producer and writing partner. That morning Sacha, purely by chance, had seen the pre-show 'trail' of me dressed as him saying, 'I is here wid mi new stylee!'

'What the fuck was that?' Sacha asked.

Downing pens and turning up the volume, they watched the sketch and fell about, which was a relief – I'd half expected a writ. Then they phoned the programme, asked for a tape, and invited Judy and me to make a cameo appearance in the Ali G feature film they were working on that morning. Naturally we accepted.

Working out of Liverpool proved to be very 'grounding' and the people there made sure no one on the show got above themselves, including us. One day Judy and I were walking along the dock after a show and we heard two women whispering behind us.

'Well,' one said, 'her teeth look absolutely fine to me.'

'You daft bugger,' her friend replied. 'That's not Esther Rantzen, that's Judy Finnigan.'

For years, people in the area would point and say, 'Look, it's that Richard Whiteley off the telly!'

Our studio had cables running all over the dock, and we used our location as a vast outdoor set to do stunts and big set-pieces.

Peter Duncan, the *Blue Peter* presenter turned actor, appeared on one of them. He was in the lead in a touring version of *Barnum*. He came on to promote the circus story and show us one of the tricks he was still rehearsing, a little stunt on a low trapeze. It was hardly death-defying stuff but we rigged up a swing and tightrope on a big flagged area about five hundred yards away from the studio. Earlier in the programme we did a standard interview with Peter from the main set, then he left to get changed into his circus outfit, and the plan was that we should join him outside during a long commercial break.

It all went horribly wrong. We had a new floor-manager that day and she didn't know the dock too well. We jumped into her car when the ads started and shot off. As she dropped us outside some big glass doors, she said, 'It's just through there,' and shot off again.

We walked through on to the dockside. No one was there, apart from a few tourists. Had they seen a film crew? No, they hadn't. But then *we* did – about a quarter of a mile away on the other side of the dock basin. Distant bright lights and a tiny figure sitting patiently on a trapeze. Peter Duncan was about to be overtaken by doom. We were completely buggered. We'd never get there, not even on a motorbike. We stood helplessly listening on our radio earpieces to the PA counting down. 'Twenty seconds to end of break. Where the fuck are they? Fifteen seconds . . .'

The director began to panic: 'We've got five minutes to fill. What am I supposed to do?' he asked the producer.

'I don't know. Somebody just tell Duncan to do his party-piece and maybe Richard and Judy will show up.'

Not a chance. 'Five seconds, four, bloody hell, three, two, one, cue Duncan!'

Looking back at the tape of what happened next is still a treat. I hope Peter Duncan has forgiven us. Surprised viewers saw the 'Welcome Back' caption replaced by the sight of a nervous actor sitting on a little swing, swaying slightly in the chilly breeze. Nothing happened for a while, and then a researcher's voice could just be heard off-camera, hissing, 'Do the trick! Do the trick!'

Peter had only been in rehearsals for a few days and the trick wasn't much more than a few swings back and forth without holding on to the ropes on either side of him. In the panic, the director forgot to cue the circus music that would have at least jollied things along a bit, and two million bemused viewers watched as the embarrassed actor swung to and fro in eerie silence, except for the wind blowing into his microphone.

Eventually he stopped, and there was another long pause.

'Do it again!' came another desperate hiss from the wings.

'What?' asked Duncan, startled. 'That's it – that's the trick.'

Another pause: 'Do it again!'

The minutes ticked away like centuries passing. Finally the credits rolled and an appalled Peter Duncan was allowed off his perch. Later, we heard that the post-programme silence in the director's gallery was the longest anyone could remember.

————

In 1993 we got our first real taste of what it's like to be 'paparazzo'ed. Judy and I had flown to Nice for a Whitsun break and were staying at a little *pension*. Judy hates me calling it that, but it is a modest little hotel overlooking the Med just outside Cap d'Antibes. There's no restaurant and you get a simple breakfast of croissants, rolls and preserves served with coffee and juices on your balcony every morning. The Alps can sometimes be seen on the horizon if there's no heat-haze. It's a fantastic little hideaway and it had been our secret for years. We never met another English person there.

That year the sun shone, we flopped out on the beach, and flew home happy and relaxed. The Sunday before we were due back at work we were leafing through the newspapers when suddenly Judy gave a little wail.

'Oh, *no!*'

There, spread across two pages in glorious colour, were telephoto snapshots of the two of us on the hotel's little private beach. Unflattering comments and captions were under each sneaky picture. Judy took most of the flak, which was about as sexist and malicious as it gets, but I came in for some too. In one shot I was shown brushing back my hair before we went for lunch. I don't know how many frames the motordrive captured of that brief action, but the one chosen made me look like a complete tart!

Worse came the next day. The photos had been 'sold on', and were all over the *Mail* and *Sun* and *Mirror*. More snide comments about Judy's appearance, but some female columnists began to rally to her support, asking which woman would be happy to be photographed in her bikini, let alone without her knowledge.

I just thought it was fantastically unfair and downright rude, but Judy, as usual, handled it all very well. In private she was mortified, but in public she smiled and shrugged it off. Neither of us could believe the paparazzi would be that interested in us. We were very minor fish in the so-called celebrity pool.

Judy had never portrayed or thought of herself as some kind of TV glamour girl, despite the fan mail she got (and which always embarrassed her). She simply saw herself as a presenter and interviewer, wife, and mother of four.

A few weeks later when we were at a party, Piers Morgan, a friend of ours and the then showbiz editor of the *Sun* (now editor of the *Mirror*), strolled up to us. 'My God,' he said, 'the papers didn't half get some stick from their readers for running those pictures of you two. We had loads of letters, mostly from women, giving us grief. Publishing those pictures really backfired on us.' He then turned to Judy and added,

'You're very popular with women, you know. They like you and felt you were very unfairly treated.'

'Well, don't quote me, Piers,' Judy replied, 'but I was really upset. I felt violated. And it's taken me ages to get over it and get my self-confidence back.'

'So you didn't plant the pictures?' Piers said in surprise.

'What?'

'It wasn't a publicity thing? A lot of people would die for that kind of coverage.'

'You're mad,' Judy told him. 'I was horrified when those pictures appeared. Do you really think I would have phoned up a photographer and said, "I'll be on the beach at Cap d'Antibes at twelve o'clock, do come"?'

Piers laughed. 'No,' he said. 'You couldn't. But you'd be amazed at who would.'

There are some showbiz people who are so desperate for publicity they would arrange such a shoot. I know at least three well-known people in TV who have done that and then cried foul. A dangerous game.

———————

About seven years after *This Morning* went on the screen, rumours that had been circulating for a while on the programme were confirmed. One December morning Max Graesser, an increasingly big cheese at Granada, made an announcement that would change the lives of everybody present.

'From September 1996,' he said, holding a prepared statement, '*This Morning* will be broadcast from a brand-new studio on the banks of the River Thames, London.'

For Judy and me this did not come as a surprise. Some months before the announcement we had decided that, much as we loved living in Manchester and working in Liverpool, we were jaded, in need of a change and ready for a new challenge. We'd been doing *This Morning* for seven years and, about twelve months into our current two-year contract, Judy and I had privately made the decision that we would probably not sign another one, and our agent, Annie Sweetbaum, quietly let Granada know.

At that time, we had nothing else in mind; we were simply feeling as if we were living out the Bill Murray film, *Groundhog Day*. Our schedule was so repetitive that one day was running into the next. We got up at six every morning at our Edwardian house in Didsbury and drove forty miles to the job in Liverpool. We'd been doing this for so long, I could recognize the faces of most of the other drivers along the way. This is not a joke!

This Morning had also hit a period when it was having endless problems with transporting guests to the studio. British Midland, which in the past had flown shuttles between London and Liverpool airports, had axed the service. The lack of direct flights had had a serious effect on our programme. The only option now was for people to fly to Manchester, then come across to our studio by limousine or taxi. Not surprisingly, they didn't like this arrangement because it was taking a much bigger slice out of their day. For a while we experimented with a little twin-prop *This Morning* plane, but those aircraft only fly at between two and three thousand feet and it's a very bumpy ride. Quite often our guests would arrive looking really queasy. Jeremy Irons, for example, came on to the set just after he'd thrown up and sat there looking green. On another occasion, a famous actress got on the plane without having a pee first. She didn't realize there wasn't a toilet on board.

'I've got to pee, simply got to pee,' she wailed.

I think one of her fellow passengers was Vanessa Feltz, who was coming up to take a phone-in, and the other was a stranger in a suit.

'Don't mind me,' he said cheerfully. 'I'm a gynaecologist so go ahead. I've seen worse before breakfast.'

A coffee thermos was hastily drained and the poor woman had to pee in that. This is not the way to waft your guests in style to the studio, and word was getting around: 'Whatever you do, don't agree to be interviewed on *This Morning*. They put you on a Sopwith Camel!'

There were two occasions when Hollywood's hottest stars, Tom Cruise and Mel Gibson, declined to come to Liverpool because it was too far away from London. It wasn't a programme-busting issue, but it was a problem.

The main issue for us two, though, was the Groundhog question. For a time we considered moving to Cornwall; and we went to look at a house, built into a dynamited terrace in the cliffs between Looe and Polperro. It had once been owned by the film star Rita Tushingham. It was absolutely beautiful, and looked like something out of a Daphne du Maurier novel. We very nearly bought it.

Had we gone ahead with this plan, we would then have moved lock, stock and barrel to Cornwall, the kids would have gone to schools there, Judy would have written her novel and, hopefully, I would have picked up some of the offers that floated around but that *This Morning* left little time or energy for.

By now there was a year left on the contract and we flew to America on our summer holiday. When we came home, there was a message to ring Annie Sweetbaum. While she'd been at the Edinburgh Television Festival, she told us, a couple of Granada executives had suddenly appeared in a hotel corridor and pulled her into a room and on to a bed.

'What's going on?' she cried, wondering whether to scream for help.

They just wanted a confidential chat, they explained. They knew we were feeling restless, and that the recent transport problems had not helped the situation. Granada had added these two factors together and had come up with a plan. Did

Annie think we would be interested in signing another contract if the show was moved to London?

'I can only ask them,' she replied.

So she did. We'd just walked into the house from the airport and were surrounded by suitcases. But we grasped what was at stake.

A move to London, we thought, would be a natural progression both for the programme and for our careers. It would give the show a shot in the arm and would resolve the guest problem. It would be the new challenge we were looking for. Three minutes after Annie's call, we were back on the line to her.

'Tell them they're on,' we said.

On the day the news was announced, there was a lot of surprise and, here and there, some resentment. Our friend Fred Talbot, the weatherman, was clearly unhappy.

'If it ain't broke, why fix it?' he asked.

To Fred and others who felt as he did we gave the same answer. There was the growing issue over getting guests, but all 'brands' have to look ahead in any case. I made a motoring analogy. 'The Ford Sierra was a bestseller but they stopped making it all the same and replaced it with the Mondeo. And that'll be updated as well.' We had to update and relaunch our product too, otherwise it would start looking and feeling stale. The programme's personality wouldn't change when we moved to London, but it would definitely be invigorated.

Around this time *This Morning* won what the newspapers cheerfully called the 'sofa wars': BBC 1's determined assault on us, using the pairing of Anne Diamond and Nick Owen. Their *Good Morning* had fought hard to overtake us since its launch four years earlier, but we worked hard to stay in front and in the end the BBC gave up the chase. We weren't sorry. We had total respect for Anne and Nick, but the corporation's naked attempt to lift our format wholesale was, I can now say, irritating.

In the very first series of *Good Morning* they even inserted funny little breaks like our commercial breaks, only made up of short 'how-to' items; if you didn't look too closely you could have been watching a Sainsbury's commercial. It was all strangely disquieting, as if new neighbours had moved in opposite and painted their house the same colour as ours, put up the same curtains in the front windows, drove the exact model and colour of car we did, and even got up and went to bed at the same time as us. Weird. But I think the seeds of the BBC's defeat were sown in the attempt to copy our show. How can you overtake someone in a race if you're constantly looking sideways at them to see exactly how they're running? You have to be creative in television, not imitative.

It was good to win and have a clear run at the morning schedule once we got to London. Because, for all the bright hopes, the move was a very big risk, and not just professionally. It was a long time since I'd left London and headed north. Judy had deep roots in Manchester. Our children were born there. We were about to head south; but what if we hated it once we arrived?

10: JUDY

Looking back now on the photographs that were taken of me in a bikini at Cap d'Antibes while we were on a Whitsun holiday in 1993, I can't believe how naïve Richard and I were. But we didn't have an inkling then that anybody would be interested in us on holiday. We'd been going to Cap d'Antibes for years and nothing untoward had ever happened. We loved the little place we'd found. It was the same hotel we went to for a week after we lost our baby, so it had many tender, bitter-sweet memories for us. It was a very romantic place that meant an awful lot to us. Whenever a series of *This Morning* finished, usually a week or two before the kids broke up for the holidays, we would grab five days alone together there before we went off for the summer with them.

When we got home on the bikini-fiasco occasion, Richard was in the bathroom having a shower and I was flicking through the papers when I suddenly saw this piece in the *Sunday People* and couldn't believe my eyes. The photographer had used a zoom lens from far away but it was not so much the pictures that upset me, it was the malice in the copy. I couldn't understand it. I was shocked and, as every story has about a week's shelf life before it dies away, the comments continued in newspaper columns for days. These were largely written by women who had never met me. Their chief bone of contention seemed to be that I was on television, married to Richard, and didn't shape up physically to the way they thought women on telly should. But that's crap. I'm not an actress, model, dancer or singer. I'm a mother and me. As far as I'm concerned, I have an obligation to look my best for the viewers, and I make sure my hair and make-up are all right, and I wear decent clothes but, as for my weight, sod it. I've never set out to be any kind of glamour girl, I'm a journalist who happens to be on TV.

I remember talking to Gaby Roslin who was also embarrassed about being snapped while on holiday. 'But why do you mind?' I asked her. 'You're much younger than I am and you look great.'

'I was looking a bit plump at the time,' she replied, 'and they just went on and on about it. I was mortified.'

I thought it was crazy that somebody as young and as pretty as Gaby should be so worried. But she then said she would never again tell anyone where she was going on holiday. It was the same for Cilla Black who was snapped in a bikini while on holiday with her husband, Bobby, some years ago. Once again the pictures were accompanied by snide copy. Cilla was a much more seasoned pro than me, had been an entertainer for a long time, and was much loved and famous, but she too was mortified. For women, such malicious personal comments are uniquely horrible. Although I got over it, it made me feel very untrusting for a long time afterwards. I hugged my four walls, didn't want to go out and, when I was on holiday in Portugal or America, I found myself looking around warily all the time. It takes away your sense of freedom, relaxation and privacy.

People talk endlessly about the freedom of the press and, as a journalist myself, I'm all for that. But I don't think the media has the right to invade people's privacy in this way. Such intrusions have a devastating effect on you, make you feel as if your soul's burning up. Richard was fantastic, kept on saying, 'You must understand, Judy, none of this has any bearing on reality. What they are saying is not what I think or what the viewers think. They're simply those kind of journalists on their own agenda.'

Some newspapers are certainly much worse than others, and sadly I have to say that some women columnists are the worst. I don't quite understand that. But presumably such copy sells their features and the papers.

For me, it was another baptism by fire, a 'wake-up call' I could have done without. Anybody in our business, Gaby Roslin, Cilla Black, Vanessa Feltz, Anthea Turner, will tell you it's always a phenomenal shock when the press suddenly turns on you. It's a loss of innocence and trust, but also a learning curve. After the first couple of times, I don't think anything ever hurts you that much again. In your heart, you know it's all nonsense and that it's crazy to allow such unpleasantness to get to you. That would be very destructive and life's too short for that. I received a lot of support from our viewers, and I remember the editor of the *Mirror*, Piers Morgan, who was at that time on the *Sun*, saying that his wife and her friends had been absolutely horrified by it all.

Afterwards, when some lady journalist wrote words along the lines of, 'Oh, I bet when she comes back after the Whit break she will have lost a lot of weight,' I thought, Stuff you; no, I won't. Get lost! So, after the initial shock, hurt and unhappiness, I got very angry and stubborn and decided, If that's what you want to believe, mate, believe it.

This emphasis on slimming, so often accompanied by eating disorders, such as anorexia and bulimia, is very much a generational thing. In our house, especially since we've had Chloe, we've always made a point of not making a big deal about food or diets. Girls are so vulnerable and some of Chloe's contemporaries are having, or have had, hospital treatment for anorexia. Chloe, thank God, has a really healthy attitude towards food, eats like a horse, and is slim. But I've met so many families where weight is made too big an issue, where the mother is constantly talking about her weight and putting herself down. It's very destructive. I remember one particular family we met. They had a little girl of Jack's age. The mother, who was as skinny as a little bird, never stopped talking about her husband being overweight. He was supposed to be on a diet and every time he ate something that was not on his list of approved foods she would get at him until it poisoned a meal or an evening. The little girl was already showing signs of anorexia and not eating, and the mother was worried about that, too. On the one hand she kept saying to the husband, 'You shouldn't be eating that,' or 'You can't have that,' and on the other, she was saying to her daughter, 'Please eat. Have a burger.' It was horrible and the atmosphere was so strained.

Frankly, I don't much care about my weight. I would hate to get absolutely gi-normous, but I've passed the stage of worrying about what I eat. One of my friends who appears on television gets absolutely furious with people who carry on *ad nauseam* about her body. She's in her early forties and is quite proud of her curves. Her husband loves them; and Richard loves me, so I don't care what others think any more. There are more important things to worry about.

———

When *This Morning* moved from Liverpool to London, and we went to live in Hampstead, I was much more homesick than I'd anticipated. I wasn't really missing anyone in particular. I was still seeing plenty of Tom and Dan, and Jack and Chloe were with Richard and me, but I was grief-stricken in a way I couldn't quite fathom at first. Then I realized I was grieving for a part of my life that was over and would never come again. This included having the babies. Tom and Dan were born in Norwich, but Jack and Chloe were born in Manchester, their toddlerhood and first schooldays were spent there; and then there was Richard and me and all the memories associated with our first meeting, becoming lovers, getting married, and the house and the neighbourhood we'd lived in. All this, given that the four of us were still together, and Tom and Dan were always coming down for the weekend, probably sounds illogical, but nostalgia was at the root of my problem.

There was also the strange feeling that we'd done things the wrong way round: that instead of the kids leaving home and going away to university while Richard and I remained in the family nest, ready to welcome them back, we had left home. The other problem was that, when we first came to London, Jack was finding it incredibly hard to settle in his new school. True happiness for a parent, I discovered, only exists when one's children are happy. Chloe was nine, Jack was ten, and both had been very upset when they learned we were moving. The last day at their old school was just awful. When we arrived to pick them up all the kids in the playground, on the tennis courts, in the gym, were in floods of tears about them going. It was a mass hysteria that spread to include all the other kids who were leaving that term to go to other schools. Richard and I felt so responsible for this tidal wave of grief, but we tried to deal with it in a very matter-of-fact way. Later that day, Chloe's friends gave her a lovely surprise party at a local restaurant in Cheshire. When she arrived there, all her classmates were hidden under the tables and, as she sat down, heads popped out everywhere and the whole place just erupted. She was *so* touched.

One way and another the tremendous build-up of emotional energy left Richard and me feeling hugely responsible for Jack and Chloe's unhappiness. Kids can be very wounding to their mums and dads when they're feeling stroppy, and both of them kept saying to us, 'How can you do this? Why is your work more important than our happiness and our friends?' We understood how they felt, and we ended up feeling we were being very selfish and self-indulgent.

In the event, Chloe, being very sociable, made friends almost immediately, settled into her new co-ed London school, and was a happy bunny within a few weeks. Jack, however, was a different matter and that worried me terribly. He was the only new kid that term at his new single-sex school, and he was up against boys who'd known each other since they were four. Being tall for his age, he looked older than he was but, contrary to appearances, was still a baby at heart. He'd go off to school clutching his little Spiderman toys and meet with derision. The other kids were so much more sophisticated than he was, and many were from mega-rich families who lived in huge mansions. I'm not pretending we were poor, but we'd never lived like that and were, by comparison, a pretty ordinary family. Suddenly there was Jack, surrounded by kids who wanted for nothing, and this was a huge shock for him.

He wasn't happy, started behaving incredibly badly, and was always looking for a fight. We couldn't have a family meal at home or in a restaurant without him causing friction. Food became one of his weapons. He'd always been a picky eater, but now he wouldn't eat anything anybody else wanted to eat. He'd sit there in a sulky silence until he'd ruined the entire meal. We tried to ignore it, but it was impossible. Then, when we were on holiday in Portugal at Easter, he even started picking terrible fights with Tom and Dan, which was completely out of character because they'd always got on so well before.

The night before the kids were due to go back to school, Richard, noticing that Jack's bedroom light was still on, went in to say goodnight and found Jack in a dreadful state.

'Daddy, it's like this,' he said between sobs. 'There's no sunshine in that school and, when I walk in, it feels like a prison. I'm only ten now and if I stay there until my A-levels, I'll be there for another eight years. I can't bear to go back to that place.'

'Don't worry,' Richard replied, shocked. 'I'll talk to Mum about it. Go to sleep.'

We were very distressed. In the beginning, we had decided not to send Jack to the same mixed-sex school as Chloe because it had seemed much too liberal in its approach for Jack. But we now knew we had made a terrible error of judgement, and decided to put this right the next day.

Fortunately Jack's deputy headmaster was a kind, wise man who, having listened to us, completely understood our reasons for wanting to remove Jack from the school and send him to the same one as his sister. We were then very lucky and managed to get Jack a place there for the coming September. From then on, Jack was a different child. I was so relieved. There's nothing worse than going to work in the morning knowing that your child is desperately unhappy, especially when I was still homesick myself.

Once we were established in London and had hit what people called 'the big-time', I was often asked what the large pay cheques meant for me. The answer was simple: security. I still worried about money. I know this was stupid, but this business is not renowned for longevity. Thus far, Richard and I had been very lucky. We were able to build up our savings and pay off long-term things like the mortgage. That was great. Before then, I always used to think that one day things would go belly-up, that our ratings would slip and the viewers wouldn't want to watch us any more. Sometimes I sat wondering what we would do when that happened because I couldn't believe we would ever get such a good job again. Then I'd say to myself, 'Don't be stupid, you can always work in Boots!'

Telling myself not to be stupid when I'm nervous, and, 'Get on with it, nobody has forced you to do this job,' are two of my commonly drawn-on catch-phrases. And when I look at what my mother exists on, her pension and the small amount my father saved before he died, I say to myself, 'What am I worrying about? It's just too silly.' Mum's eighty-eight now and manages so well. We've offered to help her a lot more than we do, but she's very independent, and won't have it.

Security is very important to both Richard and me, but then we're both Taurean and it's a characteristic of this star sign. I'm not at all extravagant. The only thing I indulge in is travel. I love going to nice places and relaxing. And that's our reward to ourselves.

We knew when we bought the house in Hampstead that it was a terrific risk because property prices are so exorbitant in that area. But because it was so ideal, we took a deep breath, gritted our teeth and went for it. We decided if things worked out for *This Morning* in London, and we were not booted out after a year or so, we could live on one of our salaries and use the other to pay off the mortgage.

I also knew when we moved to the Hampstead house that we would never live in a bigger one, that this was going to be the biggest ever. It has three bedrooms on the top floor, four on the middle, and we turned one of these into a computer room for the kids. It also has a self-contained annexe that consists of a bedroom, bathroom, sitting-room and kitchen, where Dan lives. The top floor is only ever used when Tom comes to stay or when we have friends over-nighting. The kids were – and are – very happy here. They think it's a cosy house, and I wouldn't dream of moving. It's close to our work and their school. At the time of writing, Chloe has another three years at school, Jack has another two, and then hopefully there will be university.

As far as friends were concerned, Richard and I were very lucky when we moved from the north to the south. With the exception of a few from our early days, most of our friends were in the same business, many of them were already spending most of the week working on LWT productions in

London, and lots of our colleagues on *This Morning* had made the move with us. Jane, our wardrobe girl, was even more homesick than I was. For the first twelve months or so we used to meet in my dressing-room to give each other pep talks and make each other feel better, but we usually ended up in tears. Unlike me, poor Jane had left all her family in Manchester and just couldn't stand it. At the end of the year she caved in, threw up her job and went back.

'I'm being so stupid,' I kept telling myself. 'My family's here. I'm being ridiculous.'

I didn't dare moan too much. I was only too aware that a lot of our colleagues hadn't wanted the programme to move from Manchester to London, and when you've gone along with a decision that affects so many other people you can't then turn round and say, 'I'm really unhappy. I wish we hadn't done it.'

Curiously, what helped me settle down in the end were some awful days that ended in 'bad' news! If, like me, you're on television every day for years, there are inevitably times when your health isn't as good as usual; and during those early London days I was menopausal and having a terrible time with heavy periods that sometimes made it difficult for me to work in the normal way. It is, take my word for it, fairly horrific to be sitting in a television studio, doing a live programme, while worrying about a possible stain on your skirt. Every time there was a break I would rush out to check that everything was all right. I was also experiencing a lot of pain, and feeling very tired and depressed because my hormones were all over the place. Just like the postnatal period, every day had become a battle and sometimes I literally couldn't move and make it to the studio.

Going through a difficult menopause is not like having a cold where in three days you are better, it's every damn day that ends in a peak of discomfort every damn month. Part of me really felt I couldn't cope with the daily schedule that I was on, and it crossed my mind several times to give it all up. This difficult time had been going on for years while I tried out all sorts of alternatives to a hysterectomy, but nothing, including the usual hormone pills, worked.

It's obviously not easy to talk about such personal things, especially to people you don't know, and the press began to speculate about why I was always looking so unwell and tired. Richard was great and usually pulled me through, but the endless speculation was vile and really got me down. At times when I was at home in bed, feeling utterly ill and miserable, there would be a posse of press outside my front door. I felt like a cornered animal. On the one hand I was defiant, thinking, Why should I tell these people what is wrong with me? Why do they have the right to know all my most intimate health problems? Then I'd think, The more you don't say anything, the more they're going to speculate. It was a horrible no-win situation that went on for about three years in Liverpool, and the first year in London.

The suggestion that I was taking to drink was absolute crap, and we do have our suspicions about where that stemmed from. The rumour first arose from a disgruntled former employee who was absolutely furious with us. His actual sacking had nothing to do with Richard and me, but he thought it did. This came as no surprise to us. When anybody on *This Morning* came to grief or left under difficult circumstances, the more vociferous ones usually went to the press and blamed us, and the journalists loved it because it made a better story. As a result, we acquired a reputation for being really difficult to work with, but that's unfair and untrue. We are perfectionists and quite demanding, but we have to be for the sake of good programmes. We actually get on fantastically well with good producers, researchers and editors, and have great fun with them. But on a daily show like *This Morning* there was always a lot of pressure, the deadlines were intense and some people just couldn't hack it. This doesn't mean they wouldn't have been brilliant working on a different kind of programme, simply that that particular show was very much a 'get on with it and if you can't, don't do it' affair. In the circumstances it wasn't surprising that some people, who were not right for the programme or who didn't thrive under pressure, felt incredibly mistreated and angry when asked to leave; and that journalists, always on the lookout for copy about Richard and me, made sure we were the ones to get the stick.

My so-called 'drink-problem' days also coincided with a period of intense rivalry between *This Morning* and the BBC's *Good Morning* when a lot of smear stories were circulating to add fuel to what became known as 'TV's sofa wars'. We know this because agents talk among themselves, and at a time when the two programmes were running almost neck and neck and people's jobs were on the line, our agent was well aware that at certain dinner parties in London the most outrageous stories were being circulated about Richard and me. It sounds dreadful, but I'm not being paranoid. I've heard these 'dirty tricks' stories so often from too many different people to doubt them.

'Where are the papers getting all this nonsense from?' I used to wail to our press officers. 'What the hell is going on?'

'That's the story the press wants to run. We're sorry,' they would reply.

When we were in Liverpool, I even found out that one London newspaper had sent a reporter to 'dig up some dirt' around Albert Dock, and he was going into all the local pubs to find out if I was one of their 'heavy drinkers'. But I never ever went into those pubs (other than to use the loo in the one next door in the early days). After the programme Richard and I always went home.

One day when Richard saw a reporter searching through

some of our black rubbish bags that were awaiting collection outside our house, he was absolutely furious and would certainly have thumped the guy if he could have caught him. At such moments you feel the whole world has gone topsy-turvy. You know you have no deep dark secret for any reporter to dig out, and you are totally baffled that such people cannot accept what you say. To have your privacy invaded outside your own home is a particularly awful violation, and your first impulse after such an experience is to say, 'Sod off!' to any stranger on your forecourt or doorstep. I'm a journalist, but I would never do such a thing in any circumstances. I've always had a very strong sense of what I am and am not prepared to do, and if I was ever asked to do such a thing I would refuse. I would know that I was in the wrong job, and would resign.

But enough of all that nonsense.

About eighteen months after we first came to London in 1996, I finally made up my mind to have a hysterectomy. There were two reasons why I decided to have this done in Manchester rather than in London. The first was because I was still homesick and feeling I didn't have any roots here; the second, and by no means least, was that I had a very good gynaecologist in Manchester, whom I'd been seeing for some time.

While I was in the hospital in Manchester, Richard was good enough to come up, too. It was obviously very inconvenient for *This Morning* to have the two of us off air, but the op was a big step for me and I knew I would go to pieces if he wasn't there. Having made a reasonably quick recovery, hating hospitals as I do, I couldn't wait to get out; and during the last couple of nights, I was lying awake thinking, I want to go home. I want to go home. Suddenly I realized that 'home' was the house in Hampstead and I was absolutely desperate to get back there. This moment marked the end of my homesickness. During the drive back to London, I felt nothing but relief, thankfulness and gladness to be returning to Hampstead. The homesickness, rather like mourning or bereavement, had obviously been a process that I simply had to go through. While it lasted, it was very painful and unpleasant, but once it passed there was no more looking back and all was well.

———

As far as the so-called 'north-south divide' is concerned, I experienced very little of this. The only time I recall was when I was thirteen and we came up to London for my brother Cal's wedding to Ro, a London girl. My parents were very nervous because Ro's parents were much posher than we were. Her mother was an account executive at an advertising agency and her stepfather was a professor. We, on the other hand, were unsophisticated provincial bump-kins.

The night before the wedding we had a family meal in a London hotel. This was a big event for us, and I remember ordering a porterhouse steak. It was the first time I had ever eaten one and I thought it was heavenly, but my father was a bit cross because it was so expensive. He ordered whitebait, and I was aghast when they turned up on his plate, complete with heads and tails. When my father gave me one to taste, I ate it just to please him, but I swear I could taste its eyes. I've never had one since, and I still feel revolted by any whole fish on a plate. I can only eat them if they've been beheaded and filleted! And when we're unlucky enough to be served with a whole one abroad, I look away while Richard decapitates mine for me.

During Cal's wedding my parents remained ill at ease with Ro's family, and my mum reacted with her customary northern chippiness when one of Ro's aunts, a very nice woman really, said, 'Oh, Manchester! That's the place where it always rains, isn't it.' The aunt was being chatty rather than 'catty', but my mother took it personally, was furious, and talked about it for years afterwards.

I've never been that sensitive. Having gone to university in the south, and lived and worked in London when I was young, I always thought the capital was a hugely enjoyable cosmopolitan place. Its buildings, restaurants, theatres and shops are like a lucky dip I've never tired of. But we've been so busy since we came to live here, I haven't even been to Harrods yet!

When Richard and I first arrived in London, people kept saying we must have been mad to choose a house in Hampstead that had only a small front garden to separate us from the pavement and road, but we'd fallen in love with it, loved the area and had no regrets.

'Why aren't you living somewhere with electronic gates and a long drive?' we were always being asked.

But that's not the way I wanted to live then or now. I did worry, though, when the story of our move first came out in the papers. From that time forth, we were besieged by 'snappers' hiding behind the bushes on the Heath across the road, which was very aggravating, especially when we were taking the kids to school. 'Snappers' are the worst kind of photographers to deal with because they're not there to cover any particular story. They just take endless pics in the hope of flogging them to the tabloids or magazines. I soon realized that in London we were even more public property than we had been in Manchester, but that's because London is London. We soon learned not to go to certain places if we didn't want attention. These days, for example, we can go out for an uninterrupted meal in Hampstead, but if we go to restaurants like the Ivy or San Lorenzo we know there will always be press photographers hanging around outside. So we make a decision and say, 'Okay. If we eat there, we'll have to pause and smile for the cameras before going in.' That's fine on occasion but if, like me, you want privacy, you choose local places where, although people still recognize you, it's no big deal.

————————

The only thing that had ever really worried me during our time on *This Morning* was the effect on Richard when I had to take time off from the programme. On the show, we always knew where each of us was coming from, and it was obviously harder for him to have to accommodate another presenter who'd never done the programme before. I knew that, on these occasions, he had to put a lot of extra effort into making whoever it was feel relaxed and happy.

Much of the time people thought that we could choose my replacement, but that wasn't true. It wasn't our job. Presenters were named whom Richard didn't think he would get on with at all, but he always made an effort and coped brilliantly well. Sometimes, he did come home feeling a bit down, and say that he didn't feel things had gone too well that day.

'Honestly, Richard,' I used to reply, 'just carry on doing what you are doing, being supportive and nice. That's all you can do.'

Caron Keating was one presenter who stood in for me. We hadn't met her before then, but she's now one of our closest friends. She always says that, although she was terrified of going on to the programme, it was the 'best time' for her. By then she'd already done *Blue Peter* and other TV work, but she'd never presented such a demanding programme as *This Morning*. Her mother, Gloria Hunniford, also told us that she'd never seen Caron as happy as she was when presenting *This Morning* with Richard. Caron replied: 'It was because Richard was so nice to me, and went out of his way to make me feel relaxed and happy, and was never sharp. He really was fantastic.'

There was never any doubt that I needed to take a break

from time to time, especially as too soon after my hysterectomy I'd also allowed myself to be lulled into doing a live weekly consumer affairs programme, *We Can Work It Out*. This show, ITV's answer to the BBC's *Watchdog*, was, to make matters even worse, produced in Leeds. When it first came up for discussion, I'd only been out of hospital for a week and, when the team behind it came round, I felt, 'Thanks for asking me, but I can't even begin to concentrate now, I haven't got the energy.' But they pushed and pushed and I foolishly gave in. Afterwards I was very upset and got quite cross with Richard, which then upset him. In his heart, though, he thought that I was just post-operative, and that three months down the line, when work on the new show was due to begin, I'd be as pleased as he was for me and I would do it really well. He truly regrets misreading the situation now!

When I did return to work in the April, I found I coped perfectly well with *This Morning* four mornings a week. But on Thursdays, when, immediately after that show finished, I had to drive up to Leeds, rehearse in the afternoon, do a live transmission in the evening, then get in a car and be driven back to London, I felt terrible. I got through it on adrenaline, but I wasn't at all well and I was desperate to give it up.

I'm a conscientious person and I carried on right to the bitter end with that series of *This Morning* and *We Can Work It Out*. Then, knowing that the next series of *This Morning* would come back on in the September, I asked if I could leave *We Can Work It Out*. But because it was a network programme and I was the only presenter, the answer was no and I was told that even a holiday was impossible.

I was at the end of my tether. I was feeling dreadfully overworked and tired and, by the end of May, my energy level had dropped to such a low that I told Annie, my agent, that I was not going to do it again. As it was not actually scheduled to come back until September, I felt the network had plenty of time to find another presenter. But all that came back from ITV was, 'Of course you're tired, Judy, everyone gets tired, it's the end of the run.'

'I don't want you to tell me that,' I replied testily.

Richard and I and the kids then set off to Cornwall with me not even really knowing if I wanted to sign the next contract for *This Morning*. This wasn't because I no longer loved *This Morning*; I simply couldn't cope any longer with the workload. Although by then I was only doing *This Morning* three days a week, and Richard was doing the Thursday with another presenter, I was still involved, as I had always been, with the production and editorial processes. This meant that every day after the programme I had to attend lengthy meetings to determine what was going into the next day's show, and also deal with the usual long-term planning. In addition, because I was only doing three days a week, I had to keep catching up on what had happened at the end of the previous week, and I felt the programme was running away from me.

The end-of-series eight-week break in Cornwall saved me at that point. It was a glorious summer and I made sure I kept well out of everything. I didn't answer the phone and spent a lot of time sleeping and walking, and sitting in the garden. I was determined not to go back to the consumer programme, and I had made that absolutely clear. As far as I was concerned, we didn't need the money, and I certainly didn't need the additional 'fame' or 'profile'. From then on, feeling much better thanks to Cornwall, I was now going to start enjoying my work on *This Morning* again. I did; and everything was absolutely fine. But not for long!

———

When we were first working on *Granada Reports*, Richard and I used to belong to a health club, which we had joined mainly because it was a place we could be together. We used to swim at lunchtimes, and I also joined an aerobic class. But, once we were married and had Jack and Chloe, it was impossible to fit everything in. I did enjoy it, however, and, if I hadn't been so pressed for time, I would have loved to do something like that again. It was not to be. Independent of the shortage of time, I developed a stupid knee problem which came about because of a mishap during a flight home after a holiday with the kids in Los Angeles.

During the journey, when Chloe was fast asleep in the seat next to me, I wanted to go to the loo and, as I didn't want to disturb her, I had to climb over her legs and feet to get to the aisle. During these antics my left knee was placed in a very awkward position and, as I reached the aisle, I felt something give. It wasn't agonizing at the time, I was just aware that whatever had happened had left me with a limp and I could no longer put any weight on that leg without the knee giving way. I thought I had sprained a muscle and that it would get better in time. But, one day when Richard parked the car in our drive, which is very steep, my left leg buckled and I fell flat on my face on the tarmac. That *was* agonizing. Although I realized I had to do something about the knee, I simply hadn't the time so, at work when it was at its most troublesome, I moved around the studio using a walking-stick. I couldn't go fast, and I had to wear flat shoes all the time.

As soon as the series ended, I went to see a knee surgeon who confirmed, after sending me for an MRI scan, that it was a ruptured ligament, and I needed to have an operation.

As I had so recently had the hysterectomy, I couldn't face another major operation, which involved taking tendons, which you can apparently do without at the back of the leg, and plaiting these into a new ligament which is then fixed with steel plates. The other problem was that, even after the operation, I wouldn't be able to get around immediately because it's painful, and I'd have to have physiotherapy every day. How could I manage all this and do the next series of *This Morning*? I decided I couldn't, so I put off the operation and went on limping. There then followed a period, about two years ago, when it became a bit of a nightmare. I'd get out of bed feeling okay, but then the knee would lock into position and I couldn't move for ten minutes or so. I gradually learned that if I was very careful with it, I would no longer get rooted to the spot first thing in the morning!

I know I must face up to this operation at some time in the future, and I want to because I love walking in Cornwall. At the moment I can only manage flat ground and going uphill, but I can't cope with anything steep and rugged or downhill that puts extra pressure on the knee. All I really need is a space of about six months or so, then I'll get it fixed. Apart from that, my health was then – and is now – absolutely fine!

While we were on *This Morning* it was lovely to be greeted by people who enjoyed the programme. I particularly enjoyed long-haul flights because the air crews always told us how much they loved watching *This Morning* when they were on shift work. I was amazed at how knowledgeable they were when discussing items we had covered or suggesting what they'd like us to do on the programme. Usually they went on to tell us their life story and the problems they had encountered, which was very flattering and touching. When you're on telly, people think they know you and this is an enjoyable short cut for you to be taken into their confidence.

Also, thanks to the programme, I was privileged to meet a lot of famous people whom I would never have met under other circumstances. My life was very ordinary when I was growing up but then, because of *This Morning*, my existence counted on another level. I know this is all crap really, but I got so much pleasure out of it. For example, soon after I started at

Granada Television as a gofer, I worked on *Coronation Street*. Knocking on Pat Phoenix's door and saying, 'Miss Phoenix, you are needed on set in five minutes,' was unbelievable; and I never got over walking down a corridor and seeing people such as Laurence Olivier. I still do feel star-struck by some. When Richard and I go to television awards and realize, while looking around at all the big-name actors, singers, pop stars, that we've interviewed most of them, it's fantastic. It's a huge privilege to meet such creative people on a routine basis.

Sadly, there are a few I'd love to meet who are – or were – too shy to give interviews. One of these was the wonderful John Thaw, another is David Jason. Basically such people feel they've had more than enough exposure and just want to keep their private lives private. I respect them for that, but would still have loved to have interviewed them.

The kids only found our 'fame' irritating from about the age of thirteen. Around this time, Tom and Dan chose not to come away with us very often because they found it such a bugbear at airports. When they did come, they either walked yards ahead or behind us because they didn't want to be involved with people pointing us out or staring. Jack is now getting to the same stage. He didn't used to mind, was quite proud in fact, but sadly no longer. Nowadays when he goes shopping with Richard in Hampstead, he gets really fed up when people point or whisper, 'Oh! That's Richard Madeley.'

'If you walk ahead of me, they'll be oblivious to you and you'll avoid the backlash,' Richard tells him.

We have been lucky, though, in that our kids have had no problems with their peers. As far as Tom and Dan were concerned, because we'd been on local TV in Manchester for a long time before *This Morning* came along, and because David, their father, was on TV as well, all their schoolfriends just accepted the situation. And now, as Jack and Chloe go to a school where kids have far more famous parents than we are

– people such as Annie Lennox, Jimmy Nail, Vanessa Feltz and Jonathan Ross – they don't stand out from the others. Likewise, because Jack and Chloe see celebrities dropping their kids off every day, they don't stand in awe of people who are on the telly. They only get star-struck by their favourite pop and film stars.

Chloe, I know, would kill to meet certain people. Occasionally on *This Morning* we'd get to interview someone we'd never heard of, but Chloe would know who they were. One of these was Josh Hartnett, the young American actor, who was in the film *Pearl Harbor*.

'He was gorgeous. You'd have liked him, Chloe,' I said when I came home.

'Who was it?' she asked.

'Josh Hartnett,' I replied.

As she heard this, the physical change in her was amazing. She went rigid, her face and neck went a deep red and tears sprouted horizontally from her eyes. Richard and I thought it was hilarious.

'Oooh. Why didn't you tell me? I love him,' she said. 'I'd have taken the day off school.'

'No, you wouldn't,' I said.

It was the same with the guy who played Angel in *Buffy the Vampire Slayer*. But this time we knew she had a crush on him. When she came into LWT to help out in the studio just before Christmas, we didn't tell her he was on the show. We arranged for one of the floor-managers to ask her to take a script to a guest in dressing-room four. She had no idea that we had a secret camera filming or that it was David Boreanaz sitting in there with a newspaper held up in front of his face. She knocked on the door, walked up to him and said, 'I've brought your script.'

'Thank you, Chloe,' he said, putting down his newspaper.

'Oh! Oh! *Oh!*' went Chloe.

Watching her on the screen, I thought she was going to have a heart attack and when she came back to where Richard and I were working on the script she was still trembling. It's lovely to be able to give your kids that kind of surprise and make it possible for them to meet people who mean so much to them.

Fame, then, is an extraordinary mix of pleasure and pain. In many respects, I've always found it tougher to cope with than Richard. But then, on or off telly, I've always felt quite vulnerable, always had a sense that things are transitory and that a great deal of grief awaits most of us, if not all of us, at some point in our lives. Once you're a parent you become even more aware of your own and your family's mortality. In your forties you're often preoccupied with looking back and thinking, Oh, God, that's my child-bearing years over, or My youth's gone. Will I lose my femininity and sexual attractiveness? But when you get into your fifties, which is where I am now, you stop looking back and start looking forward. That's not particularly wonderful either. You think, Oh, God, how many decades do I have left? or How many more years of good health?

Having written that, provided you let go of certain things that preoccupied you in your youth, your fifties can be quite liberating. These days, I don't exactly say to myself, 'Yes, I feel happy now I'm in my fifties,' but in a way I do because beyond your fifties are your sixties, seventies and eighties! And, as you become more aware of death, health becomes a key issue. I particularly hate reading cancer-scare stories that papers seem to thrive on; and I get really incensed when there are headlines such as CANCER SCARE IN STRAWBERRIES. It's a horrible way of keeping people obsessed with their bodies. I probably react to these things more than I used to because I've reached the age when a lot of people I know have been diagnosed with cancer.

It's also possible that my work on *This Morning* has made me more aware of human frailty. I found it impossible not to be affected by the vulnerability and grief of the people we talked to on a daily basis, especially when they were parents of children who had died in tragic accidents. All deaths are dreadful, but accidental death is without doubt the worst to come to terms with. It's just so unexpected and, even though the parents themselves are in no way to blame, they are left with terrible residual guilt feelings simply because they were not there at the end when their child desperately needed their protection.

This goes right to the heart of parenthood and even though, thank God, we haven't experienced a child's accidental death, I just know how that would feel. I am very empathic in that way and I do tend to feel another person's emotions deeply. But in my job I have had to learn to be careful. Emotion can paralyse you and there's no point in becoming so grief-stricken that you can't help in any way. I do find that extremely difficult, though. Richard is different. He's very sympathetic and can feel others' grief but, because he's a problem-solver, his first reaction in any situation is, 'Okay, that's the problem. How can we make it any easier, any better?' In truth, there's very little we can say or do, but Richard has often come up with ways of looking at a problem that can help. I admire that greatly. Despite my good intentions, I still get enmeshed in emotion, but I am a bit better than I used to be.

Many were the times when people were in floods of tears on *This Morning*. One day when I came into the studio and saw two mothers whose children had died in drowning accidents while at summer camps, my heart just missed a beat. But I had to go up to them and say, 'I'm so incredibly sorry. It must be awful, dreadful for you.' At first, you think, Oh, God, I'm talking in clichés, and they've heard all this before, but actually they really appreciate it. They say thank you, kiss you on the cheek, squeeze your hand, and all you can do is forge a sense of fellowship that conveys we're all humans in what can be a terribly sad life.

On such occasions, I was always aware that this was no ordinary interview undertaken for a programme. Our guests needed to talk about what had happened and often when we thanked them for coming in and talking about it, they would say, 'No, no. Thank you very much for giving us the opportunity.' They saw it as part of the healing process, and it was important for us to treat the interview in that way. Yes, we were dealing with such subjects for the viewers but, in those situations, my allegiance was always to the people I was interviewing.

I remember one little boy, Nicholas Killen, who was in the newspapers several years ago. He was only six or seven and had been born with a terrible incurable disease of his eyes, a kind of cancer. He'd already lost the sight of one eye when the cancer started to grow in the other. His mother had to make a heart-breaking decision. The specialist had told her that they had to operate to remove the remaining eye, which would make him blind, or else he would die. She then had to explain to her partially sighted son what was happening. When he woke up from the operation, she told the press that his first words were, 'Mum, I can't see. What's happening? Everything's dark. Mum make me see.'

When I heard that, given I've got a thing about blindness anyway, I couldn't bear it. I remember sitting there watching it on the News, before we had interviewed them ourselves, and I was just slayed, inconsolable.

'Look, it's awful,' Richard said to me, 'but he's very young. People are born without sight and still manage to have a good life. It's a horrible thing to happen, but he'll be fine. He'll grow up and will adapt to it.' He didn't add anything trite, like if he doesn't have the operation he will die. He simply said, 'Look at it positively, Judy. He's young enough to adapt.'

When we did subsequently interview the Killen family on *This Morning*, I was very impressed both by the mother who had had to make such an awful decision and by Nicholas who was a really resilient happy kid. After that we interviewed them several times to see how Nicholas was getting on and Richard was absolutely right. He was a happy little fellow and as bright as a button. He had learned braille and was busy writing and illustrating braille books. He was just fantastic.

The most embarrassing moment for me on *This Morning* was when we had Dr Ruth, the American sexologist, on the show. She had her own radio show in the USA and was used to being terribly frank. Her language was very upfront, in your face. But, despite her unreservedly forthright manner, our editor decided she should do one of our phone-ins.

'Are you sure?' we queried. 'She's very graphic. What if . . . ?'

When we met her she was, as expected, a completely unshockable, tough, New York, Jewish lady psychiatrist, with loads of chutzpah. She was also quite elderly, which was somewhat disconcerting because it was like talking about sex to your grandmother.

'I don't want to do this phone-in unless I can be completely frank,' she said at once.

'Quite,' we said nervously. 'You can be frank.'

On air, when a woman rang in and said her husband hardly ever wanted to have sex, Dr Ruth came very close to the post- let alone pre-watershed knuckle.

'What you've got to do,' she said, 'is keep a watch on him during the night. Men have lots of spontaneous erections when they're asleep, and that's how you can tell whether somebody is genuinely impotent or whether it's a psychological rather than a physical difficulty. So watch tonight.' Then, looking directly at Richard and me, she added, 'And, Judy, I think you should do exactly the same thing, so you'll know what I meant when I come on this programme again. Just keep an eye open when Richard is asleep.'

'Right, Judy,' Richard said, jumping in, 'I'm going to make absolutely sure you do that tonight.'

I was so embarrassed, I was speechless, but Richard thought it was hilarious.

When people bring your private life into things, you do have to watch it. In my view, there's a line that should not be crossed, but Richard didn't always observe it. I always had to be ready to pull him back by the scruff of his neck. In the end, though, I kind of got used to these moments and it did become less embarrassing and daunting.

That phone-in with Dr Ruth was, I suppose, a ground-breaking one. Among other things, she demonstrated oral sex on a lollipop, which was – well – entertaining but embarrassing. By then, I thought we were pretty good at judging the tone of an item and, while the lollipop was being licked, I thought the best way to react was to pretend it wasn't happening and not to take it too seriously. As I was wrapping up the phone-in, I said, 'I don't believe we did that.' The next day the TV critic Jaci Stephen said, 'Oh, Judy, I can't believe you did that, either.'

Needless to say, there were hundreds of protests from our shocked viewers.

Another of our misconceived phone-ins, although it seemed like a good idea at the time, was the age-old penile discussion: 'Does size matter?' For this we had Nina Myskow, because we thought she would be entertaining, and an elderly lady who was in the news at the time for having written her memoirs, describing her fantastically promiscuous life. She had also written other books in which she explained why you *should* be promiscuous. Fine, we'll have her in, we thought.

She proved to be a very middle-class, up-market lady. With her grey hair piled in a neat bun, she looked like butter wouldn't melt in her mouth, everybody's dream granny. But once she started talking in her disconcertingly posh voice, she said, 'Of course, size matters,' and, in case we hadn't got the message, she went on and on, becoming ever more insistent. Then suddenly she exclaimed, 'But I must say, you do get some men who are complete size queens.' It was just amazing and from such sweet lips. More complaints duly followed.

We also had an item, I remember, about a man in his thirties who had married a woman of eighty. The producer said he had talked to them both on the phone, that they were absolutely genuine and rational, and had simply said, 'Age doesn't matter, you can still fall in love,' and all the rest of it. They certainly hadn't married for money because neither of them had any. So, reassured, we decided to have them in and discuss the age-difference issue.

She proved to be very elderly, and he was a smarmy-looking so-and-so with a moustache. We felt at once that he wasn't in love with this elderly lady. He said he was and that they had a full married life in every sense of the word.

Sitting there, she kept patting him on the knee, then suddenly she said, 'Except when he starts looking at those Page Three girls.'

'What?' we both said.

'He gets these huge erections and starts nudging me. I had to tell him off this morning.'

Pretty sickening and on live TV, too! But Richard's theory was that moments like these on *This Morning* were never as bad as some people feared. Although the programme was obviously pre-watershed, he was fond of reminding us that most kids were at school and most women, watching on their own, didn't mind *risqué* items. I know there's some truth in that because in 2001, when we announced we were going to do our new Channel 4 programme at five in the afternoon, people kept coming up and saying, 'But the kids will be home from school, and there'll be so many things you won't be able to talk about any more.'

———————

In 1996, we found ourselves in a different kind of trouble with the press, a furore about not asking the 'right questions'. This arose when we interviewed O.J. Simpson, who had been sensationally cleared of murdering his wife, Nicole Brown, and her pal, Ronald Goldman. This interview was not done on *This Morning*, but on a new evening-show series which we had been asked to present, and it proved to be a bloody nightmare. The series was meant to be a half-hour weekly, topical, chat-cum-discussion show but, allowing for all the time eaten up by the titles, credits and commercial breaks, the actual interview time amounted to only twenty-four minutes. This was simply not enough time, especially as we were expected to include three guest interviews in each show. Born interviewees, composed of instant quotes, are a rare breed; and you need time to relax a person, make him or her feel comfortable, before you launch into important or controversial matters. Michael Parkinson, for instance, told us that his shortest guest interview is twenty minutes long.

It was a huge publicity coup for the production team to book O.J. Simpson for the first *Tonight with Richard Madeley and Judy Finnigan* show, but we were worried from the start about interviewing him and Neil Diamond and Bo Derek on the same show. We had a series of meetings with Granada executives and the production team to protest about this and, a few days before the transmission, I remember Richard saying, 'I can't believe you are not willing to do the whole show on O.J. Simpson.'

'It's not us, it's the network,' they replied. 'They are absolutely adamant that they want three guest items a show.'

'But it's O.J. Simpson,' we said.

'They won't back down,' they reiterated. 'You've got to do three guest items.'

There was nothing we could do. It was the first evening show we had been asked to present – a big deal for us. Both we and Granada had a lot riding on it; and nobody was prepared to say, 'We agree with you: it's too many interviews for one short programme.' The fact that we had O.J. Simpson booked, and it was his first interview in the UK was by the by.

On the day of the programme, we went up to the Green Room to meet O.J., and immediately realized that he was a fantastically articulate guy who had a strategy of his own, a filibustering technique of talking on and on to avoid answering anything he didn't want to discuss.

More concerned than ever, we went on screen to do the interview.

Considering how limited our time was, I think we managed to get in some good questions, and one subsequent headline, O.J. ON THE ROPES, seemed to bear this out. But when Roy Hattersley was asked to review the programme, it seemed to us that he hadn't actually watched it. I've never forgotten that he didn't mention one question we asked, yet described us as asking 'candy-floss questions'. This was total crap. In the twelve minutes we were allowed, we had been very direct with O.J., and were just getting to the nitty-gritty when we heard the producer, the Granada executive and the PA in the box mercilessly counting us down to the commercial break. Not one of them said, 'Let's forget the break for now and carry on,' or even, 'We've got to take a break, but we'll come back to this interview afterwards.'

Listening to the count-down, in the thick of a live programme, we were helpless. There was no way we could say to the people in the box, 'We simply can't break off here. Can somebody up there please tell us what the hell we're supposed to do?' As it was my link, the only choice I had was to cave in and say, 'Thank you, O.J. We're now taking a break and afterwards it's Neil Diamond,' and listen to the studio audience going, 'Oh, no!'

It was awful. Everybody felt so cheated.

What made matters even worse was that the Neil Diamond item on the show was pre-recorded and could easily have been dropped. Both he and Bo Derek, our next guests that night, were Americans who, having decided it was not politically correct to appear with O.J. Simpson on any television show, had decided not to be in the same studio with him. As a result, Neil Diamond had come in earlier in the day to record his number, and Bo Derek had dropped out altogether. I can't even remember now who her replacement was. It was all such a stupid mess. We were so angry – Richard even more so than me – and ever since then he has said that this experience was a learning curve for him; that if a network ever again asked him to do such a thing he would refuse and walk out.

From our point of view, it would not have been so bad if the O.J. interview had been slotted in halfway through the series, but it took place on the first night and the bad reviews that followed were very damaging. Richard, who was already furious that we had been so compromised, was then taken aback by press headlines, such as DUNCE AND JUDY SHOW in the *Observer*, others that labelled us the NO PUNCH AND JUDY SHOW, and front-page comments that picked up on Roy Hattersley's one about 'candy-floss questions'.

Afterwards, as much for Richard's sake as anything else, I shrugged it off and said, 'There you go. That's what happens in this crazy world.' Granada, though, let us down. But, at least, the executives had the good grace to admit this later.

When we were preparing for the O.J. interview, we discussed

the 'state of denial' theory with a psychiatrist. At first, we were completely dismissive of this and thought, Oh, come on, nobody could go that deeply into denial; everybody must surely know whether they have murdered somebody or not. But we were less sure as we listened to the psychiatrist talking about such cases, and saying, 'Oh, yes, people can be so convinced of their innocence that it is possible for them to block something out completely. And when they say, "Look, I didn't do it," they really mean it. Obviously, at some point, the events can come back to them in flashbacks, but I assure you that while they are in the throes of denial they are absolutely convinced of their innocence.'

O.J., I must add, was acquitted of murder by a court of law, and obviously we must all abide by that. In relation to meeting him that night, both Richard and I thought he was a very loquacious, charming man. He laughed a lot, was extremely good-looking and exuded an air of glamour. Many people in the studio's Green Room, before and after the show, including my then student sons, Tom and Dan, and some of their friends sitting in the audience, were desperate to meet him and to shake his hand.

Throughout our time on *This Morning*, we interviewed Tony Blair three times, both before and after he became Prime Minister. The first time was just before the general election and he was very nervous about appearing on our kind of programme. He knew *This Morning* was aimed at people who would be sitting in their homes judging him as a person and as a husband and father. He was disarmingly sweet when he arrived, and very insecure about what he should wear. He took off his jacket, put it on again, stood there undecided, then consulted Richard. I remember Alistair Campbell, his press secretary, standing around like a thundercloud in the background. During the interview, I got the sense of a man who had a huge respect and love for his wife, Cherie, and who was very strongly committed to family life. Some people say he has no convictions, but that was certainly not my impression. At the end of the first interview, he let out a great sigh of relief and said, 'It's much easier being interviewed by Jeremy Paxman than you two because at least he sticks to politics!'

As far as Richard and I were concerned, we were not there to establish if he would prove to be the greatest Prime Minister of our times, we simply wanted to find out about Tony, the man, and give our viewers a glimpse of the kind of person he was at home. I knew he was charismatic and charming, and I remained on the alert for this, but I didn't find him at all phoney. I thought he was very sincere, something that's hard to fake on live television. I liked him a great deal and thought the press's castigation of us for not asking all the usual tough political questions was a bit much. Exposing people and provoking them into hanging out all their dirty linen in public was not our job on *This Morning*. We were not there to hammer people into the ground, we were there to entertain, interest and leave our daytime viewers feeling happy, informed and comfortable.

Over the years on *This Morning* we must have covered every topic under the sun, and some of our interviewees included people the police were keen for us to interview because they were suspected of doing some pretty dreadful things. We once, for example, interviewed a man from the north-west of England who was suspected of murdering his wife who had gone missing. The police didn't have enough evidence to charge him, but her family was convinced he had murdered her. Despite his denials and the lack of evidence, he had been subjected to a lot of local publicity, and the police wanted him to appear on *This Morning* because they felt the more interviews he did, the more likely he was to slip up.

Tina Turner – a less controversial guest in our 'O. J. Simpson' series.

Left: One of those Madame Tussaud moments with Tony Curtis and his bride-to-be, Tony was a very funny guest on our *Tonight* programme.

Below: The best of friends. Tony Blair and Gordon Brown do a political Fred and Ginger, September 1999.

Left: Arriving at Covent Garden for *This Morning*'s 10th-Anniversary Party, October 1998.

Below: *This Morning*'s 10th-Anniversary Party's deceptively quiet, civilised opening.

The party implodes as some prat in novelty Elvis shades and sideburns attempts to cover Johnny B. Goode.

Right: A Tarantino moment with *Eye of the Storm* director, Andy Serraillier, in a Los Angeles storm drain. Only the choicest locations for us. April, 2000.

Left: The *Eye of the Storm* team smile bravely for the camera before tackling a Malibu bush fire. (Actually the thing exploded into life a few minutes later and we had to run for it.) Left to right, Richard Madeley, Ian Mills (sound), Pete Connors (producer), Gordon MacGregor (cameraman), Maire Tracey (assistant producer) and Andy Serraillier (director). April, 2000.

'The most shameless publicity stunt I've ever witnessed' – our friend John Bowe's verdict the following day.

Our Cornish garden.

A twilight shot in part of our garden in Cornwall, summer 2000.

Right: Jack and Chloe in the sitting room at our house in Cornwall before we renovated it – the summer of the eclipse, 1999.

Below: A case of hope triumphing over experience! A happy wet day on a Cornish beach with our great friends Caron Keating and Russ Lindsay, and Caron's mum Gloria Hunniford.

Our wedding blessing on 12 August 2000. Our vicar, Father William Brabiner, told us marriage was like a garden. It needed regular weeding. Hmm!

In our ancient village church in Cornwall.

After our wedding blessing, and Jack and Chloe's christening at the same ceremony, in our village church.

At lunch, after the ceremony, at the hotel next door. The cake is in the shape of a Celtic cross, with our names and Jack and Chloe's written on it.

Our great friend John Bowe with his daughters Maddie and Aimée after the ceremony.

A lovely, lovely day – after our wedding blessing.

Waving goodbye after our last edition of *This Morning*. 12 July 2001.

Girl power. Judy at our garden party the day we left *This Morning* with,
left to right, researcher Suzy Davis, producer Dympna Morrison, our P.A. Naomi
Walsch, editor Karen Smith, and former editor Sharon Powers. Dympna, Naomi and
Karen all came with us to Channel Four.

Walking out to face the press after our move to
Channel Four was announced.

During the interview, we proceeded on the following basis: 'Why do you think that, although you are strongly denying that you did this dreadful thing – and have constantly claimed that you and some of your friends have seen your wife since the alleged incident – the police still feel that you are guilty of murdering her?'

Throughout the programme he proved to be a very persuasive man, and for Richard and me it was a strange experience. Young, good-looking, middle-class, he did a brilliant job of defending himself that day, but his eyes were really creepy. Some time later when he did finally break down and confess to the police, and his wife's body was found, he received a life sentence. On the day of his conviction, we re-ran our taped interview and experienced once again the same chill we had sensed while interviewing him. His eyes were never still, always darting around as if in flight from something awful. This alone was certainly not enough for anybody to stand up and say, '*J'accuse* – you obviously did kill your wife,' but it was very telling and confirmed for Richard and me that eyes really are 'the window to the soul'.

Later, when Dr Harold Shipman was convicted of murdering his patients, we did a phone-in on the subject. During this, Dr Chris Steele commented: 'I just don't understand how he got away with it for so long. In all my years of practice, I've only ever been present at a very few deaths, yet this GP managed to be present at so many; and, in addition, he was able to acquire and stockpile so many lethal drugs. Sadly, though, I do think there are other guys like Shipman practising out there.' It was a shocking thought, but following Chris's remark, one of our phone-in girls received a call from a woman who said that her doctor husband was another Harold Shipman who had more or less admitted to her that he had done the same as Shipman.

'Doctors,' she said, 'are paid for issuing death certificates and, in the past, my husband made several allusions to receiving money for yet another one of these. He has now been struck off for drug abuse, but he's dared me to go to the police with what he has told me. I'm scared stiff of him.'

Our phone-in girl, who was worried about the legal implications of what the woman was saying, didn't put her through to us on air, but we spoke to her immediately after the show. Then, having checked out her claims with Dr Chris Steele, we handed the matter over to the police. The CID agreed there was definitely a case for this ex-GP to answer, but so far he has never been brought to trial.

There were times on *This Morning* when we got quite used to seeing police officers in the studio, and sometimes this did bother me. One of these occasions was a very complicated child-custody story which involved a father who had run away with his son. At the instigation of the police, the mother came on to the programme to make an emotional plea for the child's return. Although nobody had seen or heard from the man for months, he was obviously watching the show because he rang in.

'It's not as simple as that,' he protested. 'And here's my side of the story . . .'

After the programme, both Richard and I spoke to him at some length on the phone. 'Whatever your side of the story is,' we said, 'you must know that you can't do this; that it's bad for your son and terrible for his mother.'

We then ended the call by saying, 'Can we talk to you again tomorrow?'

'Okay,' he replied.

'Will you really talk about it on air tomorrow?'

'Yeah,' he said.

When he phoned the next day, we had another long conversation with him. Towards the end, he said he now accepted that the situation was not right and that he would return his son to his mother. But, while we were speaking, the police had traced the call and the investigating officers were knocking on his door just as we were ringing off. I really hated this, but there was nothing we could do. The mother had appeared on the show at the request of the police, and we could not negotiate with the father behind their backs. It was very unpleasant, though. Having built up a rapport with him and gained his trust, we were left feeling we had betrayed him.

Another of our so-called 'scoops' on *This Morning* concerned Charles Bronson, an American criminal who was dubbed 'the most dangerous man in the world'. While in prison, he had married a very pretty, sweet-natured Indian girl who came on to the programme to talk about why she had chosen to marry such a man. During the interview, she admitted she had been mad to do it, but said she loved him.

What we didn't know at the time, but learned later, was that, although Bronson had been in 'solitary' for something like twenty years, the governor of the prison had given him permission to watch a video of the programme. Having seen this, Bronson then sent us a long letter, saying: 'Thank you so much, you were so sweet to my lovely girl. And thank you for not automatically dismissing me as a monster and for giving her a chance to talk about me.' At the end, surrounded by doodles, he added, 'Please will you write back.'

Amazingly, it turned out that he had a PA – obviously not in jail with him – who then kept writing to us, saying: 'The boss was thrilled with you and would like to start a proper correspondence. He's hoping to get paroled soon and would like to meet you.' She also sent us some of the wedding photographs that had been taken in the jail, and I remembered these recently when I read in a US paper that his marriage had broken up.

For us, it was a very strange experience. It was also a reminder that while we are sitting there in a television studio doing cosy interviews, there are people out there living the most extraordinary lives and watching us as we are beamed into the intimate surroundings of their living-rooms, prison cells, and God knows where else.

All shows are vulnerable to hoaxes and hoax telephone calls, but what I didn't know, while I was on *This Morning*, is that agencies exist for this very purpose. Once I stopped to think about it, I realized that of course there would be unscrupulous agents who were only too happy to seek out clients who'd be willing to play along and put themselves around the chat-show circuit. In 1999 I felt very sorry for our friend Vanessa Feltz when she was subjected to an enormous amount of adverse publicity after one of these imposters slipped through the net and appeared on her BBC programme, *Vanessa*.

It's not at all surprising that programmes get caught out in this way and get taken for a ride. The pressure on production teams to come up with people who've got good stories to tell is phenomenal. I think we were very lucky on *This Morning* not to have a studio audience like *Kilroy*, *Tricia* or *Vanessa*. On one occasion, though, we did have a man who was looking for 'a wife' or 'a girlfriend'. He seemed pleasant enough to us, but we subsequently had calls from viewers saying he was a deeply unsavoury character. Fortunately, no harm resulted from his appearance, and from then on Richard and I kept a sharp eye out when looking at our guest lists and briefing notes.

My bra-baring incident on live telly in front of fourteen million viewers is funny now, but it wasn't at the time. I couldn't believe it had happened. The occasion was the National Television Awards in the year 2000. Richard and I were thrilled to be nominated for the third year running and, having worked during the day of the awards, we decided to stay at the Savoy Hotel, just across the river from *This Morning*'s studio, so that we could get to bed reasonably early before being back on air the next morning. Excited, I had bought a new dress for the occasion, a long black beaded velvet dress with a halter neck, plus a long black velvet coat which just draped down its front. I'd also bought a new black halter-neck bra, but had never tried it on. When I did, the cups were the wrong shape, it looked awful and was very uncomfortable.

'I can't wear this, it looks dreadful,' I said to Richard. 'I'll have to wear the bra I've been wearing all day. Never mind,' I said, famous last words, 'no one will ever know.'

In the auditorium of the Royal Albert Hall, the bra and dress were fine, no problem. We sat through the first awards and again everything was fine. Then it came to our award. They read the nominations, and Les Dennis and Amanda Holden, who were presenting the awards, came on stage. Amanda Holden opened the envelope and said, 'And the winner is Richard and Judy and *This Morning.*'

It's impossible to do justice to what it is like to win. When your name is read out, it feels like an electric shock at the base of your spine, and you feel so incredibly overwhelmed and grateful to everyone who's voted for you. I'm not at all surprised that so many people get tearful when they go up to collect their trophy. It's a fantastic moment. Feeling great, to huge applause, we walked up the steps on to the stage to collect our third award. Turning to the microphone we said, 'Thank you very much,' and Richard then made some remark about his Ali G impression. As the audience started to laugh, we thought they were laughing at his remarks and, as the laughter built and built, we hadn't the faintest idea that the halter neck on my dress had unravelled itself and was slyly slipping down to my waist. It could have been worse – I might not have been wearing a bra – but, because it was pale pink, it looked like my boobs had been exposed. As everybody said afterwards, when the dress first slipped, they thought, Oh, that's a bit daring, her dress is very low cut, then it dawned on them that the top half of my dress was no longer present. Meanwhile, neither Richard nor I, still looking swimmingly eyed at the audience, was remotely aware of what had happened.

It was sod's law that the dress had chosen that moment to take the plunge. It could have happened in the car or in the auditorium but, no, it waited until I was up on the stage. Trevor McDonald, who was presenting the NTA, could have said something to alert me, but he didn't. I had no idea until John Leslie, who stood in for Richard on each Friday's *This Morning*, came hurtling up from the stalls.

'What? What?' I said, shocked, as he rushed to my side, got hold of my dress and yanked it up. 'What are you doing?'

Then, looking down and seeing pink, I realized what had happened. 'Oh, God!' I said, mortified. Fortunately, I was also wearing the black velvet coat and was able to pull it tight around me.

I learned later that Fern, sitting alongside John, was the first who had 'clocked' what was happening.

'For God's sake,' she said, nudging John in the ribs, 'you've got to do something. Go up there!' It was very chivalrous of John and, as I said afterwards, the first time I had ever known him to help a woman *into* a dress.

It was all horribly undignified and the incident could not, of course, be edited out of a live show. All I could do was clutch my velvet coat, leave the stage carrying the award, and make my way with Richard to the room where all the press and the photographers wait on these occasions. As we walked there, I felt awful. Richard was busy trying to fasten my dress at the back and Amanda was trying to comfort me by saying, 'Try not to worry, Judy. It was all right really . . .'

Going into the drinks party to clink glasses with the other guests was really embarrassing. When David Liddiment came up to congratulate us on the award, I told him it had been one of the worst moments of my life.

'Sadly, it will be rather painful,' he said, 'but, to your credit, you handled it beautifully.'

That made me feel a bit better but, in truth, out there on stage I hadn't had any choice but to pretend to shrug it off with a laugh.

When I woke up the next morning in the Savoy, the humiliating scenes flooded back. I knew, before I looked, that photographs of me and my bra would be all over the papers, and there they were, front-page, on all of them. Until then, I hadn't realized how bad it was. I'd thought the pictures would just show a glimpse of bra, but the dress was down to my waist, and I was left feeling even more horrified.

'Look,' Richard said, trying to comfort me, 'it's something that could have happened to any woman wearing a halter-neck dress. I'm your husband, right? And I'm not mortified or embarrassed by any of it. Everything's fine, honest.'

When Phil, our driver, arrived to take us to the studio, I stood in the room thinking, Right! I've got two choices. I can either go to work and do the programme, or go home because I'm too embarrassed. If I go to the studio, I'll just have to be straight about it.

When I walked into the studio, all the crew were standing around looking at their feet.

'Okay, come on,' I said. 'Let's get all the jokes over and done with. Who wants to kick off?'

After that it was fine. Just let it ride, I thought.

Karen, our then editor, said, 'It's your call, Judy, but obviously I'm coming under a lot of pressure to show the clip at the beginning of the show. I won't do it if you don't want me to.'

'Go ahead,' I replied. 'It'll be much worse if I try to pretend it hasn't happened.'

I was appalled when I saw the TV footage for the first time, and I was watching a bit of film that been edited! When I saw the unedited version, it was much worse: I really did look naked.

Whenever I appeared on anybody else's programme after that – Graham Norton's, Zoë Ball and Jamie Theakston's *The Priory* – it was the first thing they covered in their interviews. Up until the New Year, when the reviews of that year's programmes were over, I simply had to put up with knowing that the NTA footage would be shown everywhere I went. There was no point in minding, the joke was on me. Loads of people wanted to auction the dress for charity but, certain that a newspaper would buy it and flog it for constant re-runs, I refused. The dress is still in my wardrobe. I only wore it once more on *This Morning*, as a joke just before Christmas, when Richard and I were covering all the highlights of the year. When I walked into the studio, all our regular team were on the set and they were gobsmacked and highly amused to see me wearing the dress that had caused me so much grief.

———

'Do people keep asking you about working together?' Mary Parkinson once asked me.

'Oh, yes,' I replied. 'Practically every day. And it's hard to convince them that we love working together.'

'Exactly!' she replied. 'Michael and I have found the same thing. Of course it works. In our line of business it's often the only way to get to see each other and, besides, it's so good to share a common line of interest. I understand his reactions and he understands mine better than anybody else in the world, and it cancels out the stress that one of you isn't quite getting the "message" or being overloaded.'

Mary, who has often worked with Michael, understood what I think most happily married couples would understand, that working together can be a positive rather than a negative situation, but I know from the way some people react to Richard and me that it can be hard, if not impossible, for some individuals to get their heads around this.

Being together all day, every day, 'joined at the hip' as one journalist described it, has obviously worked for us. But I don't deny that there were learning curves we had to go through before we enjoyed what the press is fond of describing as twenty-three hours in each other's company. I know that working as well as living together has actually helped both of us. We wouldn't have met if we were not working on the same programme and when we did, we got on very well professionally even before we got on well personally. We never once had to adapt our style to suit each other, and never suffered the nasty shock that some presenters do of finding out that the person sitting alongside us on screen was an absolute so-and-so. From day one, I always found it a huge comfort that we were there for each other, and that Richard would never deliberately trip me up. That may sound unlikely but, in our business, people can be very bitchy and territorial and do just that. With Richard, though, I always had complete trust that if I ever did get into a hole, as all presenters do from time to time, he would bail me out.

There are, however, some professional pitfalls because any two human beings are bound to disagree sometimes. Both of us are quite opinionated and, although we think alike a lot of the time, over the years we have had to come to terms with not always agreeing on how to handle a particular item or interview. We now have a very useful rule of thumb which is largely based on which one of us is the most vociferous about a specific issue! Fortunately time has proved that we don't usually disagree with equal strength or passion, and we have learned to be grown-up enough to say, 'Okay, okay. You win.' We have, in other words, learned which battles are worth fighting to the death for and when to give way to each other with reasonable good grace.

There were also times on *This Morning* when Richard – a mere male! – was inclined to see the approach to important stories differently from Judy – a mere female! But, because I am a woman and a feminist, and because the programme, let's face it, was largely intended for a female audience, I often had an intuitive empathy with how other women would relate to a particular subject. There is, I learned, as most women do, an instinctive reluctance in men to delve into and talk about emotions. Many, like Richard, are wonderfully pragmatic and excellent problem-solvers, but this can result in, 'Okay. Let's do this and that, and it'll all be solved, won't it?' But life, as the female of the species knows, is not always as simple as that or so black and white! To do Richard justice, he often allowed me to soften what would have been his more political approach to certain subjects; and I know there were many occasions when he sorted me out.

When we were first building up *This Morning*, there were often times when the stress of gaining ratings lapped into our family life. I've always envied people in our business who say, 'Oh, it doesn't matter if we win the ratings or not,' because Richard and I have never felt we can afford to take that attitude. If you are involved in commercial television, winning the ratings is a relentless pressure. We were very proud of the fact that, once *This Morning* became a top-rated daytime programme, it stayed that way. But, by God, it was harder to remain there than get there, and whenever the pressure became particularly intense it did cause some irritation between Richard and me. Also when things went wrong, or somebody was chippy on the programme, we'd sometimes have a discussion about whether it was his or my fault, and, by the time we got into the car to go home, there would be a definite *frisson* and quite a lengthy silence.

We soon, though, developed coping strategies. When we arrived home, usually mid to late afternoon, and mostly coinciding with the kids coming in, we'd go to different places in the house. I usually went to our bedroom because I'm so happy there. I still do. It's my 'bubble', the place where I read, write and work. I don't have the radio on and only switch on the television when there's a national or international crisis. Being cocooned in silence is how I unwind. Richard's approach is much more physical: he goes off on his bike and, after the ride, stops off at the shops. Then we have supper with the kids.

In the early days when we got furious with each other at work, we used to stomp off to our dressing-rooms. Once, after Jonathan Ross and his wife had stood in for us on *This Morning* while we were on holiday, Jonathan expressed some surprise that we had separate dressing-rooms. 'For heaven's sake,' I said, 'we've got to have a bit of space!' The dressing-rooms, though, didn't provide much of a haven for seething. Within minutes the editor or producer would arrive and researchers would rush in and out. But they often proved a useful distraction from whatever had caused the rift. Even if we went on air still feeling sore with each other, the adrenaline of live TV would pull us through. And, more often than not, by the end of the show the row would have evaporated into thin air.

At home, the main bone of contention has always been the phone, which never stops ringing and tends to go on into the late evening. In our work this is bound to happen. We have to deal with people at the office who desperately need decisions for the next day's programmes and this does put pressure on us. It's not unusual for Jack or Chloe to explode at some point and say, 'You've been on that phone, talking about work, for an hour now. What about us?'

These days Richard and I are much more tolerant with each

other. We recognize the danger signals, know what irritates us about each other, and we don't blow up so quickly. When you're young, you have energy to spare and often dance around shouting, but we can't bear to do that now. We've learned how to accommodate each other, and we conserve our energy. I can't actually remember the last time we had an argument but, when we do, it's usually spats about the kids. Recently, on one of those rare days, when we were alone together in our little boat in Florida, Richard suddenly said, 'Isn't this fantastic? We've run away to sea to escape the kids!' and it was. As every parent knows, much as you love them and couldn't bear to be without them, teenagers are a huge drain on one's energies. When they're babies, you can put them down for a nap, but when they're older they're always in your hair!

Richard, I know, thinks I over-indulge them, but that is one of my greatest pleasures in life. When I was a child, money was always a big issue in our home and, because I went to a school where the other girls were middle-class and had more money than us, it became an even bigger issue when I was a teenager. All my friends had Mary Quant dresses and expensive haircuts, but my parents couldn't afford these and I was never able to go on the school's skiing trips. When I started earning, my father was convinced I'd turn into a bit of a spendthrift, but I never splashed my money around and never developed a passion for flash cars and the like. The only way I have rebelled is to become a 'soft' touch for the kids. When they want something, like designer clothes and trainers, I remember how miserable I used to feel and let them have them.

One of my great regrets is that I've never really followed up my interest in classical music. Like good literature, this is one of those things you need to know something about before you really begin to appreciate it and it certainly helps if you have parents who are into it. Mine weren't, but I enjoy it none the less. Both Richard and I love Fauré's *Requiem*, Bruch's violin concerto, Sibelius and Beethoven, and we're always saying we should book for some concerts, but somehow we never get round to it. Mind you, we never get time to go to the theatre either.

The two favourite films of my youth were *West Side Story* and *Lawrence of Arabia*, and I must have seen both of them about fifty times. I also loved *The King and I*. Yul Brynner was very sexy and his dance sequence with Deborah Kerr is, I think, hugely erotic. My colleagues on *This Morning* used to groan because whenever we were discussing musicals on the programme or interviewing somebody like Josie Lawrence, who was appearing as Anna in the new London production of *The King and I*, I always insisted that we included clips of this sequence because I thought it was so sexy.

I was very amused recently when Richard and I were watching a re-run of *South Pacific*. This film used to be one of my mother's favourites but, until I watched it on TV, I never realized how 'camp' it was. All the guys were so obviously gay and there they were singing their hearts out in numbers like, 'There Ain't Nothing Like a Dame'.

I'm not really into stage musicals, but I love *Phantom of the Opera*. Richard and I first went to see this on a charity night, and we were absolutely transfixed by it. Since then we've seen it several times, and the company always knows when I'm there because I'm the first to burst into tears.

Reading is still one of the greatest loves of my life and, apart from watching the News, some documentaries, period dramas and Ruth Rendell and P.D. James, and above all *The Simpsons*, I always choose books in preference to television. I practically lived in the public library as a child, and *Little Women*, *Anne of Green Gables* and the Jane Austen novels have never dated for me. I wasn't particularly happy at Manchester High, but it did give me a very good classical education. Shakespeare still astonishes me. The 'to be or not to be' syndrome has fascinated me all my life, and my favourite play remains *Hamlet*, probably because, like him, I find making decisions very difficult. Procrastination and analysis-paralysis is me! One of the reasons I hate shopping is that I can never decide what to buy – or, for that matter, what to cook. Years ago, when I was trying to be the perfect mother and wife, I used to have huge cooking sessions at weekends and freeze everything under the sun, but not now! These days I agree with something Shirley Conran said in *Superwoman*: 'Life's too short to stuff a mushroom'!

I love food, but the older I get the more I find myself reacting to fashionable menus. I sit in restaurants looking at a plate of the latest food fad and yearn for the delicious comfort foods my mother used to cook for me when I was a child: Lancashire hot pot, Irish stews and braised liver. Mum's *pièce de résistance*, and one of my all-time favourites, was a pie made with shin of beef and sliced potatoes, stewed with onion, water and seasoning, and then covered with a very thick, golden-brown pastry crust. Served with bowls of red cabbage, this was absolutely mouth-watering. So were her broth and dumplings. Made at the last moment, the dumplings were popped into a bubbling cauldron of potatoes, carrots, pearl barley and shin of beef, and served up in a deep soup plate. Whenever I was ill or off-colour this was the best comfort food in the world.

Apart from his tuna fish dish, Richard never did any cooking until he met me. Since then, he's learned! He now makes an excellent spaghetti bolognese, one of our favourite standbys, and a good chicken stew with peppers and rice. He's good, but not as good as he thinks he is! Real cooks, in my view, don't stick slavishly to recipes. They toss the books aside, trust their instincts and get all adventurous with sherry and other seductive flavourings. When we were on *This Morning*

Richard used to get terribly enthusiastic about the cookery items, especially if they involved fish dishes which he loves. He'd bring the recipes home, rush off to buy the ingredients and set to in the kitchen. He is good in the sense that he's prepared to work very hard at it all. I, for example, can't be bothered to cook a roast every Sunday, but he doesn't mind doing it and it's always excellent.

I know some people speculate that if we were not as happy as we are, we might come to an arrangement to stay together for the sake of the job, but there is no way that Richard and I would ever do that. We've both been in marriages that didn't work, we both know how painful that is, and neither of us would ever be prepared to go through that again. Fortunately, we are still very much in love, so there's not a problem. As far as I'm concerned my relationship with Richard and the children has always – and will always – come first. He's all-important to me, the very quality of the air I breathe. He gives me the strength to do the job we do and makes all the hard work bearable. If our private life was unhappy, I'd be the first to say, 'This is a sham, I'm going'; and if any job ever threatened our relationship I'd quit the job.

One of the reasons we are such a good team and so happy to be 'joined at the hip' is because we're so different. I tend to be rather melancholic, but he has a phenomenal talent for being happy and making the most of whatever's happening. I 'ground' him, he 'floats' me. Not surprisingly, the two songs I associate most with falling in love with him are Stevie Wonder's 'I Just Called to Say I Love You' and Kylie Minogue's 'I Should Be So Lucky'.

11: RICHARD

Moving *This Morning* to London was, without a doubt, risky. For a start, there was an understandable backlash in certain quarters in the north-west who thought the show was going to become metropolitan and would lose its provincial flavour. This, however, was something that Judy and I were determined to avoid. Anyway, we'd always been careful not to 'localize' the show. All designated places seem to generate antipathy. Lots of northerners think the capital is full of metropolitan wankers; and lots of southerners are equally abusive about Liverpool and the north. Everyone else – east, south-west, Wales and Scotland – hate both of them. This happy isle!

We always knew that if we made a song and dance about *This Morning* being based in the Albert Dock, then people in Bristol, Grimsby or London would say, 'So what! We've got good docks, too. Don't keep ramming your Liverpool credentials down our throats.' So, from the beginning, we were always very careful to make the show 'stateless' and come from 'television land'. Of course, everyone knew we were in Liverpool, and that was good for the city, but we didn't want to labour the point. We called Albert Dock 'the dock'; and our announcers only occasionally said, 'Now over to Liverpool.' It was almost always, 'Over to *This Morning* with Richard and Judy.' If we could maintain that approach when we came to London, we decided, we'd be all right.

'Please don't think we're going to betray the programme's northern roots,' we told the press, 'because we will never do that. If anybody's ever snotty about the north, we'll take them on. The main reason we're going is to facilitate travel arrangements for our guests.'

Many people, however – particularly Liverpudlians – remained suspicious that *This Morning* would never be the same again; something that was confirmed when, just before we left Liverpool, the *Manchester Evening News,* a really gutsy paper that was usually a good friend of ours, ran a phone poll, asking their readers: 'Are Richard and Judy betraying their northern roots by leaving?' The answer was a hundred per cent, 'Yes.' Nobody, not one single viewer, phoned in to say we were not! Oh, well, we were just going to have to prove them wrong.

Judy and I had to find somewhere to live in London, plus a new school for Jack and Chloe. There wasn't much time. Granada had only finalized its decision in November 1995 and we were due to start transmitting the show from our new studio in August 1996. To compound the problem, nobody could tell us for sure exactly where the studio would be. First, we were told Teddington, then St Katharine's Docks. It was not until Christmas, with only six months to go, that Granada decided on the South Bank.

Annie Sweetbaum, our agent, was fantastic. With the show still on the air in Liverpool, Judy and I had no time for house-hunting in London and, as I'd been away from the capital since 1976, I hadn't a clue about where to look. Annie, who lived in Regent's Park, which we couldn't even begin to afford, whittled down the options and came up with a game-plan.

'What you need,' she said, 'is an area that has good schools and shops, a sound sense of community and a village at its centre.'

Obviously. But where?

The house also had to be big enough for Judy's mum to live with us and have her own accommodation. Her husband and all the relatives of their generation were dead. One son was in Suffolk, the other in Leeds, so, once we left, there would be nobody to keep her company in Manchester.

Annie narrowed the search down to four houses. Then, one snowy day in February 1996, with only four months to go before we were due to finish in Liverpool, Judy and I came down to London to spend the weekend at Annie's. By then, Hampstead was on the top of our list; and when we went there on the Saturday morning, it was love at first sight. The horse pond at the top of the main high road was frozen over and there were kids skating on it. Hampstead village was like an idyllic snow-covered picture postcard. If I'd been directing a romantic film I'd have had a scene written at once just to use the location.

The first three houses we looked at were too small. The fourth – the one we now live in – was perfect. One thing Judy and I have in common is the ability to make snap decisions together. We decided there and then to buy it.

The price was devastatingly high, twice what we had expected to pay; and, although after eight years on *This Morning* we'd managed to clear our debts and build a nest egg, we didn't have anything like the money to buy it. We would now be saddled with a massive mortgage, be hundreds of thousands of pounds in debt, and be back almost where we had started in 1988. It was a pretty scary moment but we reassured ourselves with the thought that if Granada was prepared to take such a huge financial gamble in uprooting the programme, we should, too.

We were also very touched that so many of *This Morning*'s team were keen to take the same risk and move south with us. In fact, by the time we arrived in London and opened for business on 3 September 1996, we were at the head of an invasion force made up of scousers and scallies. Our tough optimistic northern army set up camp on the Thames South

Bank. There was a strong *esprit de corps* and everyone was up for the coming challenge. Good days.

There was a central mantra for the editorial team: 'This show is not a London show; not a metropolitan show. It's a provincial programme.' Many people use the word 'provincial' in a derogatory way, but we said it with pride and, once we started broadcasting from the capital, we never had a shot of St Paul's, 'the Wheel' or Westminster on the set, and we rarely went up on the roof to show a panoramic view. That would have been tantamount to saying, 'We're in London. You're not.' All wrong.

A few months into the first run, we had an opportunity to show that we had meant what we'd said just before we left Liverpool. During a phone-in about marriage on the rebound, an obviously unhappy woman began to slag off our old city.

'When I got married, I should have known I was making a mistake,' she said. 'My husband was a Liverpudlian.'

'Sorry,' I interrupted, surprised, 'you are joking?'

'No, I'm not,' she snapped back. 'People from Liverpool are genetically all a bit touched – mad.'

'Congratulations on a fine display of gross ignorance,' I snapped back in turn. 'You're off the line. Goodbye.'

I wasn't being cute; in fact I was surprised at how genuinely angry I felt.

That evening's *Liverpool Echo* reported that we had obviously meant what we'd said and that we weren't letting anybody get away with snide comments about Liverpool. As far as Manchester was concerned, woe betide a guest or caller who took a pot-shot. Judy wouldn't hesitate to steam in. We were happy in London, but neither of us would take any crap about the north.

———

On the personal front, there was the kids' future to be taken into account. Tom and Dan were no problem. By then they'd been to college, were ready to leave home, and wanted to rent their own flat. They were thrilled when we sorted these out for them. Jack and Chloe, ten and nine at the time, were a different matter. They were absolutely furious with us for wanting to move to London. They were very happy at their junior school, Ladybarn House, Cheshire, thank you very much, liked its headmaster, Mr Bonner, their teachers, and their friends, and didn't want to leave just to suit us.

'Well, yes,' we kept saying, 'but when you're thirteen you'll have to move on anyway.'

'But that's three years away,' they kept wailing.

'Your *work*!' Chloe kept exploding, spitting out the words.

I felt guilty of course. We were moving because of our careers. I hated the idea of unsettling them, but I knew there would be benefits for all of us in moving to London. I did my best to comfort them and keep their chins up; and explained over and over that sometimes mums and dads did have to up sticks and move on; that we understood it was a wrench for them, but that it would also be an adventure and we would find them equally nice schools where, in no time at all, they'd be just as happy. They were not convinced and spared no effort to make sure we knew this.

Once in Hampstead, Chloe went to a school just around the corner from where we now lived. There's no school uniform there, the kids call the teachers by their first names, and goats nibble the grass of the playing field. Over-liberal and laid-back? No. It's is a small miracle, empowering its pupils to take responsibility for themselves and still enjoy their precious childhood. Chloe was settled in by the end of her first term – quite an achievement.

Jack, though, was a different matter. At that time, he was a very free spirit. He really needed to be dragooned into doing any work, and we thought he might try to take advantage of

Chloe's school's deceptively relaxed approach. So we entered him in a tough exam at a north London grammar school and he passed. We thought we were home and dry, but we weren't. For him, the school turned out to be a nightmare. He was plagued by its rules, regulations and punishments for relatively minor misdemeanours. He was totally overwhelmed.

It was not until the last night of the Easter holidays, when he'd been there for two terms, that we began to realize just how unhappy he was. That evening, listening to his tearful outpourings of why he didn't feel he'd ever fit in, I felt dreadful. This was, in many ways, a repeat of my own experience at grammar school, and something I'd always sworn I'd never put my own son through. I'd forgotten how like me Jack is. We'd obviously made a fatal error in placing him in a rigid single-sex school, and he had clearly been suffering and putting up with a great deal. Parenthood, however well intentioned, is always an inexact science, but I just couldn't believe how dumb I had been.

After Judy had spoken to him, too, we said, almost in unison, 'Fine, you're never going back there. We can't have you being this unhappy.'

'Do you really mean it?' he asked, his face lighting up.

'Absolutely,' we said. 'We'll get you a private tutor until we can get you into another school.'

'No,' he said – and I thought this was really brave – 'I think I should go back until you can find me somewhere else.'

After we explained to the school why we were taking Jack out, they could not have been more understanding. His Head of House then recommended his sister's school, which had previously offered him a place along with Chloe.

'Oh, God,' I said, still riddled with guilt, 'we could have sent him there two terms ago.'

But there were no places left. So I wrote, phoned, visited, begged and lobbied on a weekly basis. I would have streaked round Trafalgar Square if that could have helped.

By sheer good luck, a place did become available, and when Jack went there for a couple of trial days he loved it. They also loved him and he was accepted. The school worked its magic and, like Chloe, he settled in extraordinarily quickly. As I write these words, he's sitting opposite me on the other side of the table, completing an essay – they call it 'course-work' now – on the policy of appeasement in 1938. He's fifteen, focused and, thanks to his school, happy. We got away with it.

None of the kids seems to have taken too much stick because of who we are and what we do on telly. Maybe they don't tell us about remarks like, 'Your mum and dad are crap,' or 'Your mum and dad do a really crap programme.' We've always given them the same advice as Terry Wogan gave his kids twenty years ago: 'Just say, "You're right – that's what we keep telling them!"'

'If people do say anything nasty,' I've always explained to them, 'it's usually just to get a reaction. But, hey, maybe they're expressing a sincere opinion!'

Only recently Tom told me that while I was on remand, waiting to go to court on the Tesco shoplifting charges, some kids at his Manchester school told him they were 'dead impressed': 'Hey, your dad's been accused of shoplifting. Wicked, man!'

Tom said he was baffled at getting this kind of kudos. Meanwhile his own group of friends were quietly supportive. Maybe this whole thing about kids with 'celeb' parents having a hard time at school is over-hyped. Anyway, sooner or later, most kids are embarrassed by their parents; and I don't think ours are much more so because we happen to work on TV. They're certainly not blasé or over-sophisticated. When George Michael came for Sunday lunch one day, they were utterly agog. Mind you, so were we. (He'd made a huge donation to our Christmas appeal and we asked him round to say a big personal thank you.)

Anybody who winds up in the public eye takes some pre-cautions to protect their children, but we're always comforted by the thought that there are lots of people who are far more well known and well off than us, and they live perfectly ordinary unmolested lives with their kids in this country.

There was one terrible time when we thought Jack had been abducted and, for twenty agonizing minutes, we had a tiny glimpse into the hell that enfolds parents when a child goes missing. It was Christmas Day 1996. We'd been living in Hampstead for about five months. Jack was ten. It was three o'clock and Rory Bremner was about to give Channel Four's alternative Queen's speech and an impersonation of Princess Diana. I sat down to watch, and Judy was in the kitchen doing bits and pieces. Jack was getting restless, wanting to take one of his Christmas presents, a remote-controlled truck, on to the Heath opposite. We were quite happy to let him do this, provided he stayed within sight of our sitting-room windows and didn't wander off.

'Keep looking,' I said to Tom and Dan, who were watching Rory Bremner with me, 'and make sure you can still see Jack.'

'Fine,' they replied.

About fifteen minutes later, Tom suddenly said, 'Oh! Jack's gone.'

I crossed to the window and, sure enough, although there were a few people on the Heath, including parents with babies and children getting some fresh air after Christmas lunch, Jack was nowhere to be seen. It all looked perfectly friendly and safe, and I called out to Judy, 'Has Jack come in?'

'No,' she called back. 'Not through the kitchen.'

Feeling slightly uneasy, I went out into the hall and, thinking he might have gone upstairs to his room, first called then shouted his name. There was no answer.

'Are you sure you haven't seen him?' I said, going into the

kitchen. 'Are you sure he hasn't come through here and gone into the garden?'

'No,' she said. 'The door's locked. Why?'

'He's not on the Heath,' I replied.

'He must be,' she said. 'You just haven't looked properly.'

I went out of the front door and crossed over the road. It was about half past three on one of the shortest days of the year, the sky was overcast and a mist was forming. The families and people walking dogs had vanished. Jack was still nowhere to be seen.

'Jack, *Jack*,' I yelled, fighting down the beginnings of panic. There was no response.

Turning round, I saw a couple with a dog coming through some bushes and, sprinting over to them, I said, 'Have you seen a boy in a blue jumper?'

'No,' they replied. 'Have you lost him?'

'I don't know. I mean, no. He was . . .'

'Is he there?' Judy called out from behind me.

'No,' I yelled back. 'I can't find him.'

By now Tom and Dan were doing a room-by-room search of the house, just in case he was listening to a personal stereo and hadn't heard us shouting. Then, hope dwindling, we unlocked the back door and searched the garden. Nothing. We ran back on to the Heath.

Judy, who had joined up with me by then, voiced my own worst fear: 'Oh, God, Richard,' she said, 'we've lost him. Some bastard must have seen him playing with his truck, and said, "Oh, I've got one of those in the car – come and see," and Jack's been taken. Richard, he's been taken.'

We'd always warned our kids about going anywhere with strangers, but children are vulnerable to clever persuasion. I had a sickening image of Jack climbing into a stranger's car, and now being miles away. I fought back another, stronger, surge of panic.

'Let's think,' I said desperately. 'Is there anywhere else he could have gone? What about the neighbours'?'

The family who used to live in our house had only moved half a dozen houses up the road and they had sons of Jack's age. I didn't really think he would have done that without asking us. He never had before. But I ran back to our house and telephoned them.

'Hello, Richard. Happy Christmas,' the mother said.

I could hear a party going on in the background. 'Jan, is Jack there?'

'Why?' she said, startled by my brusqueness. 'What's wrong?'

'Is he there?'

'No. We've got lots of kids here, but not Jack. Hold on, I'll just double-check.'

Time stretched lazily, agonizingly, then snapped back as she returned to the phone.

'No, he's not here, Richard. He's not been round all day.'

That was that. It was as if all the doors that might have led us to Jack had slammed shut, one by one. We had checked and rechecked every possibility and now we had to accept the only option remaining.

'I'm calling the police,' I said to Judy.

As I started to punch out 999 on my cellphone I could see Tom and Dan racing about the Heath, checking shrubs and ditches. I was just about to press the third 9 when a tiny door opened in my brain. The people next door had a dog. Sometimes Jack went round to play with it. He always told us before he left and he hadn't done it for weeks, but maybe . . .

Oh, God, I thought as I ran to their front door, if he's not there, we've lost him. Please, God, let him be there.

A couple walking down the road heard me talking to myself and stared. They obviously thought I was deranged – and I was.

'Is he there? Is he there?' Judy called from our front step.

I hammered on our neighbours' door. There was no answer.

They were out. Oh, God! I pressed the bell in despair. Still nothing, but as I turned away I suddenly caught the faint sound of voices. They were all at the back of the house. An eternity later, the door opened. Our neighbour, Sandy, stood there, cracker hat on, glass in hand.

'Hi, Richard. Happy Christmas!'

'Is Jack here?'

Sandy seemed to be speaking at quarter speed. 'Yes. He's in the garden.'

I concertinaed on her doorstep, all haunches and funny breathing.

'He brought his truck round to show us. He's playing with the dog,' she said, shocked. 'Richard, are you all right?'

'We couldn't find him anywhere. We thought he'd been . . . he'd been . . .'

Her eyes widened. 'We thought you knew he was here. God, I'm so sorry.'

Jack appeared behind her.

'Hi, Dad,' he said chirpily, clutching his truck.

When I was ten there was a fire at the gasworks at the end of our road. Me and my mates snuck through the police cordon and stood happily watching the firemen desperately trying to put out the flames jetting from a pipe directly on to the biggest gasometer. Then we were spotted, bundled into a squad car and driven home. My mother's language, when she learned what I'd done, was truly unprecedented.

Let's just say that a generation later, history repeated itself on another doorstep, almost word for word.

———

All parents can become paranoid about their children, given the right stimuli. We've never felt, because we've ended up doing a job in the public eye, that ours are in any more or any less danger, in any respect. But there's no denying the *frisson* that rippled through television immediately after Jill Dando was murdered. Suddenly everyone was watchful. Oddballs and nutcases had a field day with hoax threats to individuals working in front of camera.

We'd known Jill through her appearances on *This Morning* and occasional meetings at parties and awards ceremonies. She was one of those naturally affectionate, enthusiastic people. She presented Judy and me with our first National Television Award at the Albert Hall. We both thought she looked incredibly happy and lovely that night in the sparkly red dress that she was subsequently to be shown in so often in television footage a few months after her appalling murder. We went up on the stage of the Royal Albert Hall that night to collect the award. She kissed Judy and teased me by pulling my hair, and whispered, 'I'm so chuffed for you both.' She was warm and generous and full of life. Of course, she was also engaged and obviously in love.

The day she was shot, Judy and I were having lunch in a London restaurant when Nick Bullen, our then editor, phoned us.

'Something unimaginable's happened,' he said. 'Jill Dando's been murdered.'

It was *so* unbelievable it took Nick at least a minute to convince me I hadn't completely misheard him. Like everybody else, Judy and I were left suspended in a state of shock and disbelief. The national response was so similar to the reaction to Princess Diana's death that we both felt Jill's killer, whoever he was, might have been trying in some utterly sick and disturbed way to re-create, actually cause, an echo of that response. If so, he certainly succeeded.

Like Judy, I've always felt hugely privileged to do the kind of work we do. For a start, I often meet my childhood heroes and the stars that my parents adored. Eric Morecambe died before *This Morning* went on the air, but we did interview Ernie Wise. All the time I was talking to Ernie, I was aware how pleased my dad would have been. He'd also have been thrilled to see me interviewing Denis Norden. Years before *It'll Be Alright on the Night*, Denis was one of my dad's showbiz heroes. He loved listening to his radio shows and thought he was a brilliant script-writer.

I've had my thrills, too. One of these – sadly, Judy wasn't there that day – was when the surviving members of *Dad's Army* were on the show: Bill Pertwee (ARP warden), Ian Lavender (Pike) and Frank Williams (vicar). These guys are British icons and I got a fantastic buzz out of meeting them. The best part, though, came towards the end of the interview when, through my earpiece, I was cued to take a surprise phone call: 'Someone on the line now.'

'Hello?'

'Permission to speak, Mr Madeley,' came a familiar, shaky, querulous voice.

I was blown away. It was Clive Dunn – Corporal Jones – phoning from Portugal where he runs a bar. I was still smiling happily when I left the studio an hour later.

A couple of years later some American moon-walkers came to London for a convention. One of them, the astronaut Charles (Charlie) Duke, had been with *Apollo 16* when it went to the moon. But Charlie Duke was also the mission controller who talked Neil Armstrong and Buzz Aldrin down on to the moon's surface in that first *Apollo 11* mission. That sensational landing was much hairier than any of us knew at the time: the moon capsule was almost out of fuel, the on-board computer crashed and the craft had to be landed manually. The world didn't have a clue how critical things had suddenly become, but all of us watching on TV remember Charlie Duke's southern drawl when the lunar module reported touchdown: 'You've got a bunch of guys here 'bout to turn blue!'

During his interview on *This Morning*, Charlie explained he was being absolutely literal.

When I came in on the morning of my interview with Charlie, I noticed that a very young researcher had referred to this hero of the space age, throughout the briefing notes, as 'the unforgettable Charlie Drake'! Sometimes it pays to have grown up in the seventies.

During the programme, Charlie Duke said, 'The moon smells – something that none of us guys was prepared for. It smells of iron filings.' He told us that after the astronauts had completed their first moon-walk and returned to the landing craft, their suits were covered in dust and they all smelled like 'rusty buckets after the rain'. I was entranced; I could hardly believe I was sitting opposite this guy who had walked on the moon. As a teenager I'd read everything to do with the space programme. Astronauts were my heroes and to be there talking to Charlie Duke was so unbelievable that the hairs on the back of my neck were standing up.

He was full of insights into what it's like to go into space. Until then, I'd always assumed weightlessness was a gradual process as the rocket surged further and further away from the earth into space. But Charlie explained it's not like that. As the rocket blasts off and the G-force pushes you back into your seat, you're pinned there during the rocket's acceleration into space. Once there, the motors cut out. Instantly, the sensation of weightlessness takes over: one moment you feel exceptionally heavy, the next, you're floating under your harness. Incredible. Charlie had an engineer's approach to space. He said he hadn't had any deeply religious or spiritual moments; when walking on the moon he simply knew he was poking around a rather big satellite of the earth. I loved talking to him.

When I went back to my dressing-room, there on the table

was a framed, signed picture of him on the moon, next to the lunar module. He'd signed it: To Richard, a salute from *Apollo 16*, Charlie Duke. His hand is snapped to his space helmet which reflects the grey lunar surface. The picture has pride of place in our living-room. I mean, *that's* what I call an autograph.

Speaking of personal treasures, two of our closest friends whom we owe to *This Morning* are Caron Keating and her husband, Russ Lindsay. Our friendship began when Judy was recovering from her hysterectomy and Caron was my co-presenter on the show for three months. Any way you looked at it, it was a difficult gig, but Caron handled it with instinctive and astute judgement. She did a great, yet consciously understated job, and we hit it off right away. Having quickly become good friends, we found we had a shared love for Cornwall; and soon after Judy and I had bought our place there, it turned out that Caron and Russ had decided to move permanently to a fishing town nearby, and our families have now become close in every sense of the word. Russ, who is a surfer in his spare time, keeps promising to teach me and I keep pretending I already know how to. Old friendships are wonderful, but new ones as you approach the middle years are an unlooked-for blessing.

Sometimes an interview can have a poignancy that isn't apparent at the time. After a long period in mourning for her beloved Michael Hutchence, Paula Yates made a tentative appearance with us on *This Morning*. At the time she was fronting a new TV series about boy bands and had just written a book about them. The boy band series was her first on-screen job after a string of personal tragedies: her divorce from Bob Geldof, the death of Michael Hutchence, and the amazing – but true – discovery that Hughie Green was her dad. She'd taken some really rough knocks and was struggling to come out the other side.

When she arrived, she was very tense and having second thoughts about whether to come on the programme. Paula had said she was now ready to talk about all the awful things that had happened to her, but suddenly she felt today wasn't the day. With ten minutes to go before the show was due to start, I went to her dressing-room to reassure her. When I went in, she was very nervy and pale, and her friends were looking concerned.

'Look,' I said, 'if you don't want to do this, don't do it. Follow your instincts and go home. It's only a fucking TV interview. If your heart says "no", leave now. But if it's just nerves, then you know you'll be okay. Everyone knows you've been through the mill. But if you're not ready to talk about that, it's fine. We'll just say you're stuck in traffic; we can do this another time.'

'No,' she replied, 'it's all right really. I've got to move on and I want to do this.'

So we intro'd the programme with Paula Yates, and on she came. She put on a really great show of bravado and was very funny in a dark kind of way about discovering that Hughie Green was her father.

'It's one thing to discover irrefutably through DNA evidence that the man you always thought was your father isn't, and another man is,' she said. 'But Hughie Green, I ask you! *Hughie Green?! He* was your dad?'

She also spoke movingly about Michael's death and getting her life back together again with her children, and of her hopes for a calmer, more tranquil future with them.

Weeks later Paula was dead. She'd taken heroin, but no one who knew and loved her believed it was anything other than an accident.

This Morning, then, rolled on: a daily, unceasingly changing mix of the tragic, the achingly funny, the quirky and the shocking, the headline-making and the utterly trivial.

We lived and breathed the show. But for how much longer?

12: JUDY

By the year 2000, thanks to our jobs on *This Morning*, we no longer had to rent a cottage every time we went to Cornwall because we'd been able to buy one in Talland Bay. The idea of doing this had first come centre stage in 1994. Noticing that Rita Tushingham's house was up for sale in the *Sunday Times* property section, we went to view it and very nearly bought it. Tempted though we were, we didn't actually do it because Polperro is so busy with tourists in the summer, and we were worried that, once it became known we owned the house, we'd be pointed out on loudspeakers every time the boat trips from the harbour went past. If people then started walking up to the house, we'd never again have the wonderful peace and quiet we'd experienced up till then in Cornwall.

Soon after this, having got caught up in *This Morning*'s move to London and buying our Hampstead house, we shelved the idea of buying a cottage. A couple of years later, though, thanks to a chance meeting at a Cornish crossroad during a summer break, the search for our dream cottage was once again set in motion. Pausing at Talland to let another car come across, we realized the driver was John Bowe, an actor we'd interviewed several times on *This Morning*.

'Hi, what are you doing here, John?' Richard asked.

'I live here,' John replied.

'Oh, God, you lucky so-and-so,' we said in unison.

John then told us that when the television series *Poldark* was being filmed, one of the locations was Lansallos Beach, and he and his wife, Emma, had fallen in love with the Talland Bay area and had moved there.

'Our place is just down the road,' he said. 'D'you want to come and have a look?'

'Yes, please,' we said.

We knew at once why they had bought it. The house, the garden and the setting were absolutely perfect, and our idea of a dream come true.

'You lucky people,' we said.

During the next three years, while we were settling into our new life in London, we often thought longingly of this place. Then, in 1999, when we were once again on a Cornish break, Richard, who by then was getting very itchy feet, said he wanted to start looking at some properties.

'I don't,' I said firmly. 'We're only just recovering financially from buying the London house.'

'Yes, but . . . Why don't I just pop into the estate agent's in Looe and see what's on offer?' he replied.

On the day he did this, I remained decisively in the car but, when he came out, he was buzzing with excitement and said, 'Judy, you'll never guess – John and Emma Bowe's house has just come on to the market, literally this morning. The estate agent's not even got the printed details yet.'

So seduced – as I always am by Richard! – I agreed that there was no harm in giving John and Emma a call.

'Yes,' John replied when we did, 'it is true. We're moving up to Manchester because of my work on *Coronation Street*.'

'Can we come and see it again?' Richard asked.

'Of course. Come and have dinner with us,' he replied.

We bought the cottage on the spot that night.

'We really don't want to leave this place,' John told us, 'but if we've been keeping it warm for you two, we won't mind half as much.'

Since then, John and Emma have become two of our dearest

friends; we have so much to talk about and get on with them extraordinarily well. In fact, they are now godparents to Jack and Chloe.

Once we moved into the house, we were situated just down the road from Talland Church. Built in the fifth century on a pagan Celtic hill site, overlooking the sea, this is a very holy place. The grounds have a little stream running through them, and there are ancient headstones in the graveyard. Inside the nave of the church there are some wonderfully ancient engravings and drawings. From the moment we entered this church we responded to the centuries of concentrated worship within it and to its spectacularly beautiful surroundings, and we always made a point of visiting it every time we were in Cornwall.

Neither of us is particularly religious in the sense of regularly going to church services but we do pray and, over the years, we have become increasingly aware of the spiritual dimensions to life, and this had made us regret ever more strongly that, in our haste to get married as soon as my divorce came through, we didn't get married in a church.

During the summer of 2000 we decided that this regret, which we'd shared for so many years, could be put right. This was a perfect moment to ring the vicar, the nicest and funniest man of the cloth I have ever met, and ask him to bless our marriage and, if Jack and Chloe agreed, christen and confirm them at the same time.

The vicar thought this was a lovely thing for us to do; and Jack and Chloe, who have a lot of Jewish friends in Hampstead and who are always being invited to bar mitzvahs, didn't think it at all odd to be christened and confirmed at the age of fourteen and thirteen. On the contrary, they decided it was a brilliant idea and immediately set about inviting a couple of friends down to join in the event on 12 August 2000. We, in turn, keen to keep the occasion intimate, only invited our twins, Dan and Tom, and friends, such as Emma and John and their lovely children, and Caron Keating and her husband, Russ Lindsay, good friends of ours who live in Fowey, and a few neighbours we always socialize with in Cornwall. All in all, there were to be no more than twenty of us.

When we arrived at the church which, because of its great age and beauty, and very special beckoning atmosphere, always attracts a lot of sightseers, the visitors already there were so nice. Although they were obviously aware of what we were about to do, they were never once intrusive.

Jack and Chloe were then christened and confirmed at the centuries-old font and given a Pascal candle to symbolize their commitment to Christianity. After that, and after I had mopped my eyes, we all walked to the nave of the church where everyone, except Richard and me, sat down. The blessing of our marriage could not have been more perfect and, as we knelt down before the vicar, my handkerchief was once again fully occupied.

After this, with Richard and me feeling so happy and blessed in our love for each other, we all trooped off to the little hotel just next door to our cottage, and had a lovely buffet lunch. This included a specially made cake in the shape of a Celtic cross that was decorated with the names Jack and Chloe, and Richard and Judy.

It really was a ludicrously happy day that fulfilled all our anticipations, and we brought it to a close eating fresh lobsters, drinking champagne and enjoying a very unusual, hilarious frolic. Emma, dear friend that she is, told us she'd read somewhere that if you throw eggs over the roof of a house, provided you use fresh eggs that are not taken straight from a fridge, they will land unbroken on the other side. Now, as anybody who has ever watched *This Morning* or *Richard & Judy* knows, Richard cannot be told such a thing without immediately having to put the theory to the test for himself.

Off, at his behest, went Jack and Chloe to get some fresh eggs from the farm next door. But when, on their return, they enthusiastically obliged us by throwing these over the house, every single one of them, of course, burst and splattered its yellow and white contents everywhere. Undefeated, and unknown to Richard, Caron took Tom and Dan to the kitchen to get more eggs out of the fridge and they carefully placed them here and there in the garden.

Richard had another go at egg-lobbing, rushed round to the other side to see if they'd broken, spotted the intact eggs lying on the lawn, and joyously shouted, 'It's *worked*.'

Richard can be a tease himself, but he is easily taken in.

He wasn't kidding. But it would take somebody with very specialized knowledge of eggs, or miracles, to explain why!

If this event doesn't sound surprising enough, the next may. We ended the day by levitating our son, Tom! Caron's mother, a joyous riot of an Irish woman, is the broadcaster Gloria Hunniford, who'd actually shown Richard and me on a previous occasion how this is done. She can levitate herself. I can't. The preliminaries consist of a lot of subtle stuff to do with the mind, then, if this is successfully accomplished, you start to rise up in the air from wherever you're sitting. Tom was very cynical and laid-back about all this, but Caron and Richard succeeded in levitating him. When he went up he was genuinely terrified. 'What was that?' he shouted.

It was, I had to agree with him, all rather strange and spooky. But it made a memorable finale to a perfect day.

––––––––––

What I didn't know the day of the blessing, or almost until the end of that blissful break, was that we were about to receive a phone call from Karen Smith, our newly appointed editor on *This Morning*, followed by a fleeting visit from her; and that these two events would usher in a miserable period that would last until the autumn of 2001.

By the time Karen arrived at the cottage, Richard and I, no doubt about it, had lived through some incredibly creative and fulfilling years working on *This Morning*. It's very exciting to be in from the beginning of such an innovative programme, and to be given full rein to build it up from nothing is hugely satisfying and stimulating. Then, if you're lucky enough to have one successful year follow another, the sense of attachment that grows enters deep into your psyche.

Richard and I loved *This Morning* and, even now when we're well established on our new Channel 4 programme, *Richard & Judy*, I still find the events leading up to our leaving *This Morning* a little too raw for me to get entirely into perspective and write about. What I can express is that I found the internal politics that followed the appointment of Maureen Duffy as our new controller on the programme very difficult to cope with. I know that, with her track record in marketing, she was brought in by ITV to consolidate and boost *This Morning*'s advertising revenue, but it can prove dangerous to tamper with such a successful show. In the end, although we tried our hardest to go along with the planned changes, Richard and I, unable to feel wholehearted about some of these, decided to leave.

What I prefer to remember now are the happy times: days like those we shared in Liverpool at Albert Dock, when the view from our studio window was so breathtakingly beautiful, and the water so blue on a good day that it was like looking at a Canaletto painting. The dock was equally lovely on days when it was snowing, or when the Christmas lights were all ablaze. It may sound daft, but Richard and I invested a huge part of our hearts in *This Morning*; and I'm pretty sure that, however happy we are now and whatever happens to us in the future, those days, which encapsulated so much of our personal and professional life together, will remain engraved in my memory as one of the most exciting periods of my life.

Happily, on the tenth anniversary of *This Morning*, Nick Bullen, our editor, gave us a painting, which commemorates the show's move from Liverpool to London. Painted by Ruby Drew, a contemporary Liverpudlian artist, the theme of this is water, because our new studios were situated on the south bank of the Thames. It's a beautiful painting that also has a view of St Paul's Cathedral in the background, and it means so much to Richard and me. I often stand and study it, and remember our days on the programme.

In our heart of hearts I guess we sensed, even before Karen Smith's visit towards the end of our heavenly six-week break, that things were never going to be quite the same for us on *This Morning*. This was because, just before we left London at the end of the last series, although we were thrilled that Karen, an extremely talented girl with loads of energy, had been promoted from deputy editor to editor, we were unsettled because Dianne Nelmes, our Controller of Daytime Television, had recently been promoted to Controller of Factual Programming, and was no longer a part of the show.

Any change, in what is already a frenetic lifestyle, is always an additional stress; but at least, we had consoled ourselves, we still had David Liddiment who had complete editorial control over all commissioned ITV programmes, including ours. But obviously, because David couldn't do everything single-handed, below him were a range of controllers who reported to him on each of the programme categories, such as current affairs, drama and so on, and our controller, appointed by him, was Maureen Duffy.

When we left for Cornwall, Karen, who was very excited about her new job, was working away with tremendous enthusiasm to get the programme ready for its come-back series in September. On the day we had the surprise telephone call from her, saying that she wanted to come and see us, we replied, 'Karen, for heaven's sake, you don't need to come all the way here for a chat. Just tell us over the phone.'

'No. I really think I'd better come and see you,' she answered ominously.

When she arrived, just for the day, it turned out that Maureen Duffy, whom we had not yet had a one-to-one meeting with, had made it clear to Karen that she had very strong ideas about the way the programme needed to be changed; and Karen had been shocked to discover that all her ideas for the show that had won her the editor's job were completely unacceptable, as were her plans for the set, which had been approved by our own executives at Granada. Disconcerted by all this, she wanted to discuss her situation, and some of the other suggestions that Maureen Duffy had made concerning Richard and me and *This Morning*.

At the time of Karen's visit, we felt we had to show willing and go along with the changes; and, when we returned to London, we went in for the pre-launch shooting of the new titles and other bits and pieces. By the time *This Morning* came back on air, we had still not met Maureen Duffy properly, but we were only too aware that there were some huge rows going on at executive level about the direction the programme would be taking from then on.

Basically Maureen Duffy, in order to survive what was a general decline for ITV in its share of the television market, felt the programme needed to go 'down-market'. I must say the word 'down-market' made Richard and me prick up our ears because we were unsure what this would mean for the programme's editorial content; and we also thought that description sounded very patronizing. We knew that many of the people who watched the show enjoyed tuning in to intelligent discussions about a whole range of subjects, and that they would not be happy bunnies if drip-fed too many items on lipstick, hair, cookery, make-overs and other items of a similarly undemanding ilk.

I had strong feelings about the editorial content of *This Morning*, and I had always been wary of anybody thinking that, because our viewers were mostly women, we need not concern ourselves with serious topical issues in addition to interviewing celebrities and featuring human-interest stories. In the past I'd always dismissed this as an unacceptable sexist approach, and nothing had happened since to change my mind. Our job, as we saw it, had been to make *This Morning* a programme that was as informative as it was entertaining, and to ensure that we did this in the liveliest, most enjoyable, easily accessible way.

It soon became clear, however, that this was no longer to be the programme's or, for that matter, our agenda. Instead, like a fast, unstoppable spool of film, the lifestyle element was going to become more and more predominant, while the mixed bag of goodies that had made us so different from other shows and had won three National Television Awards was to give way to the dreaded diet of fashion, hair, beauty, home decorating and other essentially feminine topics.

During the early period of Maureen Duffy's appointment, we were mostly protected from all the rows raging around us, but we were not exactly happy knowing that others were tearing their hair out. It also became apparent, as time went by, that there was another agenda: to split Richard and me up on the screen so that each of us could present items separately. This, I must confess, worried me sick. I thought we'd fought and won that battle when *This Morning* first started, and I hated the possibility that once again I would be expected to do all the 'caring' womanly items while Richard was doing what 'macho' human-interest stuff there was left. That was the last thing he or I wanted, and there was no reason to believe that the viewers would want it either. So, placed in the position of feeling we were right back at the beginning and about to be asked to repeat what years of experience had taught us would not be successful, we were very despondent.

Taking the bull by the horns on one occasion, I said to our Granada executives, 'You can't imagine what the stress is like in the mornings when we are putting the show together. It's often very loose still and both Richard and I and the team are working fantastically hard at putting in last-minute items just before transmission. If we're now going to be told by Maureen Duffy, while all this is going on, that we also have to allocate who is to do this or that interview as well as everything else, the stress on Richard and me will be intolerable.'

Our television bosses, we felt, had to take into account both sides of the coin. When Richard and I are allowed to do a show on an equal footing, we can make it work; and we had already proved that. We rub along exceptionally well together, are quite intuitive with each other, and do not cut across each other. The audience like it, and the ratings had confirmed it. It had not always been easy for us, but it had worked because we know each other inside out, better than anybody else on the planet, and we are a great strength to each other. We are aware, of course, that there are some logistical disadvantages. Somebody in the past had once said to us, 'Why do you have to have time off together?' But the answer was obvious: 'We're married and we have a family!' That may be inconvenient for our TV bosses, but that was also why they wanted us in the first place and why the programme worked.

Not surprisingly, given that all this was going on, we were becoming increasingly restless. Then, one day, when we were having lunch with Amanda Ross, a brilliant producer who, together with her husband Simon, runs Cactus, an independent television production company, we were responsive when she said, 'Do you fancy breaking out of Granada?'

'At the moment, yes,' we said. 'We're feeling fed up enough to want to do that.'

'Then why don't you let me put out some feelers, without actually mentioning your names?' she replied. 'I think I could put together a really good treatment for a show you could do on another network.'

As we had already worked with Amanda three times on the *Soap Awards*, which she'd produced and we'd presented, and had got on brilliantly with her and Simon, we said, 'Okay, fine. Go ahead and let's see what you can do.'

One day, following a couple of initial flirtations, one with Sky 1, one with BBC 1, that didn't actually come to anything, Amanda, who was at a Channel 4 meeting that had absolutely nothing to do with us, nearly choked on her coffee during a chance remark.

Jo McGrath, Head of Daytime Factual Programmes at Channel 4, who used to work as a researcher on *This Morning*, suddenly said, out of the blue, that her 'Holy Grail dream' was to have Richard and Judy doing a teatime talk-show for her network.

Amanda, remaining firmly 'mum' at this time, phoned us when she got home and said, 'How would you two feel about doing something as radically different as working on a programme for Channel 4?'

Surprised for a moment, Richard and I talked it over, then replied, 'We're happy to consider it. We're certainly not happy any more where we are.'

When Jo received this news, she was, Amanda told us, 'over the moon'. Richard and I and Amanda and Simon then put a treatment together for a teatime programme, which the Channel 4 bosses said they were 'very excited' about. After lots of preliminary talks, they were then very honest and said to Richard and me, 'You realize this will be a huge risk for you. You're very big on *This Morning* at present and our programme may or may not work. Five to six in the afternoon is a funny slot to fill, and we've never tried anything like this before.'

'We don't care,' we replied. 'If you're willing to take the risk, so are we. We're getting more and more fed up every day, and we need a new challenge.'

Throughout this discussion period, I was absolutely adamant that we should not use the Channel 4 offer as a bargaining ploy with ITV. Our direct bosses there knew we were unhappy because we'd told them so, but I was determined we'd never go in and say, 'We've been offered a slot on Channel 4, and if you don't do what we say, we're going.' Richard agreed that this offer should not be used as any kind of blackmail; and that we should be absolutely upfront and say, 'Okay, we're not happy. It's time to go,' and keep the two things entirely separate.

Day after day, before Channel 4 finally phoned and confirmed that they wanted to go ahead with us, I kept saying to Richard, 'I don't really know if we're doing the right thing. Maybe we should think more carefully about this.' But as soon as the confirmation came through, I felt one of the biggest smiles ever stretching across my face from ear to ear. I was just so pleased and happy; and when I get this kind of instinctive reaction to something, I always know we've done the right thing. After that, I never thought twice about it ever again.

We're not daft; we knew from the moment that Richard and I, and Cactus and Channel 4 agreed to go ahead with the deal that there'd be bound to be some leaks to the press; and that if we didn't get the new contracts sorted and our resignations into ITV post-haste all hell would break loose. Inevitably, then, it became a mad rush to finalize what was a complex deal between us and Cactus, and Cactus and Channel 4. In essence Cactus was to be responsible for the infrastructure, the studio, the crews and the hiring of the teams; Richard and I were to be the presenters and executive producers; and Channel 4 was to pay for it all. As if getting all this sorted in a hurry wasn't bad enough, everything then went totally berserk when Richard decided, after another call from our press office, that it had to be completed in one day by midnight to pre-empt the news breaking in the *Daily Mirror*, the *Daily Mail* and the *Sunday Times*.

On the day, the lawyers were somewhat bemused, and kept scratching their heads and exclaiming, 'It's all so sudden. Would you, please, just run through that again for us?'

At about ten o'clock that night, when the most important things had been finalized and only details needed to be settled, I decided to go home. By then I was feeling very tired and beginning to lose focus, and I was also worried about Jack and Chloe being left for so long on their own. They knew what was going on because we'd told them all about our clandestine plans and discussions, and they'd been very patient for months while we were preoccupied, but I knew by then they must be nearing the end of their tether. They'd also been brilliant. Having been sworn to secrecy, they hadn't even breathed a whisper to their best friends.

'I completely trust you, Richard,' I said as I stood up to leave. 'I know whatever you agree from now on in will be fine for both of us. I'm happy, and if there are any problems you can call me at home.'

Back at the house, I put on my dressing-gown and sat talking to the kids until they went to bed. Then, feeling exhausted, I watched a bit of telly. Richard only phoned once from the lawyer's office about holiday entitlement, then rang me again on the mobile as he was driving home.

'That's *it*, Judy,' he said, sounding very excited. 'We've done it. I've signed the contract already, and now I'm bringing it home with me for your signature. Amanda and Simon, who are coming with me, can then take it back and give it to Channel 4.'

When we finally went to bed that night in the early hours of Friday morning, not a day, thank God, when we did *This Morning*, we decided that, if we were lucky enough to sleep after such a day, we'd lie in later in the morning. But we both woke up, as usual, at the crack of dawn, thinking, Oh, my God! But even as we did so, and even though we knew we had another helluva day ahead of us, we knew we'd done the right thing.

Our first concern that day was that we had to resign from *This Morning*; and, given our bosses at Granada and ITV's chief executives were very good friends of ours, people we'd known for years, we just knew this was going to be another highly charged emotional day. Another of my priorities was to sort out Lee, the guy who did my hair and make-up for *This Morning*, so I'd be ready for the TV cameras and photographers at the Channel 4 press conference later in the day. Unable to tell Lee the truth, I'd have to fib and pretend I needed this done for a *Soap Awards* press conference.

On the way to the ITV building, when I was already feeling apprehensive, the mobile rang. It was a friend of ours who worked for ITV in Manchester.

'Richard,' he said, 'have you got a minute?'

Richard realized instantly, from the tone of his voice, that he knew something.

'No, mate, I'm really sorry,' he replied. 'I can't talk to you right now, but I'll get back to you as soon as I can.'

We then phoned Naomi Walsh, our personal assistant, whom we'd taken into our confidence, and asked her to arrange a meeting, like now, with our immediate boss, Grant Mansfield.

A few minutes later Naomi rang back. 'There's a bit of a problem,' she said.

'Why?' Richard asked.

'There's a bomb scare at LWT, and nobody, including Grant Mansfield, can get into the building. They're all stuck in a police cordon.'

Unfortunately I have just lost the toss to Richard for recounting all the dramas that resulted from this, so that will have to wait for his next chapter.

What I can say is that when we did eventually get round to resigning from *This Morning*, I did not, regardless of what the press said later, cry or end up in floods of tears. Grant Mansfield, although obviously shocked, was never once angry with us, and actually said some very kind things to Richard and me. This did catch me a bit off guard and, doubtless because I'm something of a softie, my eyes did water a little. But that's all. I was, however, very tense.

Afterwards we drove off, leaving Grant to mop up things at his end by sending people buzzing like blue-arsed flies all over the building. It couldn't, given the bomb scare, have been a worse time for us to resign. Later we were able to laugh about this, but it was a crying shame because, without that fiasco, it could have been handled so much better and avoided many of the grievances that followed.

I do regret certain things. Steve Morrison, LWT's chief executive, for example, is a very old friend of ours who lives near us in Hampstead, but we couldn't even tell him face to face ourselves, and he missed our handwritten fax because he was in a meeting, and heard the news third-hand by chance. Given the pressures created by the press leaks, we did what we could to handle it all well, but . . .

On the whole, though, despite the press coverage that claimed that ITV was absolutely furious with us, there were never, regardless of what the reporters said, any huge rows or bust-ups with any of the execs, including David Liddiment, another old friend. David was not happy – none of them was – but there was no personal animosity.

Everyone was obviously shaken by the suddenness of it all. It's not nice to be left in a state of shock, feeling vulnerable, and at a serious disadvantage with the media. But, in the circumstances, we did everything as decently as we could. I've got a strong moral conscience and I'd certainly put my hand up if I thought we'd behaved in a shitty underhand way, but we didn't. I know ITV would have liked us to give them the opportunity to negotiate another deal with us; but I also know they understood why we acted in the way we did.

At one level after we'd resigned from *This Morning*, it was all very strange and disorientating. Except for a brief period in my early career I had always worked for ITV, and now suddenly I'd left that 'family' and I was signed up for Channel 4. At least, I comforted myself, there would be some familiar faces there, including Sharon Powers, an ex-editor of ours. *This Morning* had always been a huge training ground for young people who, having started their careers on that show as runners, then researchers, then producers, had then dispersed to other networks, including Channel 4. And I was so touched when I saw so many of their faces among the people who welcomed us into the Channel 4 building after our first photo-shoot there.

Up until that moment it had been a very tense day. We knew our new bosses were completely behind us, but we had wondered how others there would react to our appointment. Channel 4 equals young, trendy, cool, hip, and we are none of those things. Would they think we were too old, too middle of the road, too 'pop' for that network? We were confident that we would be an asset to the channel and that we would make the right kind of programme for it, but how would they feel? Would they approve? The answer came in their incredibly generous welcome, a spontaneous outburst of warmth, clapping and cheers that even brought tears to the eyes of the execs.

After our first Channel 4 press conference, the *Daily Mail* claimed I looked 'strained', and this was then picked up by other papers, but I bloody didn't. I was perfectly composed and happy after such a reception by the staff. The story some of the journalists went ahead with, though, was that Richard had forced me to sign the contract! Nothing was further from the truth. I'm an independently minded woman, and a feminist, for God's sake! And, although these days I'm not nearly as dogmatic and as politically correct as I used to be, I will always be a feminist. In the sixties, like most kids in their early youth, I was much more feisty and with Germaine Greer all the way. I went to consciousness-raising sessions, and I took part in all the usual pro-abortion rallies and CND marches.

I still do believe in a lot of the women's lib issues that I championed then but, having matured, I now know there are certain things women cannot appreciate about men until they know them better and have married or lived with them. Men and women are different and, in some ways, it never ceases to astonish me that we can live together harmoniously. But I really appreciate them now. Whereas, at one time, I would have stated categorically that they are too aggressive and belligerent (which, of course, they sometimes are), I now understand that their aggression is a necessary under-belly, akin to an energy that's useful for getting things done and for supporting and protecting families.

I absolutely believe that, in spite of the conflicts that inevitably arise between men and women, it is a yin-yang relationship that, at its best, does achieve a natural balance, harmony and a happy life.

I am, I must emphasize, still a total feminist when it comes to things like equal pay and equal opportunities. I never doubted, even when very young, that some changes of attitude were essential: that women's feelings, opinions and experiences are as valid as men's; that they do have the right for their demands for equal pay and crèches and so on to be heard and not dismissed by trades union representatives and politicians; and that trades unions and politics should not be just about men's wages, men's concerns.

But, for me, it has been an eye-opener to bring up a daughter after having had three sons. Chloe, our youngest, is utterly and totally different, sometimes almost incomprehensibly different, from her brothers. I've learned so much from being with her. Chloe, in her own way, is a deeply complicated little being, with some wonderful good points. She's gentle, warm, sweet, loving and sociable, and I've no doubt she will be a very special woman. But, God help us all if the world was left to her and her friends. She'd be happy just sitting around doing nothing but gossiping with her mates! I love the natural balance of the two sexes, and how they complement each other. Good partnerships and marriages, based on mutual respect and acceptance of differences, are very hard to achieve and need a lot of sorting out in the early stages but, if it works out, a happy marriage is a glorious blessing. So, although I remain a devout feminist, I also say, '*Vive la différence*'!

There's no doubt about it, then, that many of the radical women's lib attitudes I spouted in my early twenties, especially 'I'm not going to be the little woman at home', have become more gentle. And my feelings about Chloe, my own daughter, are that if she turns out to be the world's most brilliant housewife and mother who never wants a career other than having babies and looking after them, I'll be right behind her. I certainly won't criticize or despise her for that choice. I'll think it's fantastic.

So, determined as I am to knock the absurd idea on the head that Richard forced me to leave *This Morning* and go into the

Channel 4 deal, I must stress that Richard and I always talk everything through. We may have different ways of looking at certain things, and we certainly have different strengths and weaknesses, but if either of us is ever remotely unhappy about doing something, we don't do it. It's as simple as that. What decisions we do make are, despite what anybody else says or prints, a hundred per cent mutual.

At the end of a long and tense day, we were supposed to be going out for a celebratory dinner with Cactus and some Channel 4 execs, but we were all too knackered. So, after a few glasses of champagne, Richard and I returned home, thank God, for a normal weekend.

Our next big anxiety was: would Granada/ITV let us back on *This Morning* to work out the last ten weeks of our existing contract? Or would they say, 'Sorry, we can't have you back on the programme, and continue giving you such a high ITV profile, when you've just announced you're going to Channel 4.' This would have been bitterly disappointing for us, but an understandable managerial decision. In the event, we had no need to worry because this didn't happen, and we carried on doing *This Morning*.

What did upset me, much more than it did Richard, was that we were not allowed to do the last show of the series. I thought this was a bit petty. We'd hoped that show would be a kind of celebration when we could include lots of people we had had on during our previous thirteen years. But, instead, we had to pretend it was 'business as usual' on the Thursday and not say a proper goodbye to the viewers.

George Michael was the only person who slipped through this net, and that came about because, on a past show, he had made a donation of £50,000 to *This Morning*'s first Christmas Appeal, and the money was used to hire two planes to take needy children to meet Santa Claus in Lapland. To thank him for that, we had invited him after the programme to come round to lunch at our house; and, when he accepted, I nearly died, crippled with nerves. We're not in the habit of having superstars ringing our doorbell and coming in for lunch, and George is such a huge star that Richard said it was like having a Beatle on our doorstep. But, throughout the visit, George, who came with his partner Kenny, was absolutely charming. We had a really good time, talked for seven hours and became friends.

During our last show he phoned in, taking us completely by surprise, and said, 'I'd like to say thank you very much for easing me into the day. I've been watching the show for the last ten years. You'll be sorely missed in this household, and I'm sure a lot of other people think the same thing.' There was a pause, then he added, mischievously, 'So what time is this new show you're not allowed to talk about?' To this, Richard had to say we were under orders not to say. But afterwards, when Richard and I were alone together, we laughed about George's cheek.

I found getting through that last programme very difficult. I was almost numb with disbelief that this really was the last occasion we'd be doing what we'd done for thirteen years. Half my mind knew what was happening, the other half refused to believe it; and, although every now and again I found myself clicking into normality mode, and doing what I'd done thousands of times before, I never completely forgot I'd never be doing it again.

It was a very strange experience in which I had to keep trying to remain focused and not allow my mind to stray off into any kind of emotional hinterland. Occasionally, though, I still had flashes of how momentous this last show was for Richard and me, that this part of our life was now behind us.

I couldn't quite make it through to the credits though; of

course I did cry. I was weeping when the usual end-of-series corks started to pop just as the credits were running.

Fortunately Amanda Ross, who was like a fairy godmother in our life – 'Mrs Organized' we call her – had said, 'Look, you can't just finish the show, and then go home. That would be too much of an anticlimax. Let's do something. Invite whoever you like and we'll go out to a restaurant.'

'To be honest,' I said, 'I'd rather have something at home. I'd feel more private there and we can all talk much more freely.'

'Right, fine. Done,' Amanda said, and organized caterers and a marquee on our back lawn. We then invited all our friends from *This Morning*'s production team, including as many of our ex-editors as we could locate, and some Channel 4 people. When we got home after the last show, Amanda had been at the house all morning. She'd organized the rearranging of the furniture, made a bar in the dining-room, and put someone in charge of the kitchen.

That day, 12 July, was beautifully sunny and hot, and everyone was delighted to be outside in the garden, drinking champagne and reminiscing about the past. It was a fantastic party that started at one thirty and should have been over by six when the caterers left, but people were still there having fun at nine o'clock, saying, 'Is there anything left to eat?' 'No, go home,' we kept laughing in reply. But we ended up ordering a mega take-away from our local Indian restaurant, and everybody sat around eating that at midnight.

It felt so right and so, by then, did I. It really was a smashing consolation prize for going off air the day before the end of the show, without the occasion being marked by the usual official end-of-series staff party that always took place on Fridays.

The next day, though, we did return for this, but only to find that most of our team were not present. They'd been sent up to Bromsgrove, near Birmingham, to do a live outside broadcast from a house that the programme had decorated and was giving away to a viewer who'd won it in a competition. For us, their absence was very disappointing and, although they eventually scurried back by coach to join us, the party remained a bit of a damp squib both for them and for us, which was a shame.

The following day we celebrated Chloe's fourteenth birthday, then, at the end of the next week, still feeling rather disorientated, we all went off to Florida on holiday.

During the first week in the US, doubtless due to tension and excitement, I had terrible nightmares. I do sometimes dream about going in totally unprepared for taking my A-levels or degree but, this time, I had awful work-related nightmares. Riddled with tensions and disciplinarian attitudes, these were all about presenting a programme for which I hadn't learned my lines, hadn't got an autocue, and didn't know what I was supposed to be doing. For the first couple of weeks, they usually ended with me in the *This Morning* studio, surrounded by ITV executives, saying, 'You've behaved very wickedly.' It was not nice. When I woke up in the mornings, Richard used to say to me, 'You had one of those dreams again last night.'

Thankfully, all that started to fade as we drove and flew around, and lots of new impressions started to come in. Richard and I didn't talk much about work during that holiday but, when we did, we never had the slightest doubt that we'd done the right thing; and by the time we got back to England we'd both completely recovered from all the hype. It was, though, in some respects a very strange homecoming because we arrived back at the house just as the new series of *This Morning* was coming on air.

When I'm jet-lagged from overnight flights I always need to sleep the moment I get home, and I said to Richard, 'I'm not going to watch *TM*. If I do, I'll just get all involved and worked up, so I'm going to have a sleep.'

Richard watched it, though, and videoed it and, when I got up, we sat watching it together. It felt very strange because we were still only semi- and not quite fully detached.

Then, for the next couple of weeks of our holiday, I felt as if I were skiving off school; I was actually relieved to be writing this book, and also glad that we'd taken on the double-page column for the Saturday edition of the *Daily Express*. At least that gave me the feeling that we were doing something, and it counteracted the anxiety that we'd forgotten to start school. This feeling was actually very powerful, because all the time we'd been on *This Morning* the beginning and end of each series had coincided with the beginning and end of school terms. Now this rhythm, which was firmly imprinted on my brain, had been broken.

What really helped was knowing that everything was moving ahead with our new show, *Richard & Judy*. Cactus had found a studio, an old warehouse near the Oval, south London, and construction had commenced while we were away.

About a week after our return from America, they'd just moved the offices in, and we went to see our new TV home for the first time. We'd been warned everything was still in chaos, and I wondered how Richard would cope with that! He's obsessively tidy, so much so that this has become a joke in the family. He simply can't resist putting everything in order and picking up after everybody. When the kids were little and playing with their toys, it used to drive me mad! There they'd be, happily occupied with dolls or action-men, and Richard would come into the room and, within five minutes, all the toys would be tidied away and the kids would be wailing, 'Where's my car?' I honestly don't think he realizes he's doing it. Even now, if one of us puts something down in the house, a book or spectacles, when we go back they're gone. He's moved them. So the kids are always yelling things like, 'Dad, what have you done with my homework book?'

Most of the time it's amusing, but if you really need something in a hurry and you can't find it, it's infuriating. Worse, the awful thing is he can't remember where he's put it. Domestically, that's his most irritating habit. We've all had our fair share of arguments with him about this but, in essence, we've just had to learn to live with it.

Fortunately, on our first visit to the studio he didn't, as far as I know, get too carried away tidying up the builders' spanners, wrenches, hammers, half-used packets of screws, and the like, but I bet a couple of items were back in their bags before we left!

There was, I am delighted to report, given my early days experience at Albert Dock in Liverpool, a loo at the new studios. On that first visit this only consisted of a rather superior outside Portaloo with gold-plated taps. But I was assured that the loos would be situated in the warehouse, rather than in the car park, before the show started!

It was very strange to have something like this built especially for us. It was a great compliment, but also a huge responsibility.

All these people, I thought, have a job because we have a new programme that's going to be called *Richard & Judy*.

As I stood there, reflecting a moment on our new surroundings and new life, I remembered the occasion when, like so many other people, we'd been caught out by Michael Aspel for his programme *This is Your Life*. We already knew by then that he'd tried to do us once before, but had cancelled that attempt because of a leak. Then, in late 1996, we turned around, just as *This Morning* was ending, to find him standing behind us. We knew immediately then why we'd been getting so many false count-downs during that day's show. I had smelled a rat, and I knew something weird was going on, but I hadn't guessed what.

Our then editor, Jeff Andersen, kept saying in our earpieces, 'We've got to allow a bit more time for the weather.'

'Why?' we kept replying whenever we could. 'What's going on?'

'Oh, well, there's this little child with a present for Fred who's come in specially, from miles and miles away . . .'

It all sounded pretty unconvincing to us, and we were totally astonished when, just before the end of the show, all the team, production and researchers, suddenly appeared in the studio, followed by Michael Aspel. I just couldn't believe it. I was flabbergasted, and not a little dismayed. But, on these occasions, like it or not, you have to be a good sport and go along with it. Before you have time to collect yourself, you're whisked off in a limo and not left alone for a single moment lest you do a runner. The *This is Your Life* team is very used to calming people down, and the guy who was with us did his best to do this by keeping up a non-stop stream of conversation before unloading us from the car and taking us into a dressing-room which I swear had a guard placed outside the door!

When, after being given a glass of champagne to calm our nerves, we were taken down to the studio, we discovered that Michael Aspel had left his glasses somewhere (absolutely nothing to do with Richard tidying up!) and nothing could happen until these were found. When we finally did the show, true to *This is Your Life* form, all our relatives, friends and colleagues, past and present, popped out of the woodwork, one by one, to greet us.

I was in shock, in an absolute daze throughout. It's a strange, rather creepy experience, with a huge embarrassment factor tossed in, and I completely understand why some people refuse to go through with it. That course of action, though, would have taken more guts than I've got when Michael Aspel's around! It is also, of course, a great honour.

Now, whenever I watch *This is Your Life*, I always empathize with how the person is feeling. Actors are usually fine because they're natural performers on any stage but where others are concerned I can always tell who's enjoying it and happy to be there, and who's covering up, dying of embarrassment, and longing to get off air. Des O'Connor told us that just before it was his turn to be tapped on the shoulder by Michael, he'd gone outside to have a quick fag during a recording session. As he was standing there puffing away, he saw a coach go by with almost every single member of his family on board! It was, he said, the weirdest thing. He had no idea what was about to happen and thought he was hallucinating. It was a totally surreal experience until Michael Aspel appeared with the Big Red Book.

I thought about all this showbiz stuff as I stood in the shell of our unfinished studio. I thought about the past in terms of our careers. And I thought about how unimportant it all is. In the end all that matters is love, relationships and self-respect. Whatever happens to us in the future, I've been blessed. I've had a rich life, wonderful children and a husband I love beyond measure. And, to be honest, the rest of it is just icing on the cake.

13: RICHARD

We moved into what would turn out to be our last year presenting *This Morning*. It was September 2000, and the show
was in good shape. We'd already picked up two consecutive
National Television Awards and in a few weeks would collect
the programme's third – and some choice headlines when
Judy's bra appeared on camera and made a shameless bid
for fifteen minutes of fame.

Ratings were firm and, despite a much improved opposition
line-up on BBC 1, *This Morning* was still in pole position. No
one was complacent, though; staying at the top of the heap
is actually a lot harder than getting there. We were expecting
another tough battle to win our slot.

We also expected changes. Our launch editor and old friend
Dianne Nelmes had recently overseen the programme from her
job as Daytime Controller at the ITV Network Centre, but
now she was being promoted to run all the channel's factual
programmes. Her replacement was Maureen Duffy, whom the
press later couldn't resist dubbing 'Duffy the Vampire Slayer'.
I don't know why, other than it made a play on Sarah Michelle
Gellar's TV show, *Buffy the Vampire Slayer*. I don't think
Maureen thought that *This Morning* or any other programmes
in her stable were harbouring the undead.

Contrary to anything you might have read, there were never
any personal bust-ups between Maureen, Judy and me. But
there were significant professional disagreements between our
programme team and the new boss, and we backed the team.
These differences started before the show even came back on

341

air from its summer break: there was a row about how our new opening titles should look and Maureen won it. When we saw the new sequence during rehearsals on the first day back we were stunned; all our programme experts (Denise, Chris, Raj Persaud, etc.) had been made to nod and smile at the camera in the most peculiar way, and Judy and I were featured at the end holding what was obviously an artificial conversation. We all looked as if we'd taken triple-strength Valium.

'I know it's pants,' one programme exec said later that day. 'But we've got to let the new boss try her own ideas out. We can't say no to her from the very start. Don't worry about it. Things will settle down.'

Hmm.

————

Around this time, we had what was to turn out to be a very significant lunch with Amanda Ross at the independent television company Cactus, which is part of the Chrysalis group. We'd first met her and her husband, Simon, when ITV asked us to present the first of its *Soap Awards* in 1998. We'd since hosted two more. An awful lot of people in our business get by on a combination of bullshit and luck, but it was immediately obvious to Judy and me that Amanda and Simon were real professionals. They fizzed with ideas and knew how to get them on to the screen. The four of us got on well as friends, too. By the time we lunched with Amanda at the Ivy in September 2000, we were look-ing forward to working together again on the next *Soap Awards*.

It quickly became clear that Amanda, a truly entrepreneurial woman if ever there was one, had come to lunch with a much bigger agenda.

'I keep hearing whispers that you are seriously considering leaving *This Morning*,' she said. 'I'd be absolutely delighted to come into partnership with you and come up with some suggestions and ideas for your future.'

Stuff like this happens a lot in TV, and even if you're happy as Larry in your current job you don't respond with a coy 'Sir Jasper, I am betrothed, do not touch me.' It never hurts to check alternatives out, so we said, 'Fine. Go ahead, and let's see what you come up with.'

We knew Amanda was a tenacious person who always thought 'big' and we both sensed that if anything did come from it she was the right person to do business with.

Within weeks she returned to us with a very interesting proposal. David Bergg, the then programme director of BSkyB, had an impressive strategy for the future of Sky 1. With more and more viewers going digital, he believed it was time for his channel to challenge ITV in particular with mainstream popular programmes and get stuck into a ratings war. Were we interested in coming across?

The drawbacks were obvious. Compared to ITV, Sky 1 had a tiny audience. Critics would sneer and say we'd gone nuts. But Bergg talked a good game. He was prepared, he said, to spend an ITV-sized budget to make a programme for us on Sky. The channel could only grow, and he passionately believed the moment had come to invest seriously and upgrade. We could be part of it and help Sky 1 to move forward.

Judy and I have always tried to be brave with our careers and we've never backed away from a challenge if we thought we could make it work. We were intrigued by what, on the face of it, looked an unlikely proposal, but we were still in talks about it when internal politics at BSkyB suffered a small earthquake and David Bergg departed. (He was soon, ironically, snapped up by ITV where he had already been a demon scheduler.) His vision of the way forward for Sky 1 evaporated with his departure and a fascinating (and bloody risky!) idea quietly died.

So why didn't we go to our bosses at Granada or ITV and tell them we were seriously considering other offers (including the plans we would soon be drawing up with Channel 4)? It just felt like a rather grubby thing to do, actually. We hated the idea of being seen as trying to orchestrate some kind of bidding war. We didn't want to use genuine discussions about a career change as some kind of bent weapon to give us leverage at ITV. Either we would stay with the channel and say nothing about our close encounters with other broadcasters, or we'd make a decision to leave on its own merits. Very early on Judy and I promised each other not to use the situation to put some kind of squeeze on our old friends and colleagues at Granada. We'd either stay and try to make things work with the new boss at ITV Daytime, or make a clean and honourable break. It might have been naïve or even simplistic, but we stuck to that principle all the way along.

Meanwhile Amanda Ross was, with true chutzpah, floating ideas at BBC 1. Now BBC politics makes the kind of stuff that goes on behind closed doors on other channels look like parish council meetings. I've heard three versions of what Greg Dyke, the director-general, thought about us coming over and they're all utterly different. Amanda, of course, was holding out for a fully independent production deal, whatever show or shows we might make. That would swallow a big chunk of the Beeb's budget for daytime programmes and put a lot of noses out of joint. After a lot of intense internal discussion at top level, the white smoke came out of Television Centre and it signalled 'not this time, anyway'. Amanda was undaunted.

By now it was February 2001 and Judy and I had some decisions to make. There was another one-year contract on the table from Granada which was absolutely fine, but we – and the programme – just couldn't see eye to eye with Maureen. Her background was in marketing and she had formidable knowledge of that side of television, but she hadn't had actual programme-making experience. Nevertheless she was full of ideas and many of them were good ones. Her strategy and scheduling instincts were sharp and she moved mountains to achieve her goals.

It was on the creative editorial side that the disagreements lay. Once again I must stress these were not remotely personal; at their height we had a perfectly friendly and civilized dinner with our new boss, hosted by the head of ITV, David Liddiment. David was an old friend and supporter and he's a very loyal person. It troubled him that we and Maureen couldn't seem to hit it off and he did his best to smooth things over that night. But within weeks profound disagreements arose again: about the way programme campaigns should be run, how long individual items should last, what on-screen involvement Judy and I should have with the show. It was very wearing, and our main objective – keeping the BBC in second place – began to be eroded as we increasingly, and not just the two of us, felt we were being drawn into a war on two fronts: one on screen and one behind our lines. We were still wondering quite what to do when a decisive moment came. Amanda came back to us, saying, 'I've just had a very interesting conversation with the Head of Daytime Programmes at Channel 4, a woman called Jo McGrath.'

Now that was a name Judy and I remembered with great fondness. A few years earlier Jo had been a very talented researcher on *This Morning*. Now at Channel 4 and on the lookout for fresh ideas, she'd called Amanda in for a brainstorming session and had mentioned a particular problem she was having with filling the five to six o'clock afternoon slot. Completely unaware of Amanda's current connection with us, she had then said, 'What I'd really love is to give this slot to Richard and Judy. We know from their ratings and demographic profiles that their morning show appeals to students, pensioners and every age group in between, and

I think they'd be absolutely right in the teatime slot. But they are completely tied in to ITV, aren't they?'

Amanda called us after the meeting and told us what had happened.

'Shall I call her back and say maybe we can do business?' she said.

'Yes,' we replied, 'it can't do any harm.'

Amanda phoned Jo from the car.

'I'm actually working on ideas for Richard and Judy,' she confessed. 'They've said they're happy for me to take you into our confidence. Shall we set up a meeting?'

'Yes,' Jo replied, astonished. 'I'd stab *myself* in the back to work with them again.'

Up until that moment, it had never crossed Judy's or my mind that Channel 4 would be interested in us. But suddenly possibilities were emerging. This would be a totally new challenge: a newsy, magazine slot never before tried out at that time of day; live programming set against all the other pre-recorded stuff. And – and this was no small point – we would not be up against all our friends on *This Morning*.

At first, just like the BBC's execs, the Channel 4 top brass – Michael Jackson, Tim Gardam and others – were wary, thinking we might simply be using their interest to play a bidding-war money-game with ITV. But, as March turned to April and April to May, their cynicism lessened sufficiently for Tim Gardam, Head of Programming at Channel 4, to commit to a face-to-face meeting with us, so that he could assess our intentions for himself and discuss the kind of programme we might make.

We saw it, we explained to Tim, as a catch-up on the day family programme; an arm around the shoulder for those already at home and those just coming through the door; a 'What's your day been like?' and 'Now we'll tell you how others have been spending theirs.'

This was very different to the dynamic of *This Morning*. On that programme, the emphasis was on looking ahead rather than back on the day; a kind of, 'Listen up, we know you've got a thousand things to do; you need to go out and you feel guilty sitting there, but stay with us just a bit longer because we've got stuff that'll really be worth while staying in for!'

Tim could recognize the difference and went away to think and to commission research.

One Monday in May the phone rang. It was Tim, sounding decisive, excited and confident.

'Let's do a two-year deal,' he said. 'We'll back you with the right kind of money and we'll all have a lot of fun.'

It was a good moment but pretty scary. Channel 4 were making a huge commitment and investment here. We were all betting that a teatime magazine would build an audience in one of the most turbulent hours in the television day. We would be up against three soaps; established hits such as *Blue Peter*; the TV phenomenon that is *The Weakest Link*, and God knows what else. We could take it as read that the TV critics would tear us to shreds whatever we did – failure is a much better story than success – and, of course, we'd have to change ingrained viewing habits. People would have to 'find us', and get used to a totally new kind of programming.

We'd been looking for a challenge, and now we'd got one.

Things moved very fast. It was important, now we'd agreed in principle, for us, Cactus and Channel 4 to nail down the deal before the news leaked out. And that was already happening. The *Daily Mail* rang and asked us was it true we'd just signed a contract with Channel 4? Damn, how the hell had that leaked? We were able to answer truthfully that we had not signed a contract with Channel 4, but that kind of economy with the facts felt wrong and wasn't our style at all. Anyway, it was clear the story was about to break and that could scupper everything. Granada would quite rightly move fast to head us off at the pass and it would all get messy. With nothing signed, there were no guarantees and we could end up with bad feelings all round and, as Maggie Smith once said, '*oeuf sur le visage*'.

Then we heard that the *Sunday Times* was sniffing around the story and Judy and I knew it was now or never. It was Wednesday, 2 May, and we both agreed we had three days to resolve things one way or another.

The next day we arrived at the *This Morning* studio and I telephoned Tim Gardam. He wasn't there so I left a message with his PA. Fifteen minutes later, just before our programme was due to go on air, my mobile rang. Clicking off my mike, I made my excuses to the team, said I'd only be five minutes, and raced upstairs to the roof of the building. Standing there in the wind and rain, I got straight back to Tim.

'What's going on?' he said. 'What's so urgent?'

I got my breath back and told him my concerns: that a big press splash could put real pressure on everyone. Tim agreed. So I took a deep breath and said, 'So, why don't we sign the deal today?'

There was a momentary silence at the other end of the phone, followed by a laugh, then the words, 'Go on, I'm listening.'

'If we don't sign the contracts at once,' I continued, 'the news will get out and everything will become very messy. If we try to deny the rumours by fudging the truth and saying that we may be having a conversation some time in the future and something may come from that one day, and then sign a deal just a few weeks later, it's going to look really . . . well, tacky. So, why don't we just call in the lawyers, say there's no time to play the usual games while we all jockey for positions on minor details – a bit of money here or a date there – and tell them we all want the deal done by midnight tonight.'

Again, Tim was decisive. 'Right,' he said, 'leave it with me. We'll talk again the moment you come off air.'

When I went back downstairs, I couldn't tell Judy what I'd just said because the mikes were on and the show was about to go on air. I had to wait until the first commercial break before I could fill her in.

After the programme, just as we were climbing into the people-carrier that always took us from the studio to our editorial office for the daily debrief and chat about the next day's show, my mobile rang. It wasn't Tim. It was Amanda.

'If at all possible,' she said, 'don't go back to your office, delay your usual editorial meeting and come immediately to . . .' She gave me the address of a high-powered media lawyer's practice near the Tower of London.

It all got very cloak and dagger. We made our excuses, cancelled our planning meeting, and I drove along the embankment into the Square Mile. We were directed to a discreet rear entrance of the lawyer's office. The builders were in and there were no steps up to the back doors, so we had to pile boxes up and clamber in that way.

Then we were swished upstairs in a metal and glass lift and shown into a complex of meeting rooms. The Cactus team were already present with their lawyer but, as Judy and I hadn't appointed our own yet, our first job was to go through a wish-list of media legal eagles. We chose a good one and, rather bemused by all the urgency, he rolled up slightly breathless an hour later.

Before he arrived, we sat there going through the basic bones of the three-way deal between Cactus, Channel 4, and Judy and me. It was a complex set-up to finalize in such a short time. Normally a deal like this would take weeks to put together and we had hours. Luckily, Channel 4's bosses were on an away-day conference together in a hotel in Wembley, discussing the network's future, so they could talk among themselves in one room with their lawyers and periodically we'd all hook up on a conference line and swap faxes.

God knows what the legal teams made of the cracking pace being imposed on them, but they rose to the occasion. They must have felt like drivers who usually cruise at a sedate fifty m.p.h. down the motorway in a Rover, but who've suddenly been shoved behind the wheel of a Ferrari and told to go like the clappers.

It's astonishing what can be achieved when the will to do something is so strong. By eight in the evening the deal was more or less in place. When we hit an obstacle, it was removed by all sides, with no one attempting to squeeze a little advantage out of the situation. Every time that happened little cheers could be heard from both ends of the conference line.

By now Judy was able to get back home and sort out the kids, who were patiently waiting for us there. While she climbed into a taxi I stayed behind to deal with any last-minute hitches. Finally, at about eleven o'clock, the last discussion was over and all that could be heard was the sound of pens scratching on paper. We were all signed up. There was a final flurry of congratulatory phone calls, photos were taken, toasts made in coffee and cola, and Simon, Amanda and I drove back to Hampstead so Judy could put the final signature on the contract.

Virtually at the stroke of midnight, we walked through our door. Judy was waiting in the front room.

'Well?'

I looked at her. 'With all due respect to Neville Chamberlain, I have in my hand a piece of paper. I believe it means Channel 4 in our time.'

But the long day wasn't over. There was no question of delaying an announcement, not even until after the weekend. Granada had to be told next morning – by now, this morning – and Channel 4 had planned a press conference in the afternoon. As my public-relations officer father would have advised, we must now take the initiative and break our own story, rather than risk having it broken inaccurately or even negatively. But, most importantly, Judy and I had to resign properly to one of our Granada bosses in person before the news got out, and fax all the senior people at that company as well as at ITV. As things turned out, that was easier said than done.

We worked long into the night writing personal faxes to everyone. At about four in the morning Simon took them to the Cactus offices ready for them to be transmitted later in the day. The plan was for us to seek a crash meeting with Granada's Head of Programmes, Grant Mansfield, and for the faxes to go out simultaneously. They all began with something like, 'By the time you read this, we will have spoken to Grant . . .' and then went on to explain our decision and thank them for everything over the years. These thanks were completely sincere. We were leaving friends and colleagues for whom we had a tremendous liking and respect. Excited as we were by our new move, there was a lot of sadness about leaving Granada.

We finally got to bed and grabbed two or three hours' sleep. The next day – Friday – was our usual day off so no one would be expecting us at the office. We phoned ahead and booked Judy an appointment with her hair and make-up stylist, Lee, for about eleven o'clock and I called our PA, Naomi, asking her to book us ten minutes with Grant. We knew he had a meeting at about midday with *This Morning*'s editor and planned to see him in our office just before.

By now we were driving down Whitehall towards the South Bank and I must admit my mouth was bone-dry with apprehension. It was one thing to have planned all this with such care, but suddenly the idea of actually resigning seemed incredible. What would our boss say? I began to have visions of us both being frog-marched out of the building.

My mobile rang. It was Naomi.

'Have you made that appointment?' I asked.

'Not exactly,' she answered carefully. 'A man's just walked into the main LWT/Granada building with what looks like several sticks of dynamite strapped to his head. He's locked himself in the toilets and he's threatening to blow the place into the Thames. Everyone's been evacuated and the police have cordoned the whole area off. Grant and all the other execs are incommunicado.'

'Buggeration!' I rang off.

Judy stayed calm. 'It's bound to be a hoax. It'll all be over in a few minutes. Anyway, I've still got to get my hair and stuff done for the press conference,' she said. 'It'll still be okay.'

But when we got to the office, hitch number two kicked in. Lee had been in the main building when the scare happened and he, too, was the wrong side of the cordon. Judy started to get ready by herself while I found Naomi.

'Look,' I said to Naomi, 'if we can't get hold of Grant, we need to speak to one of the other Granada executives. It's really urgent. There must be someone we can see.'

No, there wasn't. Naomi reported back that they were either trapped in the cordon, at some conference somewhere or in transit on a train. At one stage, as the minutes ticked by, I thought we'd have to resign to anybody with a bit of rank. The Head of Cleaning Services will never know how close they came to being presented with our compliments and our resignation.

Then, just as I was beginning to despair, the crisis was over: the 'bomber' – who turned out to have sausages rather than six sticks of dynamite strapped to his head – was arrested; Judy's make-up artist appeared and whisked her off; and Grant Mansfield, having suddenly arrived in our offices because he was still unable to get back into his own in the LWT Tower, was now perched on the corner of a researcher's desk making urgent phone calls as he tried to catch up on the lost ninety minutes.

Meanwhile, as more and more of our colleagues appeared in the office, they were looking at me, obviously puzzled.

'Hi. It's Friday – what are you doing here?'

'Oh, we've got something on this afternoon,' I kept saying airily. 'I'll tell you about it later.'

The moment Judy reappeared, I walked over to Grant Mansfield.

'You didn't do the show, did you?' he asked, looking up, surprised.

'No,' I said, 'we've got something on this afternoon. But can we have a quick word?'

'Yes, sure.'

'It will need to be somewhere private,' I said.

'Okay, give me two minutes. I'll see you in there.' He nodded to what was more or less a broom-cupboard, with a couple of chairs and no window.

'Fine.'

As we waited for him, I phoned Amanda and Simon and told them to send the faxes in five minutes. I rang off and stared at the phone. Bloody hell. It was starting.

By now the place was full of LWT people, made homeless by the bomb scare, and making urgent calls wherever they could. By some strange osmosis, everyone knew we had asked to see Grant and, as the three of us walked into the broom-cupboard, I felt the atmosphere behind us crackle with curiosity. What was going on?

Grant shut the door and began telling us about the bomb scare, utterly unaware of our own controlled explosion that we were about to set off. Then he must have seen how tense we looked because he stopped and asked, 'What's up?'

The room was so tiny our knees were virtually touching. This was not how I'd imagined the scene playing. I took a deep breath. (Judy had kindly allowed me to be the one to break the news. You can imagine my gratitude!)

I explained that we'd thought long and hard about whether to sign on for another year on *This Morning*, but had felt it was time to move on and seek a new challenge. That wasn't too hard to say, but now came the tough bit.

'And we have to tell you that last night we signed a two-year contract to present a new, early evening, live magazine for Channel 4. It should be on the air by Christmas. We'd love to stay and finish this series of *This Morning*, but we'll totally understand if you want us off the show.'

Grant was impressively calm. 'Just let me be clear: this is a done deal with Channel 4, is it? There's no way we can unpick it?'

'No, there isn't.'

'Hang on a sec.'

Grant opened the door and called to his PA to get a string of his fellow execs and the head of publicity on the phone. Many heads swivelled towards our cupboard. What the fuck was going on in there? Grant shut the door.

The conversation that followed is, you will understand, confidential. But my earlier fears that inside ten minutes we would find ourselves out on the pavement with a couple of bin-liners full of our personal possessions couldn't have been more wrong.

There was no doubt the news had come as a complete shock, but Grant was kind, generous and made no reproaches. We explained why we hadn't wanted to start some kind of 'contract war' and he said he understood. We said how sad we were to be leaving Granada and he made it clear he felt the same way about us. Then he smiled and said we would have to talk it all through later because, well, he had a few calls to make! So the door opened again, we shook hands and headed for the lifts, dozens of pairs of eyes boring into our backs.

'What do you think?' I asked Judy as the lift went down to the car park.

'I almost wish he'd had a go at us,' she said glumly. 'I feel awful. I know we're doing the right thing, but if everyone's going to be so nice . . .'

It was the only moment in a thirty-six-hour roller-coaster ride that our spirits dipped. Soon, though, we were pulling out of the little underpass that connected our office with the street and weaving into traffic as we headed for Channel 4 and Horseferry Road.

Halfway there, delayed in a traffic jam, we switched on the radio and heard the news of our impending departure from *This Morning* being broadcast on the lunchtime news. It had leaked sooner than we expected, then. Simultaneously our mobile phone started to go absolutely mental with calls and text messages. We switched both the radio and the phone off.

The slow, halting drive across the Thames to Horseferry Road – such a short distance – felt hugely significant. We were quite literally in transit, from one channel to another. We hadn't quite left *This Morning* – Grant had made it clear he wanted us to finish the series – and we hadn't quite joined Channel 4. We were simultaneously elated and regretful. A very odd half-hour or so.

We just beat the press pack to Horseferry Road and went up to a boardroom. Various Channel 4 commissioning editors were waiting for us, including our last editor but one, Sharon Powers, who was about to relaunch the channel's breakfast show.

'Bloody fantastic!' she kept saying. 'You'll love it here!'

We had half a glass of champagne and went downstairs again for a photo-call on the steps of the building.

There was an impressive scrum of photographers and TV cameras. We did all the usual gurning and waved a Channel 4 placard around for a few minutes and then headed back inside.

It was then that the best moment of the whole difficult, emotional and fractured day happened.

We were greeted by a sound which began as a little ripple, then swelled, wave after wave, to a deafening roar. We looked up and saw, to our astonishment, about a hundred of our now fellow Channel 4 workers – some we recognized, most we didn't – gathered on the balconies above looking down on us and clapping, cheering, wolf-whistling and banging their feet. We were being piped aboard.

It was a fantastic, heart-warming moment, a wonderful welcome and, we were told later, completely spontaneous. Heartened, we went into one of the studios for the press conference.

Judy and I had anticipated a pretty rough ride during this, with some sneering snotty questions and asides, and a general, 'what's an act like you doing in a place like this?' approach.

But actually it was okay. The questions were fair and there seemed to be a general sense of friendly anticipation about our plans. The killer question of course was, 'Channel 4 is meant to be all about innovation and risk-taking: how can your move here be compatible with that?'

Our answer was completely sincere.

'Name me,' I said, 'another channel that would have the bottle to try out a live one-hour topical magazine programme at this time of day. It's incredibly risky. But it's bloody innovative. Everything else going out between five and six p.m. is safely pre-recorded, pre-packaged and pre-edited. At least we're having a crack at breaking the mould. That's innovative and the show will be a real alternative; quintessentially Channel 4, if you stop and think about it.'

The next day's reports were thoughtful and even the *Guardian*, which I had a ten-pound bet with Simon would put the boot in, didn't.

The press conference ended, and at last we could go upstairs and have a decent drink. I switched my mobile back on and it rang at once.

'Hello?'

It was one of Granada's top people, also a good friend, who opened up with both barrels.

'How could you fuck off by fax? At least you could have resigned in person . . . disgraceful manners . . . all very let down here . . .'

It was mortifying, but I thought it best to soak up the incoming fire before making the case for the defence. Everyone in the room went silent, but someone said, 'It's —— on the phone to Richard! Shit!'

Finally I got a word in: 'Look, we *did* resign in person . . .'

I explained how the day had begun, how the bomb scare had thrown a two-ton spanner in the works, how we had managed to meet with Grant and, crucially, why we'd had to make our decision at express speed the day before.

There was a deep sigh from the other end: 'I didn't know you'd seen Grant. What with the bomb scare and half of us out of London communications haven't been great. It's only four hours since the news broke and we're all still running to catch up.'

I know business is business, but I felt very bad.

'Can I just take you through it all, please?' I said.

We talked for a while and straightened out quite a few misunderstandings, and I felt a lot better. It was suggested that Judy and I should try to get hold of Granada's chief exec, our long-time colleague Steve Morrison, to explain it to him personally.

'Of course,' I replied. 'Where is he?'

Judy and I went into another room and hooked up a conference line to Steve so we could talk as a threesome and in private. He was incredibly nice, in the circumstances, and listened closely to our story. Understandably he wanted to know why we'd played our cards so closely to our chests. We explained about the press leaks and that having agreed in principle with Channel 4 to do business it would have been madness to delay signing the contract. Having signed so close to midnight the night before, Judy and I could hardly pick up the phone to sleeping ITV bosses and say, 'Hi, guys, we've just closed a deal with Channel 4. We'll tell you all about it tomorrow.'

Steve laughed. Then, like Grant nearly five hours earlier, he said some extremely generous and kind things which was exceptionally decent of him; and that, of course, made us feel guilty again. But as a businessman used to making tough decisions, Steve signalled he understood our *modus operandi* and that meant a lot.

So that was that.

Judy and I downed one more glass of champagne with our new Channel 4 colleagues, and went home. Switching on the TV in our sitting-room, we watched ourselves on the evening news. How weird that felt, reliving moments of what had been for us a personal watershed of a day. It was official, then. We were finally leaving *This Morning*. It felt like closing a book that we'd particularly enjoyed reading and were sad to finish. But, however contradictory this may sound, neither of us experienced then or later any doubts about our decision. It had been made with eyes wide open and a cool temper. Whatever the risks, we knew what we were doing and why.

———

In the days immediately after, there was a phenomenal amount of press coverage, and this included some regurgitated stories about the so-called personal animosity that had existed between Judy and me and Maureen Duffy. TEARS, TANTRUMS AND THE REAL REASONS RICHARD AND JUDY STORMED

OUT OF DAYTIME TELEVISION was the *Daily Mail*'s headline, accompanied by a lead-in that read: 'Only now that the dust has settled can the true story be told of the bitterness and rancour and titanic clashes of egos behind Richard and Judy's departure from ITV.'

It was fuck all to do with ego on either side. In fact when we saw Maureen Duffy at ITV's summer party shortly after we left *This Morning*, we had a very pleasant conversation and wished each other well. What differences we had had in the past were, as I wrote before, purely professional ones about the kind of show *This Morning* should or shouldn't be. Now she was free to try things her way, and we were sincere when we wished her good luck. But you can hardly expect the news media to be interested in that – it's a pretty boring piece of reality, let's face it – so we remain cast as mortal foes. What the hell, what difference does it make anyway?

––––––––

It was very strange coming back in to work on Monday morning, but our production team and studio crew did the right thing in the circumstances, and took the piss. Excellent decision: it always avoids unnecessary tension and awkwardness. There were lots of congratulations, too, and it was obvious that, here at the programme's coalface, everyone had been expecting something like this for months. The tension had broken and our first show back – and the beginning of our final count-down to leaving the series – was surprisingly comfortable.

Word came down from on high that the mood should be 'business as usual', and there should be no references made to Channel 4 or our impending departure. This was understandable, but it felt a bit strange; after all, we'd always been very open with our viewers and had tried hard to 'keep it real', even during the ghastly Tesco fiasco. But this wasn't personal, this was business, and obviously we toed the line. We offered to do whatever was needed to help endorse and 'push' the show into the next season. We were – and are – very proud of *This Morning* and were willing to do or say anything to help it.

What this meant in practice was that occasionally we didn't present the show while Granada tried out alternative hosts. Again this felt odd, but as one exec told us wryly, 'No offence, guys, but you're now part of *This Morning*'s past – we're having to focus totally on the future.' He was right but the process was increasingly feeling distinctly unreal and I began actively to look forward to signing off.

Very often in life, what you expect will be a big finish turns out to be a surprisingly tame ending. We and our producers had planned our very last show ever with great care. It would be on the second Friday in July 2001 and we were going to go out with a bang. But just as the 'fireworks' – in the form of bands, big names and a trawl through the best and worst in the archives, dating back to 1988, were being put together – we were told it was all off. We would have to say a far more muted goodbye on the Thursday; ITV felt a big finish on the very last day of the series would send a signal to the viewers that *This Morning* itself was ending, never to return.

We couldn't see it but it wasn't our call, so instead of waving farewell on Friday the 13th, we slipped quietly away on Thursday the 12th. Maybe it was for the best – that last show was emotional enough as it was. Lily Savage came on and sailed dangerously close to the wind in some remarks about ITV. George Michael phoned in, asking disingenuously about the new show that we were not supposed to talk about.

The airtime slipped away and suddenly there was less than a minute left. Judy filled up with tears and I scratched my head, which people who know me very well always recognize as a sign of suppressed emotion.

I've had to go to the press cuttings to remind myself of what I ad-libbed but it was apparently this: 'It's been a privilege for us to have brought you this extraordinary thing that really shouldn't fly; this weird lovely show that's been on air for thirteen years and that people still watch. The best programmes, which people love most, are those which they truly believe belong to *them* – and this is your show. It really is, this isn't our programme. We've always known that and remembered that. It belongs to you.'

Judy added something about the show going on and suddenly we were going off air.

'Thanks everyone,' I finished. 'We will, as they say, see you around.'

There was a short silence and the studio lights flickered and went out. The house lights went up. And suddenly our boss, Steve Morrison, was walking on set with flowers for Judy and champagne for both of us. His boss, Charles Allen, was with him. It was a very warm gesture and in the short speeches that followed we felt that we had, after all, said a proper goodbye and received a proper farewell.

Then an ITN news crew barrelled in and we pulled ourselves together for an interview with Katie Derham for that night's *News at Ten*.

After that we left the studio for the last time and returned home to a huge party that Amanda Ross and Cactus had organized in our garden for Judy and me, and all our friends from *This Morning*, and lots of our new colleagues from Channel 4. It was a lovely summer's day, shared with seventy or so people, some of whom went back to our first days in Liverpool in 1988.

The next day there was another party – *This Morning*'s traditional end-of-series bash – and we had the chance to say our goodbyes to everyone else.

Then, as in a play, the safety curtain came down and there

was an interval. We knew what lay on the other side. Channel 4 was making noises about a programme launch in late November. We'd just agreed to write a double-page column every Saturday in the *Daily Express*, starting in September. We had already begun work on this book.

We grabbed the kids and took a plane to America. Let the summer take care of itself. We'd be back in the autumn.

Epilogue

Richard: The writer John Mortimer quotes his father as telling him that all advice is useless. The old boy was probably right and I think that the same can be said about predictions concerning one's own future: they're never much more than semi-informed guesses.

When I finished my O-levels I had absolutely no idea that weeks later I would leave school for ever and stake everything on a job on the local paper. Three summers on I couldn't possibly have predicted that I would shortly uproot myself from London and head north to the Scottish Borders and a seismic life-change.

When I first saw Judy on television, and then began working alongside her, it never entered my mind that a few short years later we would pledge to spend the rest of our lives together; have children; and embark on such an odd journey.

And, as I wrote in this book's final chapter, we began our thirteenth season of *This Morning* without the faintest idea that we'd finish it holding two tickets to Channel 4. And here I am, as I write this now, in a quiet corner of our new, busy production office. The new show is still not even six months old, but in the last few weeks it feels to us that it's started to fly right. Those first couple of months after we came back on air at the other end of the day and on a different channel were unexpectedly hard work. We'd forgotten just how much sheer graft it takes to get a big daily live sequence programme off the tarmac. In fact during some of the early programmes it felt as if we were still bolting on the engines halfway through take-off.

The only thing we were fully prepared for was the inevitable barrage of heavy machine-gun fire from hostile critics, even though from the word go our share of the available audience made us the third most-watched programme on the channel. *Plus ça change.* We got exactly the same treatment from time to time on *This Morning* and there's no point moaning about it and it doesn't really make much difference to anything, although it gets a bit wearing having to explain to concerned friends that, actually, everything is going fine. It's been a good and happy move. So what happens next?

When I was younger I thought the future could, with caution, be mapped out. Today I know the only certainties are what we've done, and what we do today. In *The Go-Between*, L.P. Hartley writes: 'The past is a foreign country: they do things differently there.' I've always thought that to be wrong; the opposite is surely true. It's the future that's a foreign land: mapless; hidden below the horizon. I have absolutely no idea where Judy and I will be in three, even two years from now. But as long as, wherever it is, we're together, we'll be okay.

———

Judy: Launching a new programme is like giving birth. It's hard labour, inevitably involving varying degrees of pain. As I write this, our new Channel 4 show is five months old and still needs the unrelenting care of and commitment to a baby. It's stressful and tiring, but at least we get a good night's sleep! We got off to a slightly rocky start, but that's inevitable when you launch a new format in a new (and turbulent) slot. You just have to experiment until you find the right combination. And now I'm confident we have, and the baby's becoming more independent, and we're beginning to find our new metaphorical parenthood rewarding, enjoyable and happy.

I suppose what occurs to me as I flick back through these

pages is what an extraordinary combination of luck, happenstance and strangely fated moments have brought us to where we are now. And as Richard says, where we are now is a good place. It's impossible to tell how things would have turned out had we stayed with *This Morning*, but the challenge of building something different has been totally absorbing.

Even so, some things never change, and it's no easier today to look into our futures than it was during all those years we spent presenting *This Morning*.

Life has a habit of chucking googlies at you when you least expect them, and no one with any respect for fate would claim to be set fair for total happiness. But *carpe diem*! Seize the day, seize the moment, and the moment's good. I'm content, for now. And, as long as I have my family, my health and Richard, I count myself a lucky woman.

Photographic Acknowledgements

All photographs from Richard and Judy's family albums, with the exception of the following:

© Border Television: 6 centre and below, 7 above. © Cumbrian Newspapers: 6 above. © Andy Francis: 24 above. © Granada Visual: 7 below, 8 below. © Manchester Evening News: 9 above. © mirrorpix: 16 above and below, 22 above right. © Indigo Television: 27 below (The National Television Awards, 2000). © PA Photos: 25 below and 32 /Matthew Fearn, 26 above left /Toby Melville, 31 above /Peter Jordan.

Every reasonable effort has been made to contact the copyright holders, but should there be any errors or omissions, Hodder & Stoughton would be pleased to insert the appropriate acknowledgement in any subsequent printing of this publication.

Index